BEYOND
CALCULATION

PETER J. DENNING
ROBERT M. METCALFE

Foreword by James Burke

BEYOND CALCULATION

THE NEXT FIFTY YEARS OF COMPUTING

COPERNICUS
AN IMPRINT OF SPRINGER-VERLAG

Published in the United States by Copernicus, an imprint of Springer-Verlag New York, Inc.

Copernicus
Springer-Verlag New York, Inc.
175 Fifth Avenue
New York, NY 10010
USA

Library of Congress Cataloging-in-Publication Data
ɣ-29-98
Denning, Peter J., 1942–
    Beyond calculation : the next fifty years of computing / Peter
Denning, Robert M. Metcalfe.
        p.   cm.
    Includes bibliographical references and index.
    ISBN 0-387-94932-1 (hardcover : alk. paper)
    1. Electronic data processing.   2. Computers.   I. Metcalfe,
Robert M.   II. Title.
QA76.D348   1997
004'.09'05—dc21   96-37790
                                                             CIP

Manufactured in the United States of America.
Printed on acid-free paper.

9 8 7 6 5 4 3 2 1

ISBN 0-387-94932-1   SPIN 10557481

To our grandchildren
who will live with the consequences of what we say here
and who will probably invent something better than
anything we have imagined.

CONTENTS

Foreword

In the nineteenth century, a French cleric noted the regular patterns in which crystals broke when he tapped them with his little hammer, and in consequence, a century later x-ray diffraction techniques made possible the discovery of DNA. A Scottish scientist once kept a soap bubble inflated for three years and now we have clingwrap. In the seventeenth century, Otto von Guericke rubbed a sulfur-ball model of the Earth (trying to find out why compass needles dipped) and accidentally discovered electricity.

The serendipitous nature of the "knock-on" process that follows innovation and discovery triggers a domino effect of unexpected changes that ripple through society, reshaping it in subtle ways often not observed at the time because most of what is changed tends to be local detail.

Thus, after the change, we use a car instead of a horse-drawn buggy; the postage stamp makes it easier to keep in touch; aniline dyes brighten up the world; we switch from earthenware to iron cooking pots. Almost always, in separate and apparently unrelated ways, the change makes life a little easier, healthier, more comfortable. Thanks to science and technology, we are undeniably the wealthiest, healthiest, longest-living people in history. So even though new products tend to be a surprise, the individual welcomes their short-term benefits, heedless of any larger ramifications.

The same attitude holds, in the main, among those who direct our affairs. The major public and private social institutions that provide continuity in our society are often themselves the source of these scattershot changes, since they are the ones who foster and develop innovation, initially in the interests of survival either in the marketplace or in war.

But in important ways, such institutions as decision hierarchies, the law, the sovereign community, the male-female relationship, and commercial structures have changed little since the Stone Age. There seems to be a widening gap between these essentially backward-looking, slow-to-change entities—within whose guidelines we live our lives—and the constant innovations of institution-driven technology, which in myriad subtle ways alter what we perceive those institutions' purposes to be.

It seems clear, for instance, that the rampaging speed with which recent information media have given us a new view of the world has far outstripped our educational system's ability to prepare us. And the more those same information media offer new insights into the processes of government, international relations, or global environmental issues, the more frustrated we become at our inability to gain meaningful access to our institutional "representatives."

That the institutions have survived so long almost intact is a measure of how much of our innovative efforts have so far been concentrated on providing as many people as possible with the bare necessities, and how little effort we have spent on diffusing power outward from the institutions into the community. As a result, we approach what is likely to be the greatest acceleration in the rate of technological and social change since the advent of the printing press, largely unprepared, both personally and institutionally.

It seems clear that the next fifty years will see radical changes in almost every aspect of life, and above all in the relationship between the individual and the institution. Most institutions will cease to exist in their present form. However, in a world of informed, empowered individuals, where change may be the only constant, what instruments will exist to ensure social stability? What form will they take? When communications technology removes from the individual the constraints of space and time, what will happen to community identity? Whose law will rule in cyberspace? If we use the technology to foster and preserve the immense diversity of the human race instead of molding it to a single Western model, how will we avoid confusion? With a thousand television channels, what will happen to the social glue of shared values and common knowledge? What meaning will standards have, when everybody is his or her own publisher? As knowledge-manufacture by machines speeds beyond our ability to manage it, will we give up trying and retire into cocoons of virtual reality?

The problem with these and similar questions is that they may be the wrong questions. Gutenberg's detractors worried about the way print would cause disastrous loss of memory. Mainframe makers in the 1950's were daunted by the thought of an American national market requiring at most five computers. Critics of the telegraph asked, "What would Maine want to say to Texas?" Inevitably we are constrained by our historical context. So we interpret events, trends, and the effects of innovation in the light of what we know to be the facts. Trouble is, a fact today may not be a fact tomorrow. So how do we think ourselves outside the box?

One way to start is to read this book. Here the authors look at the major areas of information and communications technology which will generate change over the next fifty years. In one sense, they are thinking backwards from the future, rather than tracing a path from here to there and becoming caught in the prediction trap. In that sense, this book is a primer for how to think about innovation and its social consequences.

One of the most exciting aspects of information technology is that as it renders the world ever more complex and fast-changing, as it reduces the cycle time between innovation and effect, and as it inextricably and interactively brings us all closer to each other on the network, at the same time making it possible for each of us to live more individual lives than ever before, the speed and scale at which the systems operate may also offer us the opportunity to look for and find patterns in the process of change.

Will that ability give us a kind of ephemeral shifting, temporary control over the social structure, so that we end up, fifty years from now, living in what might be described as continuous "balanced anarchy"? Or will it turn out differently?

Read on, and find out.

ROBERT J. DENNING
ROBERT M. METCALFE

Preface

As we write this, the field of computing is fifty years old. The ACM, Association for Computing, is celebrating its golden jubilee with a conference, an exposition, and a book. All three events have as their theme "The Next Fifty Years of Computing"—the ways in which information technology will evolve and affect society in the near future. This is the book.

The electron was discovered a century ago, by J. J. Thompson in 1895. The first electronic computers, built in the 1940s as part of the war effort, were to be used for large scientific calculations such as ballistic trajectories, the calculation of which was extremely slow and error-prone when done by hand. Electronic computers were also used for code-breaking; Alan Turing's machine at Blechley cracked the German Enigma code, a fact not known publicly until twenty-five years after the war ended. By 1950, as IBM and Univac bet that computers would become the engines to run large businesses, the news media were calling them "electronic brains" and projecting that only a few dozen would be needed worldwide. Soon other companies joined the crowd—names like RCA, Burroughs, ICL, General Electric—most of whom have disappeared or left the computer business. The first programming languages—Algol, FORTRAN, Cobol, and Lisp—were designed in the late 1950s and the first operating systems in the early 1960s. The first computer science departments were formed in the mid 1960s. Microprocessors made their debut twenty-five years ago. The first hand calculator appeared in 1972 and made the slide rule obsolete overnight. The computer chip appeared in the late 1970s, the personal computer around the same time, and the IBM PC in 1981. Ethernet was invented in 1973 but did not appear on the market until 1980. Word processing, spreadsheets, graphics, and database programs made the clerk typist, clerk accountant, graphics designer, and record-keeper obsolete by the end of the decade. The Internet, which descended from the ARPANET in the 1970s, and the World Wide Web, which seemed to appear out of nowhere in 1992 (it was actually created in 1989), joined forces with the personal computer to produce the revolution we are experiencing today. Along the way, the mainframe computer became obsolete except as a computing engine for large applications in business, science, and engineering. Computers are now in so many places that we overlook many of them, except in the fall and spring, when we must change all their clocks.

It has been a favorite pastime along the way to predict the future. The predictions have been notoriously bad. In 1950, Turing believed that by 2000 we would have computers that could not be distinguished from humans by their responses to questions. Around 1960, the founders of artificial intelligence believed that thinking machines would be a reality within a decade or two, and in particular that chess-playing machines would beat world masters by 1980. In 1968, the founders of software engineering believed that the discipline they were inventing would solve the software crisis within a decade. In 1980, Bell Labs believed that UNIX would become the world's dominant operating system. In 1982, Bill Gates thought that 640K of main memory would suffice for user workspaces in operating systems for many years to come. In 1984, IBM believed that personal computers would not amount to anything. In 1985, many people believed that the Japanese Fifth Generation project would produce intelligent machines and place Japan untouchably at the forefront of the world computing industry. None of these things happened. Many of the goals and assumptions embedded in them have been abandoned or have remained elusive.

Much of what makes up our world of computing today could not have been predicted. Who thought that most of the big names in the computer industry in the 1950s would have disappeared today? Who thought that computers more powerful than the million-dollar mainframes of the 1950s would become so cheap and small that they would routinely be built into watches, cars, radios, CD players, and scientific instruments? Who anticipated the World Wide Web or thought it would replace the Internet as everyone's focus of attention? Who thought that e-mail and Web addresses would be a regular part of every business card and advertisement? Who thought that FORTRAN and Cobol, languages of the 1950s, would still be so well entrenched today?

As we stand on the threshold of the next fifty years of computing trying to say something useful about them, we ought to be humbled by our past incapacity to make predictions that were not only believable but actually came true. Can we say anything useful about the next fifty years? We hope that ACM97 will not so much make predictions as develop possibilities, raise issues, and enumerate some of the choices we will face about how information technology will affect us in the future.

Imagine that we brought back Henry Ford to show him today's automobiles. He would not be so surprised by changes in design: cars still have four wheels, steering, front-mounted internal-combustion engines, transmissions, and the like. But he would be greatly surprised by the changes in human practices that have grown up around the automobile—for example, hot rods, strip malls, drive-in fast food, cars as status symbols, rush hours, traffic reports on the radio, and much more.

Alexander Graham Bell would be little surprised by the design of instruments and switching systems—handsets, carbon microphones, dialing mechanisms, crossbar switches, telephone exchanges, and operator services. But he would be amazed by the changes in human customs that have grown up around the phone—telephone credit cards, the Home Shopping Network, universal phone numbers, "prestige" exchanges like New York's old BUtterfield 8 or Beverly Hills's 271, public outcries over changes in area codes, electronic funds transfers, telemarketing, fax, and telephone pornography, and much more.

Edison would doubtless be little surprised by current light bulbs and generators, but he would be astonished by international power grids, night baseball, radio and television, lava lamps, electronics, computers, and much more. For that matter, can you imagine trying to explain frequent-flyer miles to Orville Wright?

The surprises lie in the way people use new technologies and the new industries that spring from them, in what people see as opportunities and what they see as obsolete.

In organizing this book, we wanted to avoid the trap of easy predictions. Instead, we asked a group of world-recognized experts to examine the current realities of how people are using computers and what they are concerned about, and then project the consequences over the next few decades. We also asked them to examine the long sweep of history and discuss probabilities. We asked them to think of a metaphor, the clearing in the forest, that represents the space in which we can move freely, delimited by dense underbrush that impedes movement. We asked them to take a serious look at the clearing—a clearing in which people are limited by their practices, habits, outlooks, concerns, and moods. We asked them to map out a portion of the clearing so that others could navigate more freely. We think that they have done this admirably.

We sent invitations to winners of major ACM awards (Turing, software systems, education, and others), ACM fellows, and others who we felt have something to say about the clearing. Even though the deadlines were incredibly tight, we still received about two dozen responses, which resulted in the twenty-one essays in this book.

The essays fell into three broad categories. The first group of six essays gives us pictures of the coming technological revolution—speculations about speeds and sizes of processors, memory, bandwidths, and networks and the consequences of these technologies for the way people live and work. The second group, six more essays, concerns the effect of cheap computers and communications on our human and organizational identities—who we say we are, how we want to be known, and who we are known as. The third group, eight more essays, concerns the effects on business and innovation—what it will take to be a leader, how to defend against attacks to the infrastructure, how to coexist with the new forms of artificial software life and with each other, how we will innovate, and how we will learn.

It is most striking that none of the writers have limited themselves to their narrow specialties. Every one of them is concerned with how the technologies to which they have devoted their lives will affect others. They are basically optimistic that the world will turn out well, but they do not hesitate to point out drifts toward worlds that we may not want to inhabit. There are no doomsday scenarios.

We are very pleased with the breadth and depth of thinking exhibited by these authors. We believe that you will find much provocation and much solace in what they have to say about the human spirit.

Peter J. Denning, Arlington, Virginia, January 1997
Robert M. Metcalfe, Boston, Massachusetts, January 1997

Acknowledgments

This book is part of a major celebration of a radical technology that has turned the world inside out. ACM, the Association for Computing, was founded in 1947. Fifty years later, ACM celebrates the field of computing by looking ahead to the next half century through the eyes of ACM97. ACM97 consists of a conference, an exposition, and a book. The conference and exposition were held at the San Jose Convention Center, March 1–5, 1997. The Web page is available at http://www.acm.org/acm97.

Major computer companies, from pioneers in the computing age to relative newcomers, have generously underwritten the ACM97 conference:

Computerworld, Inc.
Hewlett Packard Company
Intel Corporation
Microsoft Corporation
Sun Microsystems, Inc.

The fiftieth anniversary program was developed under the leadership of Bert Herzog, of the University of Michigan; Dan Lynch, of Cybercash;

ACM past president Gwen Bell, of the Computer Museum; the ACM executive director, Joseph DeBlasi; and the ACM deputy executive director, Patricia Ryan. It was vigorously supported by ACM past president Stuart Zweben, of Ohio State University; and by the current ACM president, Chuck House, of Spectron Microsystems. These people recruited Bob Metcalfe of the International Data Group as the general chair of the conference.

Bob Metcalfe put together a prominent program committee: Peter Denning (the book), George Mason University and past president of ACM; Dave Kasik (the exposition), Boeing Computer Services; David Liddle, Interval Research; Anita Jones, Department of Defense; Andy van Dam, Brown University; Rick Rashid, Microsoft; Denise Caruso, the *New York Times*.

Bob Metcalfe is especially grateful to the ACM97 underwriters, the ACM97 sponsors, the ACM97 program committee, the ACM97 speakers, the ACM97 book contributors, the ACM97 exhibitors, the ACM97 conference attendees, ACM members and staff, his assistant Gerry Desautels, International Data Group chairman Pat McGovern, and Robyn, Julia, and Max Metcalfe for their constant support after he got into ACM97 well over his head. Bob thanks Peter Denning for taking on the heavy work in editing this book, and you for reading it. And Bob may, after some time passes, be grateful to Gwen Bell, Bert Herzog, and Dan Lynch for inviting him to do ACM97 in the first place.

Peter Denning is grateful to Marcia Boalen, assistant to the executive director of ACM; to Joseph DeBlasi, the executive director of ACM; to Mark Mandelbaum, the ACM director of publications; and to Nhora Cortes-Comerer, the publisher of ACM Press Books, for their constant help with logistics of the book project. They helped to select the publisher, Copernicus, from among several offers; they helped prepare the invitation list for authors; and they followed up with all the authors who accepted the invitation to join the project. He is also grateful to Pamela Bruno, his award-winning assistant at George Mason University. He enjoyed the tremendous support of his wife, Dorothy Denning, and his two daughters, Anne and Diana Denning.

Denning and Metcalfe were the editors of this volume. They volunteered to do this work pro bono for ACM. The real work of editing, design, and publishing was accomplished by the professionals at Copernicus. Jerry Lyons, the editorial director for physical sciences, maintained a clear vision of what this book could be and of its intended audience. William Frucht, the senior editor, who Peter Denning says is the finest editor he has worked with, labored tirelessly to help all the authors cast their material to achieve the most effective communication. Karen Phillips managed the very tight design schedule and Lesley Poliner brought the editorial production process to a successful and swift conclusion.

BEYOND CALCULATION

PART I

The Coming Revolution

Try to imagine all the new kinds of computers that will arrive in the next generation or two. Imagine what we—actually our children and grandchildren—will do with them all. One thing is sure: whatever wild visions you can conjure are too tame. Our authors weave tales of amazing new technologies, sweeping changes in people's lives, dizzying distractions from the mainstream of progress, human reluctance and inertia, and arrival in a calm lagoon after a stormy trip. Fifty years ago, computer science did not exist. Today it is frothing into every aspect of life. Fifty years from now computers will be as common and cheap as paper clips are today, and as little noticed.

Buckle up for the ride of your life. Get ready to be catapulted through a dizzying array of computing technologies that will arrive during the next generation. Gordon Bell and Jim Gray are your pilots. Bell designed the VAX, started several computer companies, championed high-performance computing, and has charted the development of the Internet through "Version 3.0." Gray has designed databases of every kind from traditional to relational to object-oriented to distributed. Together, they give us a rare glimpse of the minds of creative technologists at work. What will happen, they ask, when every bit of data that ever crosses your senses is recorded and indexed forever in your personal computer? When a network of computers can be embedded in your body? Before your very eyes they invent the body area network (BAN) to connect those embodied chips, playfully extrapolating from today's WAN and LAN. And just when you think you understand, they dare to tell you that in all likelihood they are wrong about nearly everything they foresee.

Vinton Cerf takes over in midair. One of the inventors of the Internet protocols and a founder of the Internet Society, Cerf shifts attention from chips and databases to the global high-speed network. He focuses on the way our great-grandchildren will live and work with ubiquitous, unbelievably fast computers and incredibly high-bandwidth communications—when computation and communication can be wasted and distance will be meaningless.

Bob Frankston allays our fears that the accelerating rocket will disintegrate against the barriers of physical limits. Frankston, a coinventor of the first spreadsheet and a network entrepreneur, is not used to seeing limits where others see them. In his mind, the laws that tell us that chip speeds, memory sizes, transition densities, and communication bandwidths will double every eighteen months are misleading. In the backs of our minds we know that these doublings cannot go on forever, so we wonder how the projections of Bell, Gray, and Cerf can possibly be realized. Doubling laws live in a mentality of scarcity: they assume implicitly that we consume the resource with exponentially voracious appetites until suddenly it is exhausted. The evidence of history belies this theory. For centuries, technologies have been used to sidestep scarcities. They transform the meanings of resource, demand, and need. They lower the costs of alternatives and eventually render the original resource obsolete. They express the boundless human capacity to invent tomorrow's ways around yesterday's barriers.

Once we've reached cruising altitude, Edsger Dijkstra invites us to reflect on the changes and ask how much has really changed. He built his reputation around software systems that control chips and links. He built the first Algol compiler and the first level-structured operating system based on concurrent processes, and he invented structured programming. He has long been a proponent of well-designed programs that can be easily understood. He cautions against the heady optimism expressed by the previous authors and reminds us that the future belongs to those who can find simplicity where everyone else sees only complexity—as he puts it, to those who see the tide, not just the waves.

As we begin our descent, Richard Hamming asks us to reflect further on the very way we tend to think about the future. Hamming has contributed many of the most lucid explanations of coding theory (the Hamming error-correcting code is named after him), probability, statistics, and numerical computation that exist in the literature of computing and applied mathematics. He has spent much of his life watching not only the products of creative thought but how creative thinkers work and what makes them creative in the first place. He warns that we cannot understand technologies and follow their evolution until we know what people are concerned about and how they will use technologies to satisfy their concerns.

Mark Weiser and John Seeley Brown give us a smooth, soft landing. They have worked with distributed, personal computing at Xerox Palo Alto Research Center for two decades. They divide the age of computing into three eras. In the first, the era of the mainframe, computers were few and expensive; many people had to share the use of any one of them. In the second, the era of the personal computer, computers were sufficiently numerous that each person could have his own. In the third, the coming era of the ubiquitous computer, computers will outnumber people by many orders of magnitude, and each person will use hundreds or thousands of them. As our descendants learn to live with all those computers, the computers will cease to be visible or matters of direct concern. They will no longer appear to be sources of chaos and uncertainty. That final outcome will mark the age of calm technology.

These authors have left much unsaid. There is nary a word about that stuff of science fiction—bionic computers that use biochemical processes to store, retrieve, and process information; computers incredibly smaller than the chips that Bell, Gray, Cerf, and Frankston envisage; computers that are grown, not etched. Such tales will be told in another book.

GORDON BELL
& JAMES N. GRAY

The Revolution Yet to Happen

1 Introduction

By 2047 almost all information will be in cyber-space—including a large percentage of knowl-edge and creative works. All information about physical objects, including humans, buildings, processes, and organizations, will be online. This trend is both desirable and inevitable. Cyberspace will provide the basis for wonderful new ways to inform, entertain, and educate people. The infor-mation and the corresponding systems will streamline commerce but will also provide new levels of personal service, health care, and au-tomation. The most significant benefit will be a breakthrough in our ability to communicate re-motely with one another using all our senses.

The ACM and the transistor were invented in 1947. At that time, the stored-program com-puter was a revolutionary idea and the transistor was just a curiosity. Both ideas evolved rapidly. By the mid 1960s, integrated circuits appeared—allowing mass fabrication of transistors on sili-con substrates. This allowed low-cost, mass-produced computers. These technologies enabled extraordinary increases in processing speed and memory coupled with tremendous declines in price.

The only form of processing and memory more easily, cheaply, and rapidly available is the human brain. Peter Cohrane[6] estimates the brain to have a processing power of around one thousand million million operations per second (one petaops) and a memory of ten terabytes. If current trends continue, computers could have these capabilities by 2047. Such computers could be "on body" personal assistants able to recall everything one reads, hears, and sees.

For five decades, progress in computer technology has driven the evolution of computers. Now they are everywhere: from mainframes to pacemakers, from the telephone network to carburetors. These technologies have enabled computers to supplement and often supplant other information processors, including humans. In 1997, processor speed, storage capacity, and transmission rates are evolving at an annual rate of 60%, doubling every eighteen months, or 100 times per decade.

It is safe to predict that computers in the year 2047 will be at least one hundred thousand times more powerful than those of today.* However, if processing speeds, storage capacities, and network bandwidths continue to evolve in accordance with Moore's Law,[13] improving at the rate of 1.60 per year, then the computers in 2047 will be ten billion times more powerful than those of today!

A likely path, clearly visible in 1997, is the creation of thousands of essentially zero-cost, specialized, system-on-a-chip computers that we call MicroSystems. These one–chip, fully networked systems will be embedded in everything from phones, light switches, and motors to the walls of buildings, where they will serve as eyes and ears for the blind and deaf. Onboard networks will "drive" vehicles that communicate with their counterparts embedded in highways and other vehicles. The only limits will be our ability to interface computers with the physical world—that is, to design the interface between cyberspace and physical space.

Algorithm speeds have improved at the same rate as hardware, measured in operations to carry out a given function or generate and render an artificial scene. This synergistic hardware-software acceleration will further shorten the time that it will take to reach the goal of a fully "cyberized" world.

This chapter's focus may appear conservative because it is based on extrapolations of clearly established trends. It assumes no major discontinuities and

---

*The Semetech (1994) National Semiconductor Roadmap predicts that by 2010, 450 times as many transistors will reside on a chip than in 1997. This estimate is based on an annual growth in transistors per chip of a factor of 1.6. Only a factor 225, or an annual improvement of 1.16, would be required over the remaining thirty-seven years.

assumes more modest progress than in the last fifty years. It is not based on quantum computing, DNA breakthroughs, or unforeseen inventions. It does assume serendipitous advances in materials and microelectromechanical systems (MEMS) technology.

Past forecasts by one of us (Bell) about software milestones, such as computer speech recognition, tended to be optimistic, but these technologies usually took longer than expected. On the other hand, hardware forecasts have mostly been conservative. For example, in 1975, as head of research and development at Digital Equipment, Bell forecast that a $1,000,000, eight megabyte, time-shared computer system would sell for $8,000 in 1997, and that a single-user, sixty-four kilobyte system such as an organizer or calculator would sell for $100. While these twenty-two-year-old predictions turned out to be true, Bell failed to predict that high-volume manufacturing would further reduce prices and enable sales of one hundred million personal computers per year.

In 1945, MIT Professor Vannevar Bush[4] wrote prophetically about the construction of a hypertext-based library network. He also outlined a speech–to–printing device and head– mounted camera. Charles Babbage was similarly prophetic in the nineteenth century in his description of digital computers. Both Bush and Babbage were, however, rooted in the wrong technologies. Babbage thought in terms of gears, while Bush's Memex, based on dry photography for both storage and retrieval, was completely impractical. Nonetheless, the inevitability and fulfillment of Babbage's and Bush's dreams have finally arrived. The lesson from these stories is that our vision may be clear, but our grasp of future technologies is probably completely wrong.

The evolution of the computer from 1947 to the present is the basis of a model that we will use to forecast computer technology and its uses in the next five decades. We believe that our quest is to get all knowledge and information into cyberspace, indeed, to build the ultimate computer that complements "man."

A view of cyberspace

Cyberspace will be built from three kinds of components (as diagrammed in Figure 1.1)

- **computer platforms and the content they hold,** made of processors, memories, and basic system software;
- **hardware and software interface transducer technology** that connects platforms to people and other physical systems; and
- **networking** technology for computers to communicate with one another.

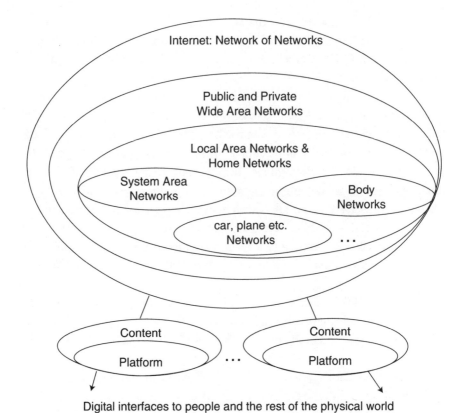

Figure 1.1. Cyberspace consists of a hierarchy of networks that connects computer platforms that process, store, and interface with the cyberspace-user's environments in the physical world.

The functional levels that make up the infrastructure for constructing the cyberspace of Figure 1.1 are given in Table 1.1.

With increased processing, memory, and ability to deal with more of the physical world, computers have evolved to handle more complex data types. The first computers only handled scalars and simple records. With time, they evolved to work with vectors, complex databases, graphical objects for visualization, and time-varying signals used to understand speech. In the next few years, they will deal with images, video, and provide virtual reality (VR)* for synthesis (being in artificially created environments such as an atomic structure, building, or spacecraft) and analysis (recognition).

---

*Virtual Reality is an environment that couples to the human senses: sound, 3-D video, touch, smell, taste, etc.

Table 1.1. Functional levels of the cyberspace infrastructure.

6	**cyberspace-user environments** mapped by geography, interest, and demography for commerce, education, entertainment, communication, work, and information gathering
5	**content,** e.g., intellectual property, consisting of programs, text, databases of all types, graphics, audio, video, etc., that serve the corresponding user environments
4	**applications** for human and other physical world use that enable content creation
3	**hardware and software computing platforms *and* networks**
2	**hardware components,** e.g., microprocessors, disks, transducers, interfacing to the physical world, network links
1	**materials and phenomena,** e.g., silicon, for components

All this information will be networked, indexed, and accessible by almost anyone, anywhere, at any time—24 hours a day, 365 days a year. With more complex data-types, the performance and memory requirement increase, as shown in Table 1.2. Going from text to pictures to video demands performance increases in processing, network speed, and file memory capacity by factors of one hundred and one thousand, respectively. Table 1.2 lists the memory requirements necessary for an individual to record everything he or she has read, heard, and seen during their lifetime. These values vary by a factor of 40,000: from a few gigabytes to one petabyte (PB)—a million gigabytes.

We will still live in towns, but in 2047 we will be residents of many "virtual villages and cities" in the cyberspace sprawl defined by geography, demographics, and intellectual interests.

Table 1.2. Data rates and storage requirements per hour, day, and lifetime for a person to record all the text they've read, all the speech they've heard, and all the video they've seen.

Data type	data rate (bytes per second)	storage needed per hour and day	storage needed in a lifetime
read text, few pictures	50	200 KB; 2–10 MB	60–300 GB
speech text @120 wpm	12	43 K; 0.5 MB	15 GB
speech (compressed)	1,000	3.6 MB; 40 MB	1.2 TB
video (compressed)	500,000	2 GB; 20 GB	1 PB

Multiple languages are a barrier to communication, and much of the world's population is illiterate. Video and music, including gestures, are, however, universal languages easily understood by all. Thus, the coupling of images, music, and video with computer translation of speech may become a new, universal form of communication.

Technological trends of the past decade allow us to project advances that will significantly change society. The PC has made computing affordable for much of the industrial world, and it is rapidly becoming accessible to the rest of the world. The Internet has made networking useful, and it will become ubiquitous as telephones and television become "network"-ready. Consumer-electronics companies are making digital video authoring affordable and useful. By 2047, people will no longer be just viewers and simple communicators. Instead, we'll all be able to *create* and *manage* as well as *consume* intellectual property. We will become symbiotic with our networked computers for home, education, government, health care, and work, just as the industrial revolution was symbiotic with the steam engine and later with electricity and fossil fuels.

Let's examine the three cyberspace building blocks: platforms, hardware and software cyberization interfaces, and networks.

Computer platforms: The computer and transistor revolution

Two forces drive the evolution of computer technology: the discovery of new materials and phenomena and advances in fabrication technology. These advances enable new architectures and new applications. Each advance touches a wider audience, raises aspirations for the next evolutionary step, and stimulates the discovery of new applications that drive the next innovative cycle.

Hierarchies of logical and physical computers: many from one and one from many

One essential aspect of computers is that they are universal machines. Starting from a basic hardware interpreter, "virtual computers" can be built on top of a single computer in a hierarchical fashion to create more complex, higher-level computers. A system of arbitrary complexity can thus be built in a fully layered fashion. The usual levels are as follows. First a micromachine implements an instruction-set architecture (ISA). Above this is layered a software operating system to virtualize the processors and devices. Programming languages and other software tools further raise the level of abstraction. Applications like word processors, spreadsheets, database managers, and multimedia editing systems convert the systems to tools directly usable by content authors. These authors are the ones who create the real value in cyberspace: the analysis and literature, art and music, movies, the web sites, and the new forms of intellectual property emerging on the Internet.

It is improbable that the homely computer, built as a simple processor-memory structure, will change. It is most likely to continue on its evolutionary path with only slightly more parallelism, measured by the number of operations that can be carried out per instruction. It is quite clear that one major evolutionary path will be the multitude of nearly zero-cost, MicroSystem (system-on-a-chip) computers customized to particular applications.

Since one computer can simulate one or more computers, multiprogramming is possible, where one computer provides many computers to be used by one or more persons (timesharing) doing one or more independent things via independent processes. Timesharing many users on one computer was important when computers were very expensive. Today, people only share a computer if that computer has some information that all the users want to access.

The multicomputer is the opposite of a time-shared machine. Rather than many people per computer, a multicomputer has many computers per user. Physical computers can be linked to behave as a single system far more powerful than any single computer.

Two forces drive us to build multicomputers: processing and storage demands for database servers, web servers, and virtual reality systems exceed the capacity of a single computer; and at the same time, the price of individual computers has declined to the point that even a modest corporate budget can afford a dozen computers. These computers may be networked to form a distributed system. Distributed operating systems using high-performance, low-latency system area networks (SANs) can transform a collection of independent computers into a scalable *cluster* that can perform large computational and information-serving tasks. These clusters can use the spare processing and storage capacity of the nodes to provide a degree of fault tolerance. Clusters then become the server nodes of the distributed, worldwide "intranets," all of which interconnect to form the Internet.

The commodity computer nodes will be the cluster building blocks, which we will call *CyberBricks*.[8] By 2010, Semetech predicts the existence of Cyber-Bricks with memories of thirty gigabytes, made from eight-gigabyte memory chips with processing speeds of fifteen giga-instructions per second.[16]

Consequently, massive computing power will come via scalable clusters of CyberBricks. In 1997, the largest scalable clusters contain hundreds of computers. Such clusters are used for both commercial database and transaction processing and for scientific computation. Meanwhile, large-scale multiprocessors that maintain a coherent shared memory seem limited to a few tens of processors, and they have very high unit costs. For forty years, researchers have attempted to build scalable, shared-memory multiprocessors with over fifty processors, but this goal is still elusive because the price and performance have been disappointing. Given the low cost of single-chip or single-substrate computers, it appears that large-scale multiprocessors will find it difficult to compete with clusters built from CyberBricks.

Semiconductors: Computers in all shapes and sizes

While many developments have permitted the computer to evolve rapidly, the most important gains have been made in semiconductor circuit density increases and storage density in magnetics, measured in bits stored per square inch. In 1997, these technologies provide an annual 1.6-fold increase. Due to fixed costs in packaging and distribution, prices of fully configured systems improve more slowly, typically twenty percent per year. At this rate, the cost of computers similar to those commonly used today will be one-tenth of their current prices in ten years.

Density increases enable chips to operate faster and cost less because:

- The smaller everything gets, approaching the size of an electron, the faster the system behaves.
- Miniaturized circuits produced in a batch process tend to cost very little once the factory is in place. The price of a semiconductor factory appears to double with each generation (three years). Still, the cost per transistor declines with new generations because volumes are so enormous.

Figure 1.2 shows how the various processing and memory technologies could evolve over the next fifty years. The semiconductor industry makes the analogy that if cars evolved at the rate of semiconductors, today we would all be driving Rolls Royces that go a million miles an hour and cost twenty-five cents. The difference here is that computing technology operates in accordance with Maxwell's equations defining electromagnetic systems, while most of the physical world operates according to Newton's laws defining the movement of objects with mass.

In 1958, when the integrated circuit (IC) was invented, until about 1972, the number of transistors per chip doubled each year. In 1972, the number began doubling only every year and a half, or increasing at sixty percent per year, resulting in improvement by a factor of one hundred each decade. Con-

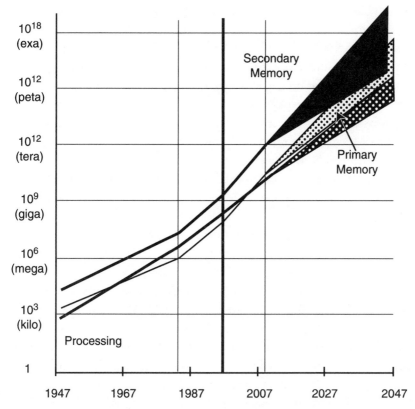

Figure 1.2. Evolution of computer processing speed in instructions per second and primary and secondary memory size in bytes from 1947 to the present, with a surprise-free projection to 2047. Each division represents three orders of magnitude and occurs in roughly fifteen–year steps.

sequently, every three years semiconductor memory capacities have increased fourfold. This phenomenon is known as Moore's Law, after Intel's Founder and Chairman, Gordon Moore, who first observed and posited it.

Moore's Law is nicely illustrated by the number of bits per chip of dynamic random-access memory (DRAM) and the year in which each type of chip was first introduced: 1K (1972), 4K (1975), 16K (1978), . . . 64 M (1996). This trend is likely to continue until 2010. The National Semiconductor Roadmap[16] calls for 256 Mbits or 32 megabytes next year, 128 megabytes in 2001, and 8 gigaBytes in 2010!

The memory hierarchy

Semiconductor memories are a key part of the memory hierarchy because they match processor speeds. A processor's small, fast registers hold a program's current data and operate at processor speeds. A processor's larger, slower cache memory built from static RAM (SRAM) holds recently-used programs and data that come from the large, slow primary memory DRAMs. Magnetic disks with millisecond access times form the secondary memory that holds files and databases. Electro-optical disks and magnetic tape with second and minute access times are used for backup and archives, which form the tertiary memory. The memory hierarchy exploits the fact that recently-used information is likely to be accessed again in the near future, and that a block or record is brought into primary memory from secondary memory is likely to have additional information that will be accessed soon.

Note that each successively lower level in this technological hierarchy is characterized by slower access times and more than an order of magnitude lower cost per bit stored. It is essential that each given memory type improve over time, or else it will be eliminated from the hierarchy.

Just as increasing transistor density has improved the storage capacity of semiconductor memory chips, increasing areal density, the amount of information that can be stored per unit area, has directly affected the total storage capacity of disk systems. IBM's 1957 disk file, the RAMAC 350, recorded about one hundred bits along the circumference of each track, and each track was separated by 0.1 inch, giving an areal density of one thousand bits per square inch. In early 1990, IBM announced that one of its laboratories had stored one billion bits in one square inch, and they shipped a product with this capacity in 1996. This technology progression of six orders of magnitude in thirty-three years amounts to a density increase at a rate of over fifty percent a year.

Increases in storage density have led to magnetic storage systems that are not only cheaper to purchase but also cheaper to own, primarily because the density increases have markedly reduced physical volume. $5^{1}/_{4}''$ and $3^{1}/_{2}''$ drives can be installed in a workstation; the smaller disks store much more, cost much less, are much faster and more reliable, and use much less power than their ancestors. Without such high-density disks, the workstation environment would be impossible.

In 1992, electro-optical disk technologies provided a gigabyte of disk memory at the cost of a compact audio disc, making it economically feasible for PC or workstation users to have roughly four hundred thousand pages of pure text or ten thousand pages of pure image data instantly available. Similarly, advances in video compression using hundreds of millions of operations per second permit VHS-quality video to be stored on a CD. By the year 2000, one CD will hold 20 gigabytes, and by 2047 we might expect this to grow to 20 terabytes.

Connecting to the physical world

Basic hardware and generic transducer-software technology, coupled with networking, governs the new kinds of computers and their applications, as shown in Table 1.3. Paper can be described as a special case because of its tremendous versatility for memory, processing, human interface, and networking. Paper was civilization's first computer.

The big transitions will come with the change in user interface from windows, icons, mouse, and pull-down menus (WIMP) to speech. In addition to speech, camera input of gestures or eye movements could enhance the user interface. In the long term, visual and spatial image input from sonar, radar, and global position sensing (GPS) with a worldwide exact time base coupled with radio data links will open up new portability and mobility applications. These include robots, robotic vehicles, autonomous appliances, and applications where the exact location of objects is required.

Speech synthesis was first used for reading to the blind and for automated telephone response in the mid 1970s. Now speech understanding systems are used for limited domains such as medical-report generation, and a useful speech typewriter is foreseen by the end of the century. Furthermore, many predict automatic natural language translation systems that take speech input in one language and translate it into another by 2010.

The use of the many forms of video is likely to parallel speech, from graphics and the synthesis of virtual scenes and sets for desktop video productions taking place at synthesized locations, to analysis of spaces and objects in dynamic scenes. Computers that can "see" and operate in real time will enable surveillance with personal identification, identification of physical objects in space for mapping and virtual reality, robotic and other vehicular navigation, and artificial vision.

Paper, the first stored-program computer . . . where does it go?

Having most information processing in cyberspace implies the obsolescence of paper for storing and transmitting money, stock, legal contracts, books, catalogs, newspapers, music manuscripts, and reports. Paper's staying power is impressive even though it is uneconomical compared with magnetic media, but within fifty years, the cost, density, and inability to search its contents quickly or to present multimedia, will force paper's demise for those uses requiring storage, processing, or transmission of data. High resolution, high contrast, rugged, low-cost, portable, variable sized displays have the potential

Table 1.3. Interface technologies and their applications.

Interface (Transducer)	Application
large, high-quality portable displays	book, catalog, directory, newspaper, report substitution and the elimination of most common uses of paper; portability, permanency, and very low power are required for massive change!
personal ID	security
speech	input to telephones, PC, network computer, telecomputer (telephone plus computer), and tv computer; useful personal organizers and assistants; appliance and home control, including lighting, heating, security; personal companions that converse and attend to various needs
synthetic video	presentations and entertainment with completely arbitrary synthesized scenes, including "computed people"
global position sensing (GPS); exact time base	"where are you, where am I?" devices; dead-reckoning navigation; monitoring lost persons and things; exact time base for trading and time stamps
biomedical sensor/ effectors	monitoring and attendance using body nets, artificial cochlea and retina, etc. and implanted PDAs
images, radar, sonar, laser ranging	room and area monitoring; gesture for control; mobile robots and autonomous vehicles; shopping and delivery; assembly; taking care of artificial vision

to supplant some use of paper, just as e-mail is replacing letters, memos, reports, and voice messaging in many environments. With very low cost "electronic" paper and radio or infrared networks, books, for example, will be able to speak to us and to one another. This is nearly what the World Wide Web offers today with hypertext-linked documents with spoken output. However, paper is likely to be with us forever for "screen dumps," giving portability and a lasting, irreplaceable graphical user interface (GUI). We know of no technology in 1997 to attack paper's broad use!

One can argue that paper (and the notion of the human interpretation of paper-stored programs such as algorithms, contracts [laws and wills], directions, handbooks, maps, recipes, and stories) was our first computer. Paper and its human processors perform the functions of a modern computer, including processing, memory storage hierarchy from temporary to archival, means of transmission including switching via a worldwide physical distribution network, and human interface. Programs and their human interpreters are like the "Harvard" computer architecture, which clearly separated program and data.

In 1997, magnetic tape has a projected lifetime of fifteen years; CDs are estimated to last fifty years provided one can find the reader, and microfilm is projected to last two hundred years (though unfortunately, computers can't read it yet) and acid-free paper over five hundred years.

The potential to reduce the use of paper introduces a significant problem:

> How are we going to ensure accessibility of the information, including the platforms and programs we create in fifty or five hundred years that our ancestors had the luck or good fortune of providing with paper? How are we even going to assure accessibility of today's HTML references over the next five decades?

Networks: A convergence and interoperability among all nets

Metcalfe's Law states that the total value of a network is proportional to the square of the number of subscribers, while the value to a subscriber is proportional to the number of subscribers. The law describes why it is essential that everyone have access to a single network instead of being subscribers on isolated networks.

Many network types are needed to fulfill the dream of cyberspace and the information superhighway. Several important ones are listed in Table 1.4. Figure 1.3 shows the change in bandwidth of two important communication links that are the basis of wide area networks (WANs) and the connections to them. Local area network (LAN) bandwidth has doubled every three years, or increased by a factor of 10 each decade. Ethernet was introduced in the early 1980s and operated at ten megabits per second. It was increased to one hundred Mbps in 1994 and further increased to 1 Gbps in 1997.

Four networks are necessary to fulfill the dream of cyberspace whereby all information services are provided with a single, ubiquitous, digital dial tone:

- long-haul WANs that connect thousands of central switching offices
- local loops connecting central offices to user sites via plain old telephone services (POTS) copper wires
- LANs and home networks to connect platform equipment within a site
- wireless networks for portability and mobility

Table 1.4. Networks and their applications.

Network	Technology	Application
Last mile (home to central office)	CATV, POTS lines, long-term = fiber	carry "one dial tone" to offices and homes for telephone, videophone, TV, web access, monitoring & control of physical plant, telework, telemedicine, tele-education
LAN: Local Area Network	wired	connect platforms within a building
wLAN: wireless local area network	radio & infrared confined to small areas	portable PC, PDA, phone, videophone, ubiquitous office and home accessories, appliances, health-care monitors, gateway to BAN;
HAN: home net (within homes)	wire, infrared, radio	functionally identical to a LAN
System x Network	wired	interconnection of the platforms of system x, such as an airplane, appliance, car, copy or production machine, or robot. SANs and BANs are system networks
SAN: System Area Network	standard, fast, low latency	building scalables using commodity PCs and "standard" networks that can scale in size, performance, reliability, and space (rooms, campus, . . . wide-areas)
BAN: Body Net	radio	human on-body net for computation, communication, monitoring, navigation

The bottleneck is the local loop, or last mile, (actually up to four miles). Certainly within five years, the solution to this problem will be clear, incorporating innovations ranging from new fiber and wireless transmission to the use of existing cable TV and POTS. In the short term (ten to twenty-five years) installed copper wire pairs can eventually carry data at 5–20 Mbps that can encode high-resolution video. Telephone carriers are trying various digital-subscriber loop technologies to relieve the bottleneck. Cable TV that uses each 6 MHz TV channel to carry up to thirty megabits per second is also being tested and deployed. Both are directed at being information providers. By 2047, fiber that carries several gigabits per optical wave length will most likely

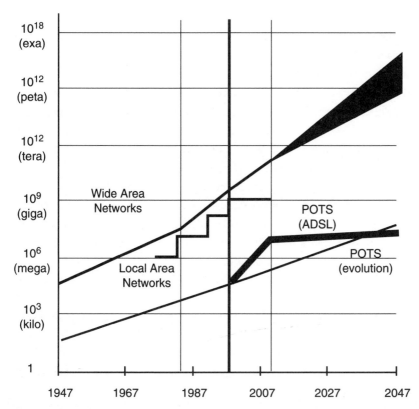

Figure 1.3. Evolution of wide area network, local area network, and plain old telephone service (POTS) bandwidths in bits per second from 1947 to the present, and a projection to 2047.

come to most homes to deliver arbitrarily high bandwidths. One cannot begin to imagine applications that utilize such bandwidths.

Once the home is reached, home networks are needed that are virtually identical to commercial LANs, but easier and cheaper to install and maintain. Within a home, the ideal solution is for existing telephony wiring to carry voice, video, and data. Telephony wiring can carry several megabits per second, but it is unlikely to be able to carry the high bandwidths that high definition TV needs.

LANs and long haul networks are deregulated, while local loops are monopolistic and regulated. By 2047 deregulation will be complete, and the local loop will catch up with its two radical LAN and WAN siblings.

The short-term prospects of "one dial tone" that can access arbitrary subscribers or data sources for voice, video, and data before 2010 are not bright.[2] Telephony's voice channels carry at most 64 Kbps and television is evolving to require 5 Mbps, or a factor of one hundred. Similarly, data files are growing from the several hundred kilobytes for an hour or so of text material that one might read to tens of megabytes of text with pictures to two gigabytes for an hour of high-quality video.

By 2047 we would hope for a "one dial tone," or single service, whereby the bits are interchangeable and can be used for telephony, videotelephony, television, web access, security, home and energy management, and other digital services. Or will there still be the two or three separate networks that we have today for telephony, television, data, and other services?

Wireless technology offers the potential to completely change the communications infrastructure. Therefore, a significant policy question arises concerning how wireless bandwidth will be allocated and potentially *reallocated* in the future. Wireless networking would allow many applications including truly portable and mobile computing, use within buildings for local and home networks, robotics, and, when used with GPS, to identify the location of a platform.

Various authors have proposed a reallocation of the radio spectrum so that fixed devices such as television sets would be wired so that telephony, videotelephony, and data platforms could be mobile.

Existing radio frequency bands capable of carrying 5+ bits per hertz could provide capacities of: 0.5Gbps (806–832 Mhz); 2.5 Gbps (<5Ghz); 1.8 Gbps (5150–5875 Mhz); and 50 Gbps (27.5–64 GHz). The actual capacity depends on the geographical cell size that enables space-sharing of a given channel that is interconnected via terrestrial cabling. Cell size depends on power, terrain, weather, and antennae location (including satellites). For example, the personal handiphone system (PHS) recently deployed in Japan can communicate at a radius of 100–300 meters with each cell carrying 268 voice channels in the allocated 1895 to 1918.1 MHz band. Digital encoding would switch about one thousand 8 Kbps connections—enough for Dick Tracy's low-resolution wrist videophone.

The following section describes potential new platforms using the computers, interface, and network technology described above.

Future platforms, their interfaces, and supporting networks

A theory of computer-class formation posited by Bell in 1975,[1] based on Moore's Law, states that computer families follow one of three distinct paths over time:

1. **evolution** of a class along a constant, or slightly lower price and increasing performance (and functionality) timeline. This path is the result of a fixed-cost infrastructure of suppliers and customers who benefit by having increased performance or other capabilities to track growth needs. More power allows computers to address and prototype new applications.
2. **establishment of new lower-priced classes** when cost can be reduced by a factor of ten. Since price for a given function declines by about twenty percent annually, a new class forms about every ten years. The class is characterized by new hardware and software suppliers and a new style of use or new applications for new and existing users.
3. **commoditization into appliances and other devices** whereby functions such as speech recognition, filing, printing, and display are incorporated into other devices such as watches, talking and listening calculators and telephones, cameras with special graphical-effects creation, and pictures that interact visually and tell stories.

This theory accounted for the emergence of minicomputers in the 1970s costing one hundred thousand dollars, or significantly less than the original million-dollar mainframes introduced in 1951; twenty-thousand-dollar workstations and two-thousand-dollar personal computers in the 1980s; several-hundred-dollar personal organizers, and ten-to-one-hundred-dollar pocket telephone-book dialers and book-substitute devices such as electronic dictionaries. It also accounts for the emergence of embedded and low-cost game computers using worldwide consumer content and distribution networks.

Most of us associated with computing use the word "revolution"* to describe something new, such as the microprocessor, the PC, or the personal digital assistant (PDA), because they represent a discontinuity. However, since the invention of the integrated circuit thirty years ago, progress in these technologies has actually been evolutionary, albeit so rapid as to look like a constant series of revolutions. The computers are all of the same species. They are all based on the basic circuit and memory technologies that process and store information. New developments of sensors and effectors (i.e., transducers) that interface to other real-world systems will determine how useful computers can be to process, control, store, and switch information. And finally, in the generation we are entering, global networking will determine the formation of new classes of computers. *Without all three components* (lower-cost computer platforms, interfaces to the physical world and users, and networks)

---

*A revolution should be a significant "leap" that produces an even more significant benefit.

today's computers would be merely scaled-down, stand-alone mainframes that consumed tiny cards and produced much paper.

New classes have formed every ten to fifteen years! Table 1.5 lists past computer classes and those that are likely to form based on platforms, interfaces, and networks. EDSAC (1949), the first useful computer, had just paper tape and a slow printer. UNIVAC (1951), the first commercial computer, was fed with cards and used magnetic tape and drums for storage. IBM evolved mainframes with the System /360 (1964) to be controlled with a batch operating system and eventually to be timeshared. Timeshared computers were controlled with keyboards of alphanumeric displays. The first minicomputers (1965) were built to be embedded into other systems for control, switching, or some other function before evolving into a downsized department "mainframe." The first personal computers (1977–1981) were controlled by single-user operating systems and command languages. PCs and workstations evolved into the WIMP interface previously described. More importantly, workstations required local area networks for intercommunication and file sharing that was inherent in a single, large timeshared computer. The first World Wide Web terminals were just PCs running browser software (1993) that accessed a global network. In 1997, various types of low-cost web access terminals, including hybrid television and telephone-based terminals, have been introduced using the World Wide Web client-server architecture.

MicroSystems: Systems-on-a-chip

The inevitability of complete computer systems-on-a-chip will create a new *MicroSystems* industry.* By 2002 we expect a PC-on-a-chip with at least 32 MB of RAM video and audio I/O, built-in speech recognition, and industry standard buses for mass storage, LAN, and communication. Technological advances will stimulate a new industry for building applications-specific computers that require partnerships among system customers, chip fabricators, ECAD suppliers, intellectual property (IP) owners, and systems builders.

The volume of this new MicroSystem industry will be huge—producing at least two orders of magnitude more units than the PC industry. For every PC, there will be thousands of other kinds of systems built around a single-chip computer architecture with its interconnection bus on chip, complete with processor, memory hierarchy, I/O (including speech), firmware, and platform software. With more powerful processors, firmware will replace hardware.

---

*Thirty-six ECAD, computer, and semiconductor firms announced an "alliance" to facilitate building systems-on-a-chip on September 4, 1996.

Table 1.5. New computer classes and their enabling components.

Generation	Platform (logic, memories, O/S)	User interface and control	Network infrastructure
The beginning (direct and batch use) (1951)	the computer, vacuum tube, transistor, core, drum and mag tape	card, paper tape direct control evolving to batch O/S	none originally— computer was stand-alone
Interactive time-sharing via commands; mini-computers (1965)	integrated circuit (IC), disk, minicomputer; multiprogramming	glass teletype and glass keypunch, command language control	POTS using modem, and proprietary nets using WAN
Distributed PCs and workstations (1981)	microprocessor PCs and workstations, floppy, small disk, dist'd O/S	WIMP (windows, icons, mouse, pull-down menus)	WAN, LAN
World Wide Web access via PCs and workstations (1994)	Evolutionary PCs and workstations, servers everywhere, Web O/S	Browser	fiber optics backbone, www, http
Web computers: network-, tele-, TV-computers (1998)	client software from server using JAVA, Active X, etc.	telephone, simple videophone, television access to the web	xSDL for POTS or cable access for high-speed data; 3 separate networks
SNAP: scalable network and platforms (1998)	PC uni- or multi-processor commodity platform	server provisioning	SAN (system area network) for clusters
One info dial tone: phone, video-phone, TV, and data (2010)	Video-capable devices of all types;	video as a primary data type	Single high-speed network access; home net
Do what I say (2001) speech controlled computers	embedded in PCs, handheld devices, phone, PDA, other objects	speech	IR and radio LANs for network access

Table 1.5. Continued.

Generation	Platform (logic, memories, O/S)	User interface and control	Network infrastructure
Embedding of speech and vision functions (2020)	$1–10 of chip area for: books, pictures, papers that identify themselves		Body net, home net, other nets
Anticipatory by "observing" user behavior (2020)	room monitoring, gesture	vision, gesture control	Home net
Body net: vision, hearing, monitoring, control, comm., location (2025)	artificial retina, cochlea, glasses for display	implanted sensors and effectors for virtually every part of a body	Body network, gateway to local IR or radio nets everywhere
Robots for home, office, and factory	general purpose robot; appliances become robots	radar, sonar, vision, mobility, arms, hands	IR and radio LAN for home and local areas

The MicroSystem industry will consist of:

- customers building MicroSystems for embedded applications like automobiles, room- and person-monitoring, PC radio, PDAs, telephones, Internet TV boxes, videophones, smart refrigerators
- about a dozen firms that manufacture MicroSystems
- custom design companies that supply "core" IP and take responsibility for the systems
- existing computer system companies that have large software investments tied to particular architectures and software
- IP companies that supply designs and are paid royalties:
  - ECAD companies that synthesize logic and provide design services (e.g. Cadence, Synopsis)
  - circuit wizards who design fast or low-power memories (e.g., VLSI Libraries), analog for audio (also a DSP application), radio and TV tuners, radios, GPS, and microelectromechanical systems (MEMS)
  - varieties of processors from traditional RISC to DSP and multimedia
  - computer-related applications that require much software and algorithm understanding such as communications protocols and MPEG

- proprietary interface companies like RAMbus developing proprietary circuits and signaling standards (old style IP)

Like previous computer generations stemming from Moore's Law, a MicroSystem will most likely have a common architecture consisting of instruction set architecture (ISA) such as the 80xx, MIPS, or ARM; a physical or bus interconnect that is wholly on the chip and used to interconnect processor memory and a variety of I/O interfaces (disk, ethernet, audio, etc.); and software to support real-time and end-use applications. As in the past, common architectures are essential to support the myriad of new chips economically.

Will this new industry be just an evolution of custom microcontroller and microprocessor suppliers, or a new structure like the one that created the minicomputer, PC, and workstation systems industries? Will computer companies make the transition to MicroSystem companies or will they just be IP players? Who will be the MicroSystem companies? What's the role for software companies?

Web computers

The World Wide Web, using Internet, has stimulated other computer classes to emerge, including network computers for corporate users, telecomputers, and television computers that are attached to phones and television sets. These near-term computers use existing networks and interfaces to enhance the capability of telephone and television. In the longer term, they will be integrated with all communications devices, including mobile computers and phones.

By building Web computers into telephones, TV set tops and TV sets (e.g., WebTV), and TV-connected games, much of the world will have instantaneous access to the Web without the complexity associated with managing personal computers that limit use.

Scalable computers replace nonscalable multiprocessor servers

Large-scale systems will be built that consist of clusters of low-cost, commodity, multiprocessor computers that communicate with one another through a fast, system area network (SAN). Clusters enable scalability to thousands of nodes. A cluster can operate as a single system for database and online transaction processor (OLTP) applications. The cluster can exploit the parallelism implicit in serving multiple simultaneous users or in processing large queries involving many storage devices.

Clusters will replace mainframes and minicomputer servers built as large multiprocessors with dozens of processors that share a common, high-speed bus.* Personal computers with only one to four processors are the most cost-effective nodes. They are dramatically less expensive than mainframes, yet scalable in size, performance, location, and reliability. In 1996[8] a PC cluster of several dozen nodes can perform a billion transactions per day. This is more transaction throughput than can be achieved on the largest mainframe cluster.

One need for scalability comes from serving World Wide Web information, because Web traffic and the number of users doubles annually. Future Web servers will have to deliver more complex data, voice, and video as subscriber expectations increase.

It's unlikely that clusters that are no more than a collection of loosely connected computers will be a useful base for technical computing because these problems require substantial communication among the computers for each calculation. Exploiting the underlying parallelism of multi-computers is a challenge that has escaped computer science and applications developers for decades, despite billions of dollars of government funding. More than likely, for the foreseeable future scientific computing will be performed on computers that evolve from the highly-specialized, Cray-style, multiple vector–processor architecture with shared memory.

Useful, self-maintaining computers versus users as system managers

As the computer evolves to become a useful appliance, we must remedy today's software paradox: more software provides more functions to save time, but its increasing the complexity and maintenance costs cause time to be lost. One of two paths may be followed: far greater complexity or simplicity. The path of complexity will yield specialized functional computers and components that know how to install and maintain themselves; this means that once a computer or a component such as a telephone, videophone, or printer arrives in an environment, such as a room, it must operate with other components reliably and harmoniously.

Choosing the path of simplicity, on the other hand, will result in dynamically loading software from central servers to small, diskless computers such as a web terminal.

Telepresence for work is the long-term "killer" application

"Telepresence" means being there while being here at possibly some other time. Thus, telepresence technology provides for both space and time shifting

---

*A bus is a collection of wires used as a switch that allows processor, memory, and input-output components to communicate with one another.

by allowing a user to communicate with other users via text, graphics, voice, video, and shared-program operation. Communication may be synchronous with a meeting or event, or it may be asynchronous as in voice mail or electronic mail. Computers also provide for time compression, since prior multimedia events can be "played back" in nonlinear fashion at rates that match the viewer's interest.

Telepresence can be for work, entertainment, education, plain communication that goes beyond telephony, videotelephony, mail, and chat. Telepresence for work is most likely to have been the "killer app" when we look back in the year 2047. The question is, can mechanisms be invented that will make telepresence nearly as good as, or even better than, presence?

Bell characterized telepresence in four dimensions:[10]

- mechanism: synchronous, e.g., phone, chat, videophone distributed application sharing; and asynchronous such as voice mail, electronic mail, video mail, web access to servers via direct use and agents. Various channels include program transfer and shared control, phone, videophone, chat windows, and blackboards.
- group size & structure: one-to-one and small group meetings, one-to-many presentation events
- purpose: meetings and broadcast events to interview, problem-solve, sell, present, educate, operate a remote system
- work type segmented by professional discipline: engineering, finance, medicine, science, etc.

Given the modest growth in teleconferencing and the past failures of videophones, one might be skeptical of my prediction that telepresence will be a "killer app." Yet we are quite certain that within a decade, users will spend at least one-fourth of their time, not including the time they access static Web information, being telepresent. This is based on the cost of time, travel, and Web access terminals coupled with the ubiquity of built-in, no-extra-cost voice and video that can utilize POTS. In 1997 video encoding standards and products using POTS that are compatible with telephones have just been introduced. The final telepresence inhibitor, lack of a critical mass of common platforms, explained by Metcalfe's Law, will be almost entirely eliminated within a few years. Until videotelephony becomes ubiquitous, so that everyone can communicate freely, it will have little value.

Computers, devices, and appliances that understand speech

In 1960, after one year of working on speech research, one of us (Bell) decided to work on building computers because he predicted that it would take twenty years before any useful progress could be made. Progress has been almost two times slower than this prediction. In 1997, speech input is used for interface control and context-sensitive report generation, although speech dictation systems were available in 1990.

We believe that we can optimistically assume that by 2010, speech input and output will be ubiquitous and available for every system that has electronics, including cars, computers, household appliances, radios, phones, television, toys, watches, and home or office security and environment controls such as heating and lighting.

Video: Synthesis, analysis, and understanding

The ability to synthesize realistic video in real time is the next human-interface barrier. This will allow entire plays and movies to be synthetically generated. It will also allow a face-to-face Turing between a computer synthesized image and a person. It would seem unlikely that a computer posing as a person will be able to interact visually with a person without detection within fifty years.[11]

To illustrate the possible evolution of a constant cost, increasing-performance computer, we can look to the time when it will be possible to "render and view" a movie at film resolution (approx. 20 Mpixels), in real time. Using 1994 SUN computers,* each high resolution frame of the motion picture *Toy Story* took seven hours to compute on a 165-million-instruction-per-second (Mips) processor. Real-time rendering would require a 605,000-fold speedup (7 hours/frame × 3600 seconds/hour × 24 frames/second). Such capacity would require 100 million Mips (or 100 Teraops), and a computer of this speed will likely not be available until about 2030. However, rendering video for high-definition television would require only 6 Teraops, which will probably be attained six years earlier. Image-synthesis algorithms speed up improvements and are almost certain to be equal to hardware improvements, so that only half the projected time will be required, the goal being reached by 2010. Similarly, the use of special-purpose rendering hardware can reduce the cost to PC price levels, provided there is a consumer desktop market, e.g., games. In fact, the first products using Microsoft's Talisman rendering architecture promise to generate high-resolution video of natural scenes by 1998, enabling the desktop production of television programs, not merely from systems that store, manipulate, and play back video.

---

*The entire movie required two hundred computers that ran two years (0.8 million hours) at a combined rate of 33 Gips.

Robots enabled by computers that see and know where they are

The assimilation of real-world data of every form, including video, global position, and radar, enables new computers, including home, office and industrial robots. Radio networks and GPS opens up more possibilities by having objects that know where they are and can report their state and that are not just adaptations of cellular phones. Nothing—from keys to cars to people—need be lost.

Can useful, general-purpose robots that work with everyday home or work appliances and tools such as dishwashers, brooms, vacuum cleaners, stoves, copiers, filing cabinets, construction tools and equipment, and office supply rooms be built in this short time? Or will we simply make each specific appliance that actually does the work more helpful? We will see a combination of the two approaches? Initially, specialized but compatible appliances and tools will be built, followed by robots that can carry out a wide variety of activities.

Body Nets—Interconnecting all the computers that we carry

A wide range of prosthetic devices are being designed, deployed, and researched including artificial eyes.[9] It is unclear when the computer will interface with humans biologically with implants in the visual cortex for artificial vision, rather than the superficial, mechanical ways they do now.

The range of applications can vary from personal health care, control, assistance, and enhancement of human functions to security and communication. Wearable computers are built today to help workers operate in complex physical and logical spaces such as an airplane or a wiring closet.

We can even imagine building the ultimate personal assistant consisting of "on body" computers that can record, index, and retrieve everything we've read, heard, and seen. In addition to dealing with information, the body-networked monitoring computer could act as a "guardian angel."

The World Wide Web offers the most potential for change at all levels of health care through standardization and universal access, including: online information; linking human- and machine-created information, medical equipment, and body-networked computers; caring for people by communicating with them; and onboard monitoring that would warn of an event such as an impending heart attack.

Computers disappear to become components for everything

Within five years, a new MicroSystems industry will emerge. It will be based on intellectual property that designs highly specialized nearly zero-cost systems-on-a-chip. Semiconductor firms will build the one-chip computers that have been specified by customers such as "smart appliance" manufacturers and designed by the intellectual-property computer companies. These one-chip, fully-networked systems will be available to be customized so that they may be used everywhere.

In 2047, the computer population is likely to be one hundred thousand times larger as they infiltrate everything! The challenges of ubiquity through embedding into every object can positively influence the computer's direction towards higher human productivity and enjoyment.

Some examples of objects into which computers will be embedded are appliances, books, pictures, and toys that communicate with one another and with us by voice, vision, and action in the context of their function. One can imagine that a smart and helpful "computerized" kitchen would be a dietitian, food manager (shop and control inventory), cook, server—and cleanup crew. If a device can be cyberized, it will.

On predictions . . . and what could go wrong

Mis-predictions are legend: in 1943 Thomas Watson Sr. predicted that only five computers would be needed for the entire country; in 1977, Ken Olsen, former CEO of Digital, predicted that there would be no use for home computers. In July 1995, Bob Lucky, vice president of Bellcore, stated "if we couldn't predict the Web, what good are we?"

The 1962 special issue of the IRE Proceedings ventured predictions for the next 50 years. Since 2010 is the year when semiconductor density improvement is predicted to begin to decline or even to end, we can observe the progress needed to meet these early predictions.

Camras predicted a small, nonmechanical, ubiquitous memory pack that would hold 10^{20} bits. This still appears unattainable even in 2047 without some new material. He hypothesized that telephony would be used to update and communicate among the packs. He predicted home shopping, home education, and electronic payments using individual memory packs. He also predicted that consumable everyday items like food, drugs, and fuel would be delivered in pipelines in suspension.

Harry F. Olson, who headed speech research at RCA's Sarnoff Labs, predicted, "There appears to be no doubt that these [speech] systems will be developed and commercialized because all significant steps have been made toward this goal." Three systems he described were speech to text and speech in one language to either written or spoken speech in another language:

- Microphone → analyzer → code → typer → pages
- Microphone → analyzer → code → translator → code → typer → pages
- Microphone → analyzer → code → translator → code → synthesizer → output speech.

Simon Ramo, Founder of TRW, predicted a national network and a system of selective databases that could be accessed by scholars, lawyers, and health care consumers and providers. The simulation he prophesied for engineering design has occurred, as well as reservation and electronic-payment systems.

One 1969 report for the Naval Supply Command,[3] using the Delphi Panel of Experts, forecast the following:

- For spoken inputs, a computer will interpret simple sentences by 1975
- Some form of voice input-output will be in common use by 1978 at the latest
- Computers can be taught, thereby growing in utility by 1988
- Personal terminals will simulate activities in functional departments by 1975
- Advances in cores, wire, and thin film will provide large memories with one million words by 1976
- Terabit memories at a price of one million dollars may be possible by 1982
- Card readers will peak at 1500 cards per minute by 1974 and then their use will decline
- Computer architecture will have parallel processing by 1975

Raj Reddy and one of us (Bell) have two near-term (2003) bets: Artificial Intelligence will have had as significant effect on society as the transistor, and a production-model car that drives itself will be available.

Moore is unwilling to make predictions about growth beyond 2010, when various limits will have been reached in both materials that can resolve a bit, and processing. Moore once predicted[12] that packaging and power supply voltages would not change from dual in-line and 5 volts.

In another case, one of us (Bell) wrote about the future[1] yet failed to predict the Internet, which was brought about by the serendipity of research that created a workable client-server architecture due to the standardization around the WWW, HTML, and the Mosaic browser. Predictions about computer performance, structure, and applications were correct.

In predicting, the major question for 2047 is whether the technology flywheel will continue with new useful applications to sustain the investment to find more useful applications.

Acknowledgments

The author is indebted to colleagues at Microsoft, especially the Bay Area Research Center (BARC) researchers, and the writings and ideas of Bill Gates and Nathan Myhrvold. Sheridan Forbes of SGI was helpful with content and form. David Lyon of Cirrus Logic's PCSI division provided information about wireless networks.

References

1. Bell, G. and McNamara, J. *High Tech Ventures: The Guide to Entrepreneurial Success.* Reading, Mass.: Addison-Wesley Publishing, 1991.

2. Bell, G. and Gemmell, J. "On-ramp Prospects for the Information Superhighway Dream." *Communications of the ACM* 39, no. 7 (July 1996): 55–61.

3. Bernstein, G. B. "A 15 Year Forecast of Information Processing Technology." Naval Supply Command Delphi Study, AD681752 (1969).

4. Bush, V. "As We May Think." *Atlantic Monthly,* July 1945. (http://www.isg.sfu.ca/ ~duchier/misc/vbush/vbush.shtml).

5. CNRI, "Vision of the NII: Ten Scenarios." Reston, VA, 1996. See also papers on future networking. (http://www.cnri.reston.va.us/).

6. Cochrane, P. (1996) Many papers on future computers, including their use for caring for the aged (http://www.labs.bt.com/people/cochrap/).

7. Gibson, W. *Neuromancer,* (1984): 4–5.

8. Gray, J. "Scalable Servers." (http://www.research.com/research/barc/), 1996.

9. Dagnelie, G. and Massof, R. W. (eds.) "Towards an Artificial Eye." *IEEE Spectrum* (May 1996): 20–68.

10. Krankel, Karen A. "A Conversation with Gordon Bell," *ACM Interactions* II, no. 4 (1995): 66–79.

11. Kurzweil, R. "The Age of Intelligent Machines." Cambridge: *MIT Press* (1990): 448.

12. Moore, G. Electronics 53, no. 9. (April 17, 1980), 633.

13. Moore, G. "Nanometers and Gigabucks—Moore On Moore's Law." University Video Corporation Distinguished Lecture, 1996. (http://www.uvc.com/).

14. Olson, H. F. "Processing of Sound." *Proceedings of the IRE* (Fiftieth Anniversary Issue, predicting 2012) 50. no. 5 (May 1962): 599–600.

15. Patterson, D. "Microprocessors in 2020." *Scientific American* 273, no. 3. (September 1995): 62–67.

16. Semetech. *The National Semiconductor Roadmap.* Semetech and Semiconductor Industry Association (1994).

VINTON G. CERF

When They're Everywhere

2 | Premise

In 2047, Internet is everywhere. In seventy-four years it has grown from an idea to interconnect heterogeneous packet-communication networks to a world-wide, ubiquitous communication web joining people, businesses, institutions, appliances, and all forms of electronic equipment in a common communication framework. Like electrical power, it is assumed to be available whenever and wherever needed. The little vignette below suggests some of what I believe will be commonplace.

Prologue

Friday, April 12, 2047

Robert was awakened by the warbling of birds outside his fifty-fourth-story window in Taos, New Mexico. They weren't real birds, of course. They were programmed by the house computer and, at Robert's whim, could be drawn from the fauna of every habitat in the world. Today he was hearing kookaburras from Australia. The sun crept over the mountains and as its rays were detected by the sensors built into the windows, the window controllers depolarized to allow a diffuse morning light to enter the room. The window controllers responded to commands from the central computer, which exchanged brief messages from thousands of built-in sensors, controllers, and appliances scattered throughout the house. The sound was generated by small piezoelectric speakers mounted on the windowpanes

Robert stretched. "What time is it?" he asked, idly. "It's nearly seven A.M., sir," replied the house computer in a pleasant baritone with a decidedly British accent. Robert's friend Charles had sent him the accent plug-in over the Internet as a surprise birthday present the year before. As detectors noted Robert's weight lift from the bed, the computer shut down the gentle heating that it had supplied and broadcast messages around the house that Robert was up.

The bathtub controller started to fill the tub with the 98°F water that Robert preferred. "Stop the bath, Jeeves, I don't have time for it today." "Yes, sir," replied the house computer, and the bathtub drained itself. "Caffè espresso, please, wheat toast, and orange juice," ordered Robert. Messages flashed to the kitchen, where the kitchen subsystem analyzed the order and signalled the appropriate appliances.

Robert wandered into the bathroom, which turned on its lights when it detected his arrival. "Your sugar level appears to be satisfactory," announced the house computer, having received the urinalysis from the instrumented toilet in the bathroom. Robert was a diabetic whose condition had been corrected with autogenetic therapy, but the house computer had been programmed at his doctor's orders to monitor his condition and to report daily results to his computer-based assistant and to Robert.

"What is on my calendar today, Jeeves?" asked Robert, finishing his ablutions and walking over to the clothes closet. "You have a teleconference at 0805; e-mail correspondence at 0915; a lecture to give at 1000 in New York; then free time until noon, when you are lunching in Los Alamos with Sir Arthur Clowes; tennis at 1430 and a massage; consultation with your financial advisor at 1615; free time again until 1930, when you are scheduled to dine with Randy Gregg here in Taos."

Robert slipped on a shirt, comfortable pair of slacks, and lightweight slippers. Strolling into the kitchen, Robert drained a tumbler of orange juice, then took his coffee to the breakfast table, where the toaster had begun toasting two slices of bread once his presence had been detected in the kitchen.

Robert strapped his personal computer to his wrist and donned a pair of reading glasses. The latter represented the evolutionary descendants of the "heads-up displays" of the previous century. High-resolution images presented themselves at a convenient virtual distance. When inactive, the glasses were merely transparent. Upon activation, they substituted for the CRTs and flat-panel displays of an earlier era. Flat panels were still in use—for example, the door of the microwave oven contained such a display to permit convenient interaction in the kitchen with local, neighborhood, national, and global information resources, as well as local control of the various appliances around the house.

A small, fitted earpiece and a "finger mouse" completed his kit. Robert was amused by the so-called finger mouse because it didn't look anything like the animal it seemed to reference. Nearly eighty years before, a small device about the size of a mouse had been invented by a man named Douglas Engelbart. It was attached by a wire to a computer and was used to signal X-Y locations as a way of "pointing" at the display screen in a way that was meaningful to the program with which one was interacting. The small, thimble-like device on his finger now accomplished a similar objective, but its location was detectable in three dimensions and keyed to the images displayed in his "reading glasses."

The ear piece, finger mouse, display glasses, and wrist communicator were linked to each other by very low-power, 60 GHz radio signals that propagated only a short distance before being absorbed into the oxygen of the atmosphere.

Activating his wrist computer, Robert examined the images now ranged before him within easy virtual reach. Selecting his personal information page with his finger mouse, he watched as that image filled the display area. He selected the "entertainment" heading and then the "restaurants" heading. Scanning the options, the Red Sage caught his eye. He hadn't been there in a while. The microphone in his earpiece caught the sound of his voice and relayed it to his wrist computer.

"Call Randy Gregg, please." "Calling," answered the wrist computer through the earpiece.

"Gregg here," answered the familiar voice of his friend. "Hi Randy, it's Robert calling. I've been thinking about dinner tonight. Have a look at the Red Sage menu." Robert dragged the restaurant icon over to the telephone icon and dropped it. It popped up on Randy's display, and a bright blue cursor marked where Robert was pointing.

"Looks like the chef is getting even more adventurous than I remember," said Randy. "OK, I will plan to meet you there at 1930 hours. Let me know if there is a change in plans."

"No problem. 'Bye for now," said Robert as he ended the call. Activating the voice-mail icon in the Red Sage display page, Robert dictated a brief message, asking the restaurant to confirm reservations both to himself and Randy Gregg. The message joined the hundreds of others that winged their way to and from Robert's wristcomp via low-power radio links to the house computer.

"Nearly time for your conference call," reminded Robert's wristcomp. A teleconference window popped up and filled the display. Munching the last of his toast, Robert washed the morsel down with a final swallow of espresso and headed to his working office with the large picture window. One of the few luxuries he permitted himself, the window was actually a super-high-resolution (and rather expensive) display capable of reproducing at five hundred lines per inch. Removing his reading glasses, Robert sat down in a comfortable chair facing the window and picked up a simple infrared pointing device. The wristcomp, alerted to the change by sensors in the chair and in the reading glasses, vectored its output to the display window. As 8:05 A.M. approached, images of his correspondents began to appear on the display. His own, picked up from a small video camera mounted at eye level, was included.

With a few moments to spare, Robert selected the "news" icon on the display and brought up the *New York Times*. Glancing through his personal edition (news selected by his resident knowledge robot running at the *New York Times* server), Robert updated his watch list to include any articles on implants, then turned to the teleconference at hand.

Future thoughts

One of the more difficult challenges in trying to predict the future of technology is to distinguish between what will be commonplace from what may be merely feasible. That which is feasible may not be economical for any but the most special of circumstances. Most infrastructure evolves and emerges in an incremental fashion. Each increment is, in effect, economically self-supporting on some basis. Complex infrastructure, such as the Internet, does not happen all at once. It develops in steps, each one of which has some economic support (whether from the government, private sector, for-profit or nonprofit). Indeed, it can be a long time between steps. For example, facsimile concepts were around in the mid 1800s but did not form a significant infrastructure until costs per device dropped precipitously and standards were established to achieve universal interoperability over 125 years later. Television was demonstrated in the late 1920s but did not become marketable as a product until the late 1940s and really took off with color television in the 1960s.

The Internet has moved forward in steps as well, first with support from the Advanced Research Projects Agency of the U.S. Defense Department, then through the National Science Foundation and other government agencies such as the Department of Energy and the National Aeronautics and Space Administration. More recently, the expansion of the Internet has been fueled by the telecommunications and software industries, finding enormous interest in the World Wide Web in the business and residential sectors. In 1997, we are seeing rapid development of Internet-based radio, television, and telephony and mixtures of these that result from the programmable nature of the devices that carry these new media. We can thus expect the future of Internet growth to be stimulated by new applications made feasible by reduced cost of programmable devices, which in turn will build infrastructure for more complex and integrated services.

Interoperability is a keystone, if not the keystone, to the creation of infrastructure. Telephone interworking is fundamental to that system's value, and its existence formed a foundation supporting facsimile, computer communication via modem, as well as conventional voice telephony.

In the case of the Internet, the basic IP layer, however it evolves through the year 2047, will still be a key element in the utility of that system. The common address space provided by that layer will be crucial. Even now, we can see that bindings and mappings from other address spaces, such as the telephone numbering plan, will be needed to make it possible for Internet-based and telephony-based systems to interwork. Creation of an extremely large address space (whether flat or hierarchical) will be important because of the large number of terminations that one might anticipate will need to be serviced in fifty years' time. The full 128-bit address space of IP version 6 may well be needed by then, if every light bulb, light switch, power socket, and appliance is on the net, in addition to personal computing and communication devices, online information services, radio and television transmitters and receivers (so-called, even if they no longer go "over the air"!), telephones, and sensors of all kinds.

I had a modest taste of what's ahead in composing this chapter. A part of it was written while I was driving across country from Virginia to Santa Fe, New Mexico. Thanks to an inverter and a cellular telephone, it was possible to keep a laptop humming all the way across the country and to occasionally check in for e-mail exchanges and even look up a few necessary facts on the Internet. The freedom to work virtually independent of location was exhilarating.

Far more self-organization will be needed for such a huge system to function. Dynamic adoption of addresses in the common space and binding of them to more fixed identifiers will be the norm. For example, one's e-mail address may well continue to look something like "vint.cerf@mci.com," but this "handle" will merely be an entry into a directory service that caters to all forms of communication. One will be able to telephone this "address," which will be mapped as needed into a conventional telephone number, an IP address, a voice mail box with its audio response capability, or a pager identifier. Depending on circumstances, attempted communication may be signalled in several different ways. Since one cannot easily enter "vint.cerf@mci.com" into a conventional telephone, it is to be expected that an international telephone numbering equivalent will be created. Perhaps Internet will have its own country code so that numeric "identifiers" will be usable from an ordinary touch-tone telephone. Longer term, of course, one expects telephones to become Internet-capable.

One will be able to specify in simple terms how e-mail, fax messages, pages, telephone calls, and voice mail messages are to be captured, brought to one's attention, and stored. Background processes, or intelligent agents, will interpret these specifications as needed. Directory services keyed to standard identifiers, like e-mail addresses, will be useful for associating other information such as digital signature parameters that can be used to authenticate various transactions.

Just as the term "horseless carriage" fails to fully convey what the automobile has become, such phrases as "Internet telephony" do not and will not convey the richness of communication options that will emerge as various communication devices and appliances become Internet-capable and therefore subject to a variety of forms of interworking.

Statistics

The world's population will be about 11.5 billion by 2047, compared to about 5.8 billion in 1996. Internet will probably achieve penetration rates similar to television and telephony, at least in the parts of the world that have suitable power generation and other technology infrastructure. Indeed, by that time, penetration may exceed that of television, with the use of personal and vehicular devices adding to conventional office and residential units. Instant demand for communication capacity will be satisfied in large measure by a combination of fiber optics and optical switching as well as very broadband radio communication and perhaps infrared links over relatively short distances. Broadcast communication via digital satellite will also play a role, and conventional over-the-air media will carry Internet packets. Conventional television and radio may by that time have become as quaint as crystal radio is today.

If the average penetration of the networking technology reaches thirty percent by 2047, this suggests on the order of three to four billion devices, possibly more if the "ubiquitous computing" appliances predicted by Mark Weiser of Xerox PARC actually proliferate. There might be hundreds of such devices in a residence, vehicle, or office. Moreover, wearable devices could inflate the total even further. Such scales are dramatically more than the present-day telephone network of 660 million terminations, which has already had a material impact on all aspects of the global economy and social structure.

Data rates will have reached the limits of optical fiber technology in the 38 THz range per fiber. End-user data rates will be in the gigabit range and backbone rates in the tens of terabits range. Optical switching will be the norm. At these rates, the flow and congestion control mechanisms of TCP/IP will have had to adapt significantly or will have been supplanted by entirely new methods appropriate to the speed-and-delay regime implied by such high data rates. The speed of light will become the dominant factor in the design of new protocols.

Multiplexing of data streams from end-user devices into the global network will be essential, since most devices will be capable of performing many functions concurrently. Both packet and circuit-like services will be provided over a common channel (which may be optical, radio, or wireline).

Sensor networks

Sensor systems have become an integral part of our world, so much so that we don't even think about them. I predict that an inhabitant from 1997 visiting 1947 would almost certainly get a black eye or broken nose from walking into doors that did not automatically open. One can just imagine, then, what would happen to a visitor from 2047 to our fair decade. Room lights would not automatically turn on upon entry. Car doors would not open at the press of a finger tip to a print-reading device built into the door. Appliances would not respond to spoken commands. Houses would not provide you with an e-mail report on security status while you are away. Chairs would not conform to your shape upon recognizing who you are (perhaps through the ID device you are not wearing in 1997).

Generally, sensor information will become far more integrated into our daily lives than it is today. Global positioning information will be readily available to answer questions like "Where am I?" or "where are other things in relation to me?" In fact, the display glasses in the fictional account that opened this article will certainly be able to ask "where am I?" and get back an answer from the residence computer: "You are in the blue bedroom on the second floor" or "You are in room 5A125" and thus respond to the broadcast question "where are my glasses?" This would be achieved not by putting GPS in the glasses, but simply by allowing the glasses to ask the room, "what room am I in?"

Global positioning system data will be used to locate buildings and geographic points with high accuracy, all keyed to a common, global grid. Regular updating can deal with cataclysmic events such as earthquakes. As buildings are constructed, key GPS locations can be recorded for future use. Real estate records will be far more accurate and more easily searched than at present. The impact of geocentric indexing will be dramatic. Things, people, and events will become related merely by their current proximity or, in the extreme, because they were once nearby—or will be nearby, as in collision detection and avoidance.

The incorporation of sensor data into the normal computing stream will make computers and networks far more "aware" of surroundings and local activity. To the extent that one wants to speculate, the emulation of self-awareness may be quite impressive in the computing world of 2047.

Media integration

With Internet or its successor(s) proliferating dramatically and offering unprecedented data rates, it is predictable that the existing, conventional communications media will find themselves merging in a powerful mixture of functionality.

Internet will not, at first, replace radio, television, telephone, and print media. Instead, it will emulate their functions and interwork with them, augmenting existing capabilities. At the same time, conventional media will begin to carry Internet traffic (in television vertical retrace intervals or in FM sideband, for instance). Eventually, the juxtaposition of these media in the Internet framework will lead to integration and mixing of functionality that would not otherwise be easily achieved.

In the simplest forms, one would be able to initiate a telephone call in the midst of viewing a World Wide Web page, just as one can initiate e-mail today. In fact, it won't take until 2047 for Internet telephony to show up, since it is already happening in small quantities today. Television broadcasts (or cable casts or satellite casts or net casts) will contain Internet content that can be displayed separately. Thus, during a conventional television program, Web pages will be sent that can be examined and interacted with independent of the TV program. Private discussion groups could be formed around particular programs, in real time, taking today's newsgroup discussions one step further. The technology will permit casual creation of multicast communications groups—with obvious applicability to business communication, emergency command and control, and the like.

Convenience is a powerful driving force in consumer electronics. A single device that will allow one to make telephone calls, watch television, surf the Internet, do e-mail, listen to radio, play interactive video/computer games, and handle a variety of other personal computing and communication needs sounds very attractive. The humble laptop is moving rapidly towards that goal.

Individual devices designed to do one thing (e.g., television), if they are also on the Internet, can be subject to management and control from the network. For example, one could use a personal laptop (or personal digital appliance) to select television programs to watch, record, or otherwise process, and convey that information via the Internet to the target television. There is an obvious need for authentication in effecting such applications, or the fifteen-year-old next door will reprogram your appliances while you are away at work or on vacation!

At last, our VCRs will be programmable via the Web! And the clock in the VCR can be automatically reset after a power failure! That's progress!

By embedding so many appliances into the Internet environment, we can anticipate that the power company will want to stop the water heater during peak power demands—one hopes this doesn't lead to microwave oven failure while you are hosting an important dinner party. Perhaps one could program the microwave to negotiate priority for power during such events.

Interposing computing power in the middle of communications also leads to the potential for speech recognition, transcription, translation, and understanding, all of which seem likely to be achieved in various degrees by 2047 if not before. Limited vocabulary, speaker-independent recognition is already fairly reliable and is in use with voice-response units for placing telephone calls, directing calls to appropriate parties, and so on. One can hope that Internet telephony will lead to increasingly useful automatic translations, at least between commonly used languages. One can now emulate some of this functionality either in real time by including a human interpreter in the loop or in delayed fashion as in the translating of business correspondence via e-mail. So for some instances, we can already see what such services could be like, if they could be made automatic and less costly.

Mobile software

Platforms for the support of mobile software will be commonplace. Security problems associated with ingesting and executing such itinerant programs will have been dealt with through digital signatures to authenticate origin and filters and interpreters that control the scope of action of such software. The side effects will be that the rate of accretion of new functionality in Internet-enabled devices will escalate dramatically. We are already seeing some of these effects with readily downloadable software from prominent vendors. The process will become even more automatic. End devices become "smarter" merely as a result of interacting with services on the network.

Many such downloads will be effected on a scheduled basis—for instance, the 2047 tax software will be broadcast via satellite or other Internet multicast segment to computing devices that have been alerted to receive and store the transmission. Since many appliances will be operated under computer control, the 2047 models may well be simply downloads of new software into the 2040 chassis!

Virtual worlds

The virtual reality experiments of the late twentieth century will find fruition in a cornucopia of applications in the twenty-first. Multiparty games will be common. One will be able to visit virtual stores, banks, schools, and government offices and interact either with computer-driven simulacra or, if need be, with real people via video teleconference. The seeds of these capabilities are already apparent, and they will surely evolve in unpredictable ways in the future.

Final note

The two great networks of the twentieth century, the telephone network and the Internet, will be joined by and merge with all the other electronic distribution systems of the twentieth and twenty-first centuries. We will be surrounded by a sea of computing and information, interacting with one another and with intelligent software in ways that might astonish us from our twentieth-century perspective but which we will take as much for granted in the twenty-first as we do doors that open automatically as we step through them.

BOB FRANKSTON

Beyond Limits

3 | Introduction

The first million was easy. Computers have improved by a factor of millions in price, performance, capacity, and capability in their first fifty years.

We've come to expect such improvement. Memory prices, for example, halve every eighteen months (according to Moore's Law), CPU's get faster, and software does even more. Today's desktop computers are far more powerful than the mainframe computers of twenty-five years ago.

Are we running into natural limits?

In the excitement about what we've accomplished we should remember that we have not fulfilled many of the promises of very intelligent machines. If anything, we've come to see the computer as a fancy calculator or word processor and little more. Shouldn't we expect more from these systems? More to the point, why are computers so hard to use?

While we might reach limits on particular technologies, we are far from the limits on what we can do with computers. The pace of change is limited only by our ability to innovate. This pace has been accelerating because the computer itself is our key tool. As we improve computers, we increase our ability to improve them.

As we innovate, we keep changing the nature of the computer. The "computer" itself is a device that performs computations. The next stage shifts the focus from what we can do in the computer to what we can accomplish with it as part of the larger infrastructure. The computer itself will "disappear into the woodwork." Our challenge is to learn how to master this new arena—one in which we are not writing programs but adding intelligence to everything around us. The limit is in our ability to manage complexity. It is a world in which resiliency is more important than perfection. A resilient system is one that can continue to function in the midst of the chaos and failure that are the norm.

As a developer, I'm very concerned with how we evolve computing. The challenges of complexity are overwhelming. When we back up and observe the history of computing, the individual changes fade into the grand forest of innovation. Stepping further back, computing itself is a part of, as opposed to apart from, the evolutionary process of innovation.

If we step too far back we fail to see that the evolution of computing has not been uniform. What we got isn't necessarily what we asked for. But it is in the nature of systems to exploit unexpected advantages.

The history of computers has also been rife with failed promises and frustrated expectations. Yet these tend to be forgotten in the excitement of what we can (almost) do.

Once again, we are at a transition point. (When are we not?) We are leaving the confines of the isolated computer and becoming the infrastructure, an infrastructure of intelligent elements. And we have no idea where it will lead but we can be sure that the pace of change will continue to accelerate.

The first fifty years

Rapid change and innovation

When four-function calculators were first introduced they cost $1000 (in 1997 dollars), and now they are given away free, the cost being covered by the advertisements on the back. Not only does a wristwatch contain a computer, but it plays music and soon may also be a telephone.

The first half century of computers has been a period of rapid advancement in hardware and software design.

This rapid pace was driven by many innovations. Core memory was created to meet the needs of the early computers. Semiconductors were invented separately but were crucial to the ability to create large systems. But even before transistors became widely available, vacuum-tube technology had been advanced beyond anything believed possible in the days of radio.*

Equally important were the improvements in software. Operating systems were created to make efficient use of expensive hardware, and software tools were created to make programming simpler. These innovations used existing hardware. Only after the software was available was the hardware tuned to meet the needs of the software. The improvements in software are characterized by Corbató's law, which states that the number of lines of code is the same, independent of the language used. The more we can leverage programmers with tools that make it easier to express their algorithms, the more productive they are.

Projects that required innovating in too many areas at once were unlikely to succeed. The IBM 360 and the Multics project were notable exceptions and both experienced long delays in delivering on their promises. The lessons of why these projects were so difficult are still relevant today. Fred Brook's *The Mythical Man Month* applies to any complex system, not just a large pride of programmers.

After the success of these first fifty years, are we running into the limits of what computers can do? What if we can't make circuits much smaller than they are now? What if we can't dissipate the heat? The size of an atom hasn't shrunk, and you need at least one to make a wire.

This mood of uncertainty about our ability to overcome limits is not new. In 1798 Thomas Robert Malthus wrote his *Essay on the Principle of Population as It Affects the Future Improvement of Society.* His basic claim was that we were doomed to starve because population increases exponentially, but food sources increase linearly.

This pessimistic view fails to take into account the nature of change and innovation. It is necessary to be flexible and build upon the innovations available rather than just improving already available technologies. While there have been many technological advances in food production, it has also been necessary to improve distribution and to limit population growth. The innovations build on each other but are not rigidly dependent upon each other. If we have better distribution we can transport food from farther away, or we can im-

---

*This is from a talk by Jay Forrester at the Computer Museum. He explained that the requirements of getting eighteen thousand tube systems working reliably led to research in why tubes failed. The solutions, such as preheating the tubes, were relatively simple and greatly extended their reliability.

prove the local crop yield. If we have higher agricultural productivity we can move to the city.

With computers we have an additional element—the computers themselves are direct agents in the process of innovation.

The marketplace and creative solutions

The evolution of personal computers was accelerated because electronic spreadsheets appealed to investors. The marketplace directly funded the development of the technology. This is a particularly dramatic example of the value of a marketplace in driving innovation.

The size of the marketplace was also important for a variety of approaches to coexist and flourish, enriching the store of concepts available for reuse.

The development of graphics processors is a good example of a sufficiently large specialized market. 3-D graphics processors can be targeted at consumer games and then used for commercial visualization while retaining the low price of the large consumer marketplace.

Innovations are typically accomplished in service of a need. In the case of communications, a major need is increased bandwidth. We can increase bandwidth by improving signal processing or by compressing the data. As we run into the limits of the signal speed, we improve compression. Voice compression reduced bandwidth requirements from 32Kbps to 9.6Kbps or less in a few years. Some of this has been due to faster processors and some due to algorithms, such as those modeling the constraints of the human mouth.

To the user, communications simply became better (cheaper? more capable? faster?). What seems to be a uniform process of improvement is composed of disparate elements.

The evolving nature of programming

The dramatic changes in hardware often obscure changes in software. We've gone from wiring plug-boards for each calculation to drawing a description of what we want them to do. In some cases the computer watches what you do and tries to offer its own suggestions, which are not always appreciated.

Using the computer itself as the tool for its own programming has been central. Assemblers allowed machine instructions to be coded symbolically; later, compilers converted program descriptions into machine instructions; and development environments became available to manage the process. Note that these terms, "assemblers," "compilers," and even "computers," come from human jobs with similar functions, but the machines have become the agents for these tasks.

The meaning of programming has itself evolved. Initially the focus was on coding the steps involved in solving an identified problem. As the tools became more powerful, the coding aspects became automated, and the focus has been on the description of the problem itself. In fact, original programming languages were called Automatic Programming tools since they automatically generated the program from the description—we now refer to the description *as* the program. But as our capabilities have grown, so have our expectations and thus our requirements. The term "coding" moved from specifying machine instructions to writing in a language such as COBOL or FORTRAN. Later generations of tools allowed for describing the desired result rather than an algorithm. One might specify a report by giving a sample rather than the details of how to construct the report.

The challenge has shifted from providing the professional programmer with tools to providing the "users" with the tools to interact directly with the computer. The original users of FORTRAN saw themselves as, and they were, scientists and engineers solving their own problems. As their needs grew, they had to choose between focusing on programming computers or on their area of professional expertise. For many, programming was more seductive.

As we've expanded the set of "programmers" to include, potentially, anyone using a computer, we've also changed the nature of programming. Rather than specifying a series of steps, one can give examples or a description of what should be done rather than the detailed steps for how to do it.

Even if these users approach the computer as an improved version of an earlier device such as a typewriter, the real power comes from understanding the new capabilities. Rather than "typing," one uses rule-based "styles." Instead of being concerned with the attributes of each "section head," one tags (or "codes") each header as such and then can set at once the properties of all heads and, perhaps, subheads as well. Later one can add some rules to describe what happens if the head is stuck at the bottom of a page or how to handle odd pages differently from even pages. It is not necessary to have this understanding to use the computer to type, but those who do are rewarded with a more effective tool. Of course, the software vendors are trying to garner the largest possible market and so have an interest in making the capabilities more accessible. Features understood by only a few are liable to be discarded.

Likewise, the spreadsheet is not just a digital analog of a calculator but a tool that allows for experimentation. (Only later did it become a presentation tool, but that's another story). In fact, the electronic spreadsheet derived its power from allowing a user to specify an algorithm by "doing it" and then being able to repeat the operation with new values. The name "VisiCalc" emphasized the visibility of this process. We were, in fact, getting people to program without their realizing that that is what they were doing.

It is this ability to use the computer as an agent by "programming" it with behavior that is central to the power of computing. It is important to realize that we have converted the user into a programmer, just as the phone dial converted people (users?) into phone operators. In the 1930s there were some estimates that by the 1950s we'd need to have everyone be a phone operator in order to satisfy the demand. The effect of automating the phone system can be viewed as not eliminating phone operators but making everyone a phone operator.

Requiring a separate class of programmers who translate user requirements into algorithms is not only expensive, but it ultimately frustrates our ability to make effective use of the technology. It is this requirement for the specification of behaviors and effective algorithms that is at the heart of societal change. Just as there weren't going to be enough phone operators, there aren't going to be enough programmers to add all the little bits of intelligent behavior we are going to expect of the infrastructure. And it is this limitation imposed by the need to specify behavior that is part of the upcoming challenge.

The ability to be descriptive is an important twist on programming in both the spreadsheet and the telephone system. Rather than specifying programming as a series of step-by-step operations, the user describes the behavior in a "language" that is shared with the computer. This allows the computer to do more than blindly execute the steps. It can also explain what is happening and recover from many possible problems. But there is still enough freedom left to the user to "reach a wrong [telephone] number" or specify an incorrect formula on the spreadsheet.

From programming to problem solving

One way to characterize problem solving is as the process of making the complex simple.

Computer systems come from a heritage of extremely complex systems built with seeming perfection. Error rates in the trillionths and better are not unusual. Initially this was achieved by careful engineering. Programs were carefully audited to be seemingly bug-free. We even had the notion of proving programs correct.

At best, one can prove that two representations of an algorithm are equivalent, but that doesn't address the question of whether the program meets a vaguer requirement. The question is whether the program works properly in service of some larger goal. There may, in fact, be multiple conflicting goals.

Rather than proving programs correct, we must make them simple enough to understand.

The Copernican heliocentric solar system was more than a mathematical reformulation of the geocentric Ptolemaic system. It represented a better understanding of the motion of the planets. The heuristic is that the simpler solution is better (Occam's Razor). We can take this one step further and argue that simplification *is* our goal.

But this begs the question since it just shifts the problem to finding the right representation, which is unsolvable in the general case, both because it reminds us that the nature of the solution is a function of the context in which the problem is being solved (ambiguity) and simply because it is a restatement of general problem solving.

But there are elements of a solution here. While we can't necessarily find the right decomposition, we can iterate on the problem and redecompose the problem as we improve our understanding. In practice, if we start out with an initial structure we can recompose the set of elements, or objects, as our understanding is refined. In terms of object-oriented systems, as long as we have control over our set of the problem space, we can iterate on the system design. This is an effective technique, but it becomes more difficult as the scope increases. Fred Books addressed some of the implications of scale in *The Mythical Man Month*. The same issues that arise with adding people to a task also arise when building a large system where iterating on the whole design becomes increasingly difficult.

When we have independent, interacting systems we don't necessarily have the option of recomposing them. This places a premium on getting an effective representation the first time, but inevitably, the initial solution will need to be adjusted as the situation changes. To the extent we can, we must be prepared for such change.

Communications and computing

The impact of the Web has been dramatic—more than the Internet itself. In the "calculator era," computers stood entirely alone. They took input on paper tape or cards and produced results on a printer or maybe punched out some result for later use. That was a long time ago. In the 1960s time sharing became common, and in the '70s and '80s, the Arpanet, later the Internet, started to link systems together. Local Area Networks (LANs) became common in the '80s. The impact of the Web was dramatic because it brought connectivity to the center of computing.

Like VisiCalc, the Web came at just about the "right time." More to the point, there was a waiting ecological niche. The Internet was sufficiently ubiquitous to be the basis for a global infrastructure. What was needed was an effective way to name elements in this network. The key to the URL (Universal Resource Locator) is that it is a pragmatic name that indicates not only where a resource is but how to access it. The "http" in the URL could also be "ftp," for example, for File Transfer Protocol. Thus we absorb the old protocols into the new without giving up any of the old capabilities. A graphical browser (Mosaic) for the widely available consumer platforms made the power available beyond the scientific community for which the Web was originally created.

Once again we have a positive feedback cycle with the Web growing in scope because of the Web. Not only do we have the tight loop, with the Web being the means of improving the Web, but each iteration brings in more participants and their contributions. The result is very rapid growth, or hypergrowth.

The Internet protocols were themselves built upon simple standards, with the main tools being a terminal program (Telnet) and the text editor. The Web came about during a period when the Internet seemed to be getting saturated and was suffering from slowdowns and other problems of overextension.

Yet the Internet is now much larger, with many times more users. Of course, there are the standard predictions of collapse. The difference is that the Web has transformed the Internet from a tool for the cognoscenti to one of the fundamental engines of society.

It won't fail, because we can't let it fail. Our ability to learn to be resilient in the face of failures will allow us to avoid the collapse that is characteristic of rigid systems.

In the earlier example, we saw that there was a tradeoff between bandwidth and communications speed. With the Internet we have another communications tradeoff in the ability to use a very jittery and not fully reliable medium (the Internet) as an alternative to the well-engineered, isochronous PSTN, or Public Switched Telephone Network. The impact will be profound, because we're selling telephony components linked together with software rather than a single "dial tone" service. The threat to the phone network is not just in the dramatically better economics of the Internet; it is also in the ability to define new telephony services purely in software.

Generations

We have a tendency to group together a set of changes into arbitrary "generations." There is a reality to this in that small changes aggregate to form larger trends. Operating systems for mainframes serve to dole out scarce resources. Minicomputers, being less expensive, were tuned for particular purposes. Personal computers started out as an extreme simplification of earlier computers for a very low price with limited utility.

Generational change serves a necessary function of clearing the underbrush of complex ideas so that new ideas can flourish. The radical simplification of computers in the form of PCs has allowed the growth of new operating systems with great emphasis on the ad hoc integration of applications. The term "application" itself represents a shift from emphasis on the isolated program to its role in service of a task.

Though the various hypergrowth phenomena seem to come just in time out of nowhere, if we look closely we can see their antecedents. VisiCalc had screen editors and calculators, the Web had the WAIS, FTP, Telnet and Gopher, and simpler access tools. CISC hardware had the RISC experience to draw upon. The hardware, software, and especially networking growth are building upon themselves.

For the last twenty-five years the Internet had been growing in importance, until it was unleashed by the Web. The interactions between applications over the Internet are an extended form of the cooperation among applications within the personal computer itself. This is setting the stage for the next change in the nature of computing.

Becoming the infrastructure

We are in the midst of a fundamental change in the nature of computing and its role in the world. We are creating a global communications medium that supports digital connectivity among computing agents throughout the world. We are also deploying bits of intelligence throughout the infrastructure.

The growth of the Internet (often confused with the Web, which is just a set of capabilities riding the Internet) is dramatic in its own right. What is less obvious is the growth of intelligent elements such as light bulbs that implement their own lighting policies or cars that use a local area network to coordinate their components and the global network to report diagnostic information and get traffic updates.

The traditional approaches to system design posit that there is a system being designed. We are adding to a complex system without any overall coordination. Once again we've introduced major sources of complexity without the corresponding means to deal with it. We need to learn how.

In a sense, the overwhelming scope of the problem contains the seeds of how to approach a solution. Techniques that seemed sensible in a well-understood system just don't work. There is no single version of software to be updated. But alas, cleverness allows us to keep up the illusion that we are still operating in the old world of self-contained systems. Remote procedure calls allow us to pretend that we are invoking a local subroutine when we might be using arbitrary resources on the network.

The deception fails when something goes awry, even something as simple as a delay. The result appears as just one more case of the computer being unreliable rather than as a symptom of a fundamentally flawed approach embodied in the programming tools.

The file system interface for a disk drive doesn't have the semantics for reporting that the network cable fell out. And the network itself fails to detect this since it is a mechanical problem and not a "network" problem.

The problem of naïve extensions of existing solutions should sort itself out as we develop alternative approaches that focus on the interactions between systems. New methodologies will have to be resilient enough to survive in a constantly changing, inconsistent environment by bending rather than failing.

Interactions

What happens between or among applications can be more important than what happens within them.

A system consisting of a million well organized parts is not complex in the sense that a system of a hundred autonomous subsystems is. The real measure of complexity is not the number of elements but the number of (nonuniform) interactions. The way of dealing with this complexity is to reduce the number of interactions. In psychology this is called "chunking," and humans seem to be able to process fewer than ten such chunks at once. This represents an extreme but effective simplification of the world. In programming, this can be a matter of finding a representation that allows us to factor the problem into subproblems with limited numbers of interactions.

Techniques such as structured programming, modular programming, and object oriented programming (to observe the evolution of the concepts) have been attempts to provide the programmer with structuring mechanisms. But they have mostly focused on interactions within a set of programs. By finding the proper structuring of a program, we can decompose it into elements and then manage the interactions among the elements. Solving a problem by finding an effective representation is a recurring theme.

The challenge is not simply to create programs in isolation, but to create independent systems that interact. The interactions are not preplanned. Furthermore, failures must be bounded and their propagation limited. In the world of the Internet, all systems are potentially interconnected. Ideally, local failures do not lead to failures of the entire system. Within a single computer, we can be very ambitious in designing interactions among systems and must sometimes completely reset the entire system to clear out the knots that form among these interactions. This is not an option for the systems that form the global infrastructure.

What makes the problem of managing the interactions even more difficult is that the systems are not necessarily well managed—if they are managed at all. Increasingly, "programs" are being provided by people who do not even view themselves as "programmers," and the linkages are not well understood. Mix in a little Internet and we have a powerful brew.

Scalability

In order to scale systems it is necessary to be able to regenerate reliability. Normally, when you multiply probabilities of success, the result is to decrease the reliability at each stage. We've been able to defeat this phenomenon by having a way to "understand" the constraints of a system and use this understanding to regenerate the likelihood of success. Active elements operating independently without sufficient defense against failure of other modules and without a description of how they should work together lack this regenerative property.

We've pushed the limits of hardware by determining how to make locally reliable devices. Initially, for example, we could use a modem to send data across the country at ten characters a second simply by shifting between two frequencies for the 1's and 0's. But now we send 28.8Kbps (or more!) across channels designed for 3KHz voice.* We are using complex algorithms to make up for the unreliability of the channel. We hide this complexity within the modem.†

---

*For the information theorists, we are preserving more bits of information than necessary for a 3KHz wave form.
†A modem is an incredibly complicated device that takes a digital signal and transmits it over an analog phone network. As the phone network became digital, modems took a digital signal, converted it to analog, sampled it, sent it as a different kind of digital signal, reconstituted the analog signal at the other end, converted it back to a digital signal, and wrote all sorts of error recovery code around this. Why? Because technological change slows down dramatically once one has to deal with an infrastructure with many participants and ruled over by a multitude of regulatory fiefdoms. ISDN is supposed to provide an end-to-end digital connection, but it is likely to be too little too late because it is beholden to the other assumptions of the PSTN. Native digital connectivity will ride Internet protocols.

Problems that are not amenable to a localized attack are much more difficult to solve.

An important change is to shift from algorithmic programming (traditional) to descriptive programming. The description limits the "program" to the common understanding between the describer (or user) and the computer. Describing the interactions between elements allows an observer (the computer) to assist in maintaining the integrity of these interactions and in regenerating reliability.

The description is only in terms of the common understanding and, like the railroad, can only go where track is already laid. We are thus limited by the speed at which we can lay tracks or define the language. It is the nature of the frontier for the attention to be focused at the leading edge. In a sense, the trailing standards setting is a form of track laying. As with railroad tracks, the descriptions are limited to the route, or language, chosen.

The standards process itself must adjust to the pace of change and be made more adaptable. In fact, standards setting is a competitive effort to deliver solutions. The ability of the fleet-footed IETF (Internet Engineering Task Force) to deliver sufficient, even if overly simple solutions, has given it an advantage over the slower-moving organizations that either standardize the past or create inflexible standards for the unknown.

The IETF also has the further advantage of codifying practice rather than prescribing practice. X.400 embodied many assumptions about how e-mail should work, whereas the primitive Internet protocols of the Internet, SMTP (Simple Mail Transport Protocol) coupled with domain naming, worked. Some of the limitations were later addressed with MIME encoding. This might be kludge layered upon kludge, but it got the job done.

There is not fear that the IETF itself has become too laden with its own history.

Social systems

Cooperating independent systems are, in effect, social systems. The participants try to interact by following rules that benefit them all. Norms are ideally derived by consensus after experience. Ultimately, each individual must take some of the responsibility for its own behavior and fate.

The Web is a good example. It spans continents and travels through (near) space. And it normally works!

The reason that it works is the unreliability of the world wide Internet. Each element of the Web is constructed on the assumption that it will encounter errors and surprises over which it has no control. The Web, despite its spectacular growth and the vast number of services built on top of its protocols, is simple and shallow—simple in the sense that its architecture is understandable (so far) and shallow in that it isn't built layer upon layer, but only using a simple transport protocol over a fairly robust connection protocol (HTTP on top of TCP/IP with HTML as a simple markup language).

There is a normal progression from the simple and viable to the complex and fragile that endangers the very robustness of the Web. But its core functionality will sustain it. The Web has also invigorated the Internet as a medium. The increased market size of the Internet due to the Web has spawned efforts such as Internet telephony. The Web is built upon the Internet, but the Internet is not limited to Web protocols.

This meandering path of change and innovation leaves us without a simple rule when we want to go in a specific direction and are not willing to wait passively for accidents to deliver solutions.

The basic principle of building a system out of cooperating elements applies. The key is to preserve robustness by having each element not just preserve reliability, but regenerate it. Ideally, it should be possible to recompose capabilities among their elements and subelements. This is difficult in arms-length relationships, though even there, negotiation should be part of the normal interaction, at least at the design level.

But what is most important is the attitude from which the problem is approached. Change and surprise are the normal state. To expect one design to continue to work is naïve and dangerous. The term "bit rot" describes the process by which a seemingly stable set of bits or programs degenerates over time. The bits don't change but their relationship with their environment changes because of normal drift.

The nature of the problems we are trying to solve has changed and so have the tools. Rather than writing programs, people are specifying rules or policies or local behavior as part of their normal interactions with the world. Yet we don't understand how to compose these into coherent and explicable systems. We have had to learn the pragmatic debugging when theoretical debugging was proven impossible. Now we need to learn the heuristics that apply to compositing systems. To the extent that a system of those local rules can be observed and "understood," we can assist the user in understanding the behavior of the system.

This understanding needn't be full, just sufficient to manage the interactions. In fact, we should expect that our understanding is incomplete and wrong so that we can adapt to surprises.

In general, a descriptive approach to specifying behavior is much better than an algorithmic one, since it allows for an overseer to "understand" what is being requested, whereas a procedural description must be evaluated step by step without an overview. One is able to be descriptive precisely because the procedural elements are so well understood that they are incorporated into the larger system, and we are simply calling upon these known elements of behavior. So we are back again to this cycle of building upon our previous understanding. The rate at which this process can propagate and iterate limits the rate of progress.

Towards resiliency

The old goal was bug-free. The new goal is resiliency. It is much more important to recover from exceptions than to avoid them. The term "bug" is useful in describing a behavior in the purview of a single designer or design team. Failure to respond to the external failure or even simply the surprising behavior of another element is really different from a bug within one's own program.

This requires a shift in our thinking: from techniques for building programs to the integration of independent and partially defined elements. The programs are still there, but so are other forms of specification such as policies and constraints. This is an environment in which surprises (aka exceptions or failures) will be the norm. Since this *is* the infrastructure, there is no option for a complete "reboot," though local resets are allowed.

This resiliency applies as well to the "programs" by people providing specifications for behavior.

We are learning how to build resilient systems. The model of social systems provides some clues. At each scale there are organizations that define the limits of the interactions with other organizations. These organizations also have mechanisms for regenerating local reliability. This is one of the tenets of the American federal government.

Conclusion

The world is full of limits imposed by physics and by the complexities of interacting chaotic systems. With cleverness and with the computer as tool for effecting computation, we've pushed against these limits with great success. We'll continue to create faster and better systems.

The challenge, now, is to shift our thinking from improving systems in isolating to how to create an infrastructure of interacting intelligent elements. We need to move from the goal of precise, bug-free but isolated systems to resilient cooperating systems. Naively extending the rigid models of computing will fail. But we can apply the lessons from earlier models of computing as long as we design them for this new arena. The solutions will be as much by discovery as by design. And we need to realize that it has always been so.

The rapid changes we've seen in computing systems have been due to our ability to quickly create tools that extend our capabilities. We've now gotten to the point where these changes are no longer confined to isolated systems.

The growth we've seen in the capabilities of computer systems is indeed remarkable, but it can also be seen as the expected continuation of the hypergrowth that occurs whenever there is a strong positive feedback cycle.

This feedback cycle is fed by the computer's ability to serve as a tool in its own advancement. It is also a means to leverage innovation from a large number of people.

Classic hypergrowth phenomena run out of resources or simply reach an insupportable scale. We've avoided these limitations so far because the systems are becoming increasingly resource efficient. We've been able to scale the systems because we've been able to regenerate reliability at each level.

This isn't always the case. We've been very unsuccessful in mastering the complexities of interactive systems, and these complexities continue to increase as we interconnect systems and add intelligent elements throughout the systems.

We are not limited in what we can do with the systems. Innovation will continue to surprise us, the Web and Internet telephony being but two of the most recent examples.

The Malthusians are very aware of the problems and challenges they confront. It is not reasonable to simply accept the premise that things will get better. There is no certainty, and the advancements may be disconcerting to those looking for answers in terms of the current circumstances.

But it is the very uncertainty and chaos that allow new ideas to vie for superiority. This can be disconcerting for those who are looking for obvious solutions. But it is an exciting environment for innovation.

System design in the connected chaotic world requires resiliency. And we must regenerate reliability by discovering new simplicities.

EDSGER W. DIJKSTRA

The Tide, Not the Waves

4

When the idea to write about the next fifty years of computing first entered my head, I wrote it off as utterly preposterous: what sane scientist purports to be able to see so far into the future? But then I realized that in a way that is precisely what educators do all the time: when designing our courses, we do dare to decide what to teach and what to ignore, and we do this for the benefit of students, many of whom will still be active forty to fifty years from now. Clearly, some vision of the next half century of computing science is operational. To this I should add that it is all right if the crystal ball is too foggy to show much detail. Thirty-five years ago, for instance, I had no inkling of how closely program design and proof design would come together, and in such a detailed sense my life has been full of surprises. At the same time, these surprises were developments I had been waiting for, because I knew that programming had to be made amenable to some sort of mathematical treatment long before I knew what type of mathematics that would turn out to be. In other words, when building sand castles on the beach, we can ignore the waves but should watch the tide.

Fortunately, there are a few things that we can learn from the past, for instance, that the rate at which society can absorb progress is strictly limited, a circumstance that makes long-range predictions a lot easier. Earlier this decade I was told of a great invention called "the register window"; my informant was very young, but in my ears the invention sounded very familiar because I remembered the Burroughs B5000 of thirty years before. So, if you have a bright and sound idea now, you can expect it to be hailed as a novelty around the year 2025.

Another thing we can learn from the past is the failure of characterizations like "computing science is really nothing but X," where for "X" you may substitute your favorite discipline, such as numerical analysis, electrical engineering, automata theory, queuing theory, lambda calculus, discrete mathematics, or proof theory. I mention this because of the current trend to equate computing science with constructive type theory or with category theory.

Computing's core challenge is how not to make a mess of it. If people object that any science has to meet that challenge, we should give a double rebuttal. Firstly, machines are so fast and storage capacities are so huge that we face orders of magnitude more room for confusion, the propagation and diffusion of which are easily inadvertently mechanized. Secondly, because we are dealing with artifacts, all unmastered complexity is of our own making; there is no one else to blame, and so we had better learn how not to introduce such complexity in the first place.

In this connection the history of the real-time interrupt is illuminating. This was an invention from the second half of the 1950s that enabled the completion of a communication with the external world to interrupt the execution of one program in favor of another. Its advantage was that it enabled the implementation of rapid reaction to changed external circumstances without paying the price of a lot of processor time lost in unproductive waiting. The disadvantage was that the operating system had to ensure correct execution of the various computations despite the unpredictability of the moments at which the interrupts would take place and the central processor would be switched from one computation to another; the nondeterminism implied by this unpredictability has caused endless headaches for those operating-system designers who did not know how to cope with it. We have seen two reactions to the challenge of this added complexity.

One reaction was to enhance the debugging facilities, as IBM did for the design of OS/360. (This was the operating system IBM tried to design for its 360-series of machines, which were introduced in the first half of the 1960s; IBM's problems with this design facilitated in 1968 the recognition of the worldwide phenomenon that became known as "the software crisis.") IBM built, in fact, special-purpose monitors that exactly recorded when the central processor honored which interrupt; when something had gone wrong, the monitor could be turned into a controller, thus forcing a replay of the suspect history and making the "experiment" repeatable.

The other reaction could be observed at the THE (Technological University Eindhoven), viz., to determine the conditions under which one could feasibly and safely reason about such nondeterministic programs and subsequently to see to it that these conditions were met by hardware and software.

The difference was striking, showing once more that debugging is no alternative for intellectual control. While OS/360 remained a mess ever after, the Multiprogramming System designed at THE was so robust that no system malfunction ever gave rise to a spurious call for hardware maintenance. Needless to say, the whole episode has made a lasting impression on me.

One moral is that the real-time interrupt was only the wave, whereas the tide was the introduction of nondeterminism and the development of the mathematical techniques to cope with it. A wider moral is the constructive approach to the problem of program correctness, to which we can now add the problem of system performance as well. It is only too easy to design resource-sharing systems with such intertwined allocation strategies that no amount of applied queuing theory will prevent most unpleasant performance surprises from emerging. The designer who counts performance predictability among his responsibilities tends to come up with designs that need no queuing theory at all. A last, and this time fairly recent, example is the design of delay-insensitive circuitry, which relegates all timing difficulties in clocked systems to the class of problems better avoided than solved. The moral is clear: prevention is better than cure, in particular if the illness is unmastered complexity, for which no cure exists.

The above examples point to a very general opportunity, in broad terms to be described as designs such that both the final product and the design process reflect a theory that suffices to prevent a combinatorial explosion of complexity from creeping in. There are many reasons to suppose that this opportunity will stay with us for a very long time, and that is great for the future of computing science because all through history, simplifications have had a much greater long-range scientific impact than individual feats of ingenuity.

The opportunity for simplification is very encouraging, because in all examples that come to mind the simple and elegant systems tend to be easier and faster to design and get right, more efficient in execution, and much more reliable than the more contrived contraptions that have to be debugged into some degree of acceptability. (One of the reasons why the expression "software industry" can be so misleading is that a major analogy with manufacturing fails to hold: in software, it is often the poor quality of the "product" that makes it so expensive to make! In programming, nothing is cheaper than not introducing the bugs in the first place.) The world being what it is, I also expect this opportunity to stay with us for decades to come. Firstly, simplicity and elegance are unpopular because they require hard work and discipline to achieve and education to be appreciated. Secondly, we observe massive investments in efforts that are heading in the opposite direction. I am thinking about so-called design aids such as circuit simulators, protocol verifiers, algorithm animators, graphical aids for the hardware designers, and elaborate systems for version control: by their suggestion of power, they rather invite than discourage complexity. You cannot expect the hordes of people that have devoted a major part of their professional lives to such efforts to react kindly to the suggestion that most of these efforts have been misguided, and we can hardly expect a more sympathetic ear from the granting agencies that have funded these efforts: too many people have been involved, and we know from past experience that what has been sufficiently expensive is automatically declared to have been a great success. Thirdly, the vision that automatic computing should not be such a mess is obscured, over and over again, by the advent of a monster that is subsequently forced upon the computing community as a de facto standard (COBOL, FORTRAN, ADA, C++, software for desktop publishing, you name it).

In short, the opportunity to simplify will remain with us for many years, and I propose, in order to maintain our sanity and our enthusiasm, that we welcome the long duration of that opportunity rather than suffer from impatience each time the practitioners deride and discard our next successful pilot project as a toy problem—and they will do so, even if you have achieved what shortly before, they had confidently predicted to be impossible.

By now we all know that programming is as hard or as easy as proving, and that if programming a procedure corresponds to proving a theorem, designing a digital system corresponds to building a mathematical theory. The tasks are isomorphic. We also know that while from an operational point of view a program can be nothing but a manipulator of abstract symbols, the designer had better regard the program as a sophisticated formula. And we also know that there is only one trustworthy method for the design of sophisticated formulas, viz., derivation by means of symbol manipulation. We have to let the symbols do the work, for that is the only known technique that scales up. Computing and computing science unavoidably emerge as exercises in formal mathematics or, if you wish an acronym, as an exercise in VLSAL (very large scale application of logic).

Because of the very close connection between program design and proof design, any advance in program design has a direct potential impact on how general mathematics is done. Since the time computing scientists have built compilers, they have been very used to the idea of mechanical manipulation of uninterpreted formulas, and I am sure that they will significantly contribute to a further realization of Leibniz's dream of presenting calculation, i.e., the manipulation of uninterpreted formulas, as an alternative to human reasoning. The challenge of turning that dream into reality, however, will certainly keep us busy for at least five decades.

It is not only that the design of an appropriate formal notational and conceptual practice is a formidable challenge that still has to be met; the challenge is worse because current traditions are hardly helpful. For instance, we know that the transition from verbal reasoning to formal manipulation can be appreciated as narrowing the bandwidth of communication and documentation, whereas in the name of "ease of use" a lot of effort of the computing community is aimed at widening that bandwidth. Also, we know that we can only use a system by virtue of our knowledge of its properties and similarly must give the greatest possible care to the choice of concepts in terms of which we build up our theories: we know we have to keep it crisp, disentangled, and simple if we refuse to be crushed by the complexities of our own making. But complexity sells better, and so the market pulls in the opposite direction. I still remember finding a book on how to use "Wordperfect 5.0" of more than 850 pages, in fact, a dozen pages more than my 1951 edition of Georg Joos's *Theoretical Physics!* It is time to unmask the computing community as a Secret Society for the Creation and Preservation of Artificial Complexity. And then we have the software engineers, who only mention formal methods in order to throw suspicion on them. In short, we should not expect too much support from the computing community at large. And from the mathematical community I have learned not to expect too much support either, as informality is the hallmark of the Mathematical Guild, whose members—like poor programmers—

derive their intellectual excitement from not quite knowing what they are doing and prefer to be thrilled by the marvel of the human mind (in particular their own). For them, the dream of Leibniz is a nightmare. In summary, we are on our own.

But that does not matter. In the next fifty years, mathematics will emerge as the art and science of effective formal reasoning, and we shall derive our intellectual excitement from learning how to let the symbols do the work.

Calculemus!

R. W. HAMMING

How to Think About Trends

5

It requires a brave person, or else a fool, to attempt a detailed, and accurate prediction for the next half century of computing. But without a vision of the future we will tend to wander like the proverbial drunken sailor and will not successfully attack many of the important problems facing us. As impossible as accuracy may be, it is nevertheless necessary to make some predictions. Of necessity, this is more of an essay than a technical report.

The future of computing depends on three things:

1. The internal state of the field: what appears to be its main problems and the tools used to attack them. Only occasionally does the main paradigm of a field get changed; most of the time most of the workers in the field are pursuing and elaborating the accepted ways, and rarely do they search for radically new approaches. We cannot expect many major changes in the field.

2. The technical support from other fields: some examples are, How fast and how

small can the components of a computer be, what will be the price of a computer, and what restraints will be imposed on the field by the supporting technologies?

3. The surrounding society; will it continue to support us as we believe we need to be (physics is experiencing the loss of government support already), will society provide the needed kinds of people to study computer science (enrollments in computer science are no longer rising rapidly), and will we have social and political rules that restrict us in direct and indirect ways? For example, the probably legal restraints on doing medical diagnoses by computer, followed by the needed prescriptions for drugs, seem to be enormous; and it is doubtful whether they can be overcome in the next fifty years.

Furthermore, there are really three questions to ask:

1. What can happen → science.
2. What will happen → engineering and economics.
3. What should happen → morals, ethics, or whatever you want to call it, including what society is prepared to accept or reject.

And these are three very different questions indeed.

There are many rules for predicting the future. One well-known rule is that most short-term estimates are optimistic, while long term predictions are pessimistic. As illustrations, the time to get a program working is generally much longer than was first predicted; while for long-term predictions the geometric progression of improvement in speed and decrease in cost is hard for the human mind to grasp. There are counterexamples; in Artificial Intelligence most of the long-term predictions have not yet been realized. For example, in the 1950s it was claimed by the experts that within ten years the chess master of the world would be a computer, but again (1996) we missed! In the hardware domain, both superconducting and bubble technologies did not result (so far) in much that is in widespread use in computers.

1. Hardware, software, and applications

Everyone knows that the cost of setting up a new production line for computer chips is steadily increasing and is now at the point where companies combine rather than try to go it alone. True, when finally running, the production lines result in cheaper computing for the users, but the time is clearly coming when the next technology may be too expensive to start the mass production of the corresponding chips; the risk will be too great.

While one reads about transistors that will change state with the passage of a single electron (maybe), further reductions in line widths, occasional articles on thermodynamically reversible computers (to absorb the heat), and for chemical and molecular computers, one has to wonder about the delivery of these innovations *for general-purpose computing* within the next fifty years. And can anyone foresee the equivalent of the invention of the transistor, which moved us away from vacuum tubes?

We should also examine more closely how long the Turing machine model, or if you wish the Von Neumann model, will last in the area of algorithms, since it no longer models the hardware we use all the time. Many texts on algorithms dwell on the need for a "halt" instruction in the program, but a "halt" instruction is generally not on the modern chip! It is evident, even now, that the classical algorithm books, which so lovingly compute bounds, are out of date (since most chips now in use have cache memories and one or more pipelines built into them, and whose operation is not directly under control of the programmer) but they can greatly alter the estimates based on the models of computers being used in the algorithm courses. Parallel computing is here to stay!

In our pursuit of speed can we have machines that are *basically* object oriented, and not mere simulators of it? And again, is it possible that some of the machines of the future might include functional programming? The history of gradually incorporating software into hardware is very long—we simulated index registers (B boxes), floating point arithmetic, and vector processing, until finally the engineers saw the wisdom of putting them into the hardware. How much more of our software will be incorporated into the hardware? No matter whether or not you like C++, there is a large amount of code written in it at present; will machines be made in which these instructions are the machine language and the rest of the details to the machine are in microcode? Or some language other than C++? The use of a widely used language means that there is no need to provide the enormous libraries of the useful tools we expect to have at hand when we buy a computer. The efforts to speed up computing will surely not ignore this avenue. It was tried years ago for LISP, but apparently the development of the general-purpose personal computers displaced them, and the corresponding companies went broke. Long ago there were proposals that we build computers that operated at the machine level in FORTRAN or in APL, but they were not built because they seemed, at that time, to limit the machines too much. It is more a question of economics than it is of the logical possibilities; the long-term trend of going from software to hardware will surely not stop with pipelines and cache memories. Thus we can confidently expect to see much more of what we now call programming being incorporated into the computer as delivered to the user; but this will not solve "the programming problem." The desire for more speed had driven us for a long time; after all, a machine ten times faster than some other machine can do ten times the work in a given time.

I have often used the analogy of novel writing with the writing of software; in both cases the essence is first clear thinking followed by the straightforward writing of the actual words. To what extent can great writers be taught? Shakespeare and Jane Austen did not take creative writing courses, and most people who take creative writing courses do not end up among the greatest writers. All that programming courses can do, apparently, is to make poor programmers a bit better. Experience, while necessary, seems not to be enough. Indeed, I suspect that the bureaucrats in Washington, after years of writing proposals and instructions for the public, merely get worse, not better! And there is little evidence that experience with many programming languages and many years of writing programs makes people much better at programming. Nor do we see major amounts of novels copied into other novels; hence, while I expect reusable software (libraries?) to help to some extent, I doubt that it will become a major part of essentially new programs.

Recent reports suggest that software writing has improved over the years at a rate of four and one-half percent per year, meaning that in the past fifty years it is about a factor of ten easier to write a program (compared with the speedup of the computers, which is more than a millionfold). The observation that for large programs the speedup is less than for small ones merely underlines that it is more the time for the human brain to process the data defining the problem and the algorithms to be used than it is the actual program-writing effort itself. Thus, until we have languages that help us think about the original problem and its proposed algorithms, there will be only slow improvements in programming effort. This flies in the face of the regularly reported speedups in the literature—indeed, while walking to the office the other morning I decided that if the savings in elapsed time (not in percent improvements) were really true, then we would have the running programs before we had the problems! Optimism, and the neglect of the well-known Hawthorne effect, are the reasons for this phenomenon of reported improvements not actually being widely realized in practice. The four and one-half percent improvement rate will probably continue for perhaps all of the next fifty years, and we will never really "solve the programming problem" regardless of what you may read in the future literature of great breakthroughs in programming, of silver bullets, etc.

A point to notice is that the field of neural networks promises some alleviation in programming—we simply write the underlying program to simulate the neural net, pick what seems to us to be an appropriate structure, and let the machine find how to solve our problem without we ourselves having to undertake the detailed programming. How many other ways are there to escape broad areas of programming? Are such approaches inevitably restricted to comparatively narrow fields?

Automatic programming can be seen as a variant on Huffman coding. The strings of bits that the machine needs to solve the problems we want it to are apt to be long, while most of the short strings solve problems we are not interested in; we want therefore a language that has short strings of bits for the problems we want to solve and long strings for the problems we seldom, if ever, want to solve.

The programming problem is more a matter of getting rid of the poor programmers than anything else—it has long been true that good programmers outperform poor ones by more than a factor of ten, and the poor ones are a burden on the good ones! The way we teach programming does not in any way resemble how sports and other art forms are taught, and we had better look at how programmers learn to program rather than trying to fix the bad habits they develop in class and on their own. But unfortunately, many of the current professors of programming are themselves poor programmers with no real sense of taste and style; they tend to think that it is a matter of cute, accurate, fast programming; hence it is a matter of slowly upgrading the whole profession, lifting ourselves up by our own bootstraps.

Highly parallel computers are coming in, and will persist, but they have one nasty feature: many of them have basically different structures and require correspondingly different software. Can reasonably efficient software be written to generate the corresponding compilers? Or are we doomed to a lot of special work for each family of parallel computers?

Speech recognition is currently a hot topic, but again I have grave reservations. I lived through IBM and Harvard independently reporting that they had machine programs that would translate from Russian to English, but somehow they faded out and were forgotten. Speech recognition is a difficult problem since there are many words with the same sound but different spellings, *led* and *lead* (metal), for example.

Speech generation from text may be a bit easier, but local context will not help much in going from characters to spoken language, as the following sentences show:

> A tear was in her eye.
> A tear was in her dress.

Almost no one has any trouble reading these sentences, yet when you come to the word "tear" you must have already processed, to some extent, the final word in the sentence so you can give "tear" the right pronunciation. The idea that local clues will be enough is clearly false. There is also a classic sentence:

> Time flies like an arrow.

There could be a breed of flies called "time flies" that like to eat arrows as food instead of bananas. The actual ability to parse sentences, at least as I was taught in school, is not a real algorithm at all—the parsing I was shown depended frequently on understanding the meaning of the sentence, something no one really has much of a clue on how to attack (in the above sentence "flies" can be a noun or a verb).

The effort, especially in AI, to escape from "meaning," "ideas," and "understanding" will leave us at best only partially successful in speech recognition, speech production, language translation, and many other AI fields. The history of AI is a lesson in what happens when you try to evade them; you get some apparent successes that really evade meaning, ideas, and understanding, with a continuing list of failures. At present we have no decent ideas of how to write algorithms for such words. Indeed, we seem not to actually understand what we mean by the word "understand," nor have we any idea of what an "idea" is, nor the meaning of "meaning." Yet we use these three words constantly as we try serious communication with each other! Will the next fifty years produce the needed progress? I doubt it!

Graphical data seems to be on a course that has not yet reached its end and often represents the way we ourselves go about things (apparently), but it can tax a moderate-sized computer. In fifty years graphics will be both commonplace and still a field of research (probably), though less active and more highly developed than now.

We are now having great discussions and anxiety over the matter of privacy—another fifty years will not settle the matter to most people's satisfaction. It is less a technical problem than it is a social one. Security has many of the elements of cryptography, whose long history shows that practical systems have weaknesses and that secure systems are hard and expensive to use; it is not likely that the verdict of time will change suddenly, much as we wish it would.

2. Support from other fields

As noted above, engineering progress can do only so much to improve computers, and to lower the costs still more, but essentially new discoveries can change the picture almost overnight and simply cannot be anticipated.

Most great advances in a field come from outside. Thus the transistor was invented by the telephone company to improve their service, and computers were seldom thought of by them in the late 1940s. In archaeology the dating of remains is basic, but carbon dating, and similar advances, came not from the experts in archaeology but from the physicists. The telephone came, apparently, from a teacher of the deaf and not from the telegraph companies, who would not pay $100,000 for the patent when offered it!

The nature of the problem of where we can expect significantly new things to come from means that at present we do not know where to look for them! Indeed, can we reasonably expect another fifty years without large changes in the way we see our problems in computer science? Who is to make them if they are to occur? Probably not the current experts!

There is at present an ambiguity in the view that the public adopts towards computers. There is the comic "nerd" programmer view, and there are devotees of computers who promise the end of all troubles. What many of the enthusiasts fail to realize is that the mere supplying of information that is not given any support as to its truth or falsity is of little value. And offering large amounts of unorganized and not carefully selected information is also not what is widely wanted. A large menu of possible selections from which the user must make a choice is often an annoyance. When, having chosen the entree in a restaurant from an all too large menu, the waitress asks the diner, "soup or salad," and if salad is the answer, then another multiple choice awaits the person. Looking at the faces of my friends in such situations, I have come to believe that the average human animal does not like to spend a lot of time choosing. Thus many of the claims of the great contributions of computers to the spread of information will not be realized.

With computer networks, we are already seeing what happened to us with radio and TV; the promises of the idealists are not realized, and the distribution is taken over by commercial organizations who have the money to pay, and it becomes commercialized rather than the idealistic thing we hoped for.

3. Society

At the base of most human activities is economics, though there are exceptions, such as cosmology. Economics controls much of what will be accepted and be paid for by society.

Some of the ways society will affect the evolution of computing have already been noted, since you cannot separate computers from society. I have already mentioned the question of the extent to which the image we will have in society will restrict the kind and growth in the number of people entering the field, as well as the economic support for expensive projects. Our efforts at "user friendly" interfaces are currently under erosion—too many people are now getting a machine at the front end of a phone call with instructions to dial further digits for what you want, followed by music and a long, long wait, and all too often being left with nothing after half an hour, or at best an unsatisfactory response.

Intellectual property ownership will also not be solved in the next fifty years, but we will probably have come to some better conventions in this delicate matter than we have at present. The original reason for forming the patent system in America (and probably elsewhere) was to get the inventor to reveal the secrets so others could build on top of them, thus producing long-term progress—the inventor was promised safe protection for a limited time as payment for revealing things. It was for the good of the whole to have information in the open, but there had to be rewards for finding the new things or else the source would soon dry up. High quality information is no different—the effort to organize a body of knowledge, remove the false, eliminate the irrelevant, and lay down an easily understood, fairly direct, approach to the heart of the matter is costly in effort for the individual to do, and hence they need to be rewarded for this effort—else it will not be done.

Let me return to privacy. Apparently, in primitive tribes there is little individuality; you are a member of the tribe, you behave as the tribe does, and neither novelty nor creativity is wanted most of the time. Tribal behavior is inculcated in you at all stages of living; while you are hunting with the group, sitting around the campfire, participating in group dances, etc. With the rise of civilization has come the rise of the individual. I have a book that claims that in Western Europe the idea of the individual, as an individual, rose in the late Middle Ages. Cities help one to feel like an individual, yet it is easy transportation that most enables us to escape our neighbors. As a result we now have more privacy, but we are also more isolated from each other than previous generations of humans were. The computer nets of communication will simply continue this trend—we will have still more acquaintances but fewer friends. As a result there is less need to learn the difficult art of compromise in our behaviors, more room for fanaticism; you must be for (or against) abortions if I am to vote for you, for gun control, for the environment, for this or that, and this is dividing our American society into small fragments. The consequences you can work out for yourself, but it will be one of the effects of computers on our society. The cumulative effects on our society in the next fifty years are hard to imagine, but they will probably not go away and could seriously affect the environment in which computers will evolve.

Growth of knowledge

Knowledge has been doubling about every seventeen years since the time of Newton (1642–1727). We have coped with this growth mainly by specialization, to the point where we now have around ten thousand specialties. It is always the last doubling period that is the hardest to cope with, and which we are in now. To continue another 340 years at this rate would mean a million-fold increase, and ten billion fields of specialty is not really believable! Hence there is no argument that the doubling cannot go on indefinitely; we are only haggling over when it will become a severe problem. Indeed, so far as I can see, we are now near the end of the exponential growth. Yes, computers can help us, but they are also helping us to generate the very data itself! Computers may ameliorate the situation, but without "meaning," "ideas," and "understanding" in our programs they will be merely skirting around the main problems. The mass processing of data, using statistical studies, will merely confuse things since statistical tests give typically ninety to ninety-five percent reliability, and in doing a large number of studies they will, ipso facto, give the corresponding number of false leads! We are already in that period!

The solution to this problem of the growth in details, which is so often proclaimed in computing circles, is "information hiding." And we have done a remarkable job in the integrated circuit area—for the modern chip many of the details have passed through no human mind, nor will they ever, probably. We have been able to design, build, and use complex integrated chips and successfully hide the details! How far this information hiding can go is not known. Many years ago (1960) in a textbook on numerical analysis I wrote, "It is better to regenerate than to retrieve," and I presented ways of finding any formulas of a wide class, whether or not they had ever been found before. Increasingly, in mathematics we are seeing systematic methods for finding results in some fields such as binomial identities, and we can expect this search for methods to replace the sea of details to continue indefinitely. There are, of course, things that at present cannot be easily regenerated, such as our current social security numbers and airplane reservations, but there is the approach to organizing knowledge in such a fashion that the computers can generate what we want when we want it, rather than trying to retrieve it; this is clearly a viable path to go down.

I have sketched out a number of likely developments in the future of computing; there must be many others that I have not foreseen. I have tried hard to avoid predicting what I wish would happen and to avoid wishful thinking, but of course I have not been perfectly able to do so. I think I have come closer to the fundamentals than most predictions of fifty years into the future. Time will tell, but being old, I will never find out whether mine are anywhere near correct; the younger people in the field will have to do the checking!

Technology suggests to many people a glamorous, unlimited future, but the very slow evolution of the human animal suggests a far more restricted future. We are the result of eons of evolution, and we have innate drives, a limited bandwidth of input and output, a modest rate of internally processing bits of information, rather fixed patterns of mental activity, apparently highly specialized brain structures, etc. While much can be done to supplement the form we are born with, wishful thinking will not do it. Unless you think you will be able to make great changes to the insides of our minds, then the externals, including better education, can do only a limited amount for advancing us along the paths some people wishfully dream of. Social evolution, while more rapid than biological evolution, is also rather restricted in its possibilities. They, more than technology, limit our future.

MARK WEISER
& JOHN SEELY BROWN

The Coming Age of Calm Technology

6 Introduction

The important waves of technological change are those that fundamentally alter the place of technology in our lives. What matters is not technology itself, but its relationship to us.

In the past fifty years of computation there have been two great trends in this relationship: the mainframe relationship and the PC relationship. Today the Internet is carrying us through an era of widespread *distributed computing* towards the relationship of *ubiquitous computing*, characterized by deeply embedding computation in the world. Ubiquitous computing will require a new approach to fitting technology to our lives, an approach we call "calm technology."

This article briefly describes the relationship trends and then expands on the challenges of designing for calm using both the center and the periphery of our perception and the world.

Table 6.1   The Major Trends in Computing.

Mainframe	many people share a computer
Personal Computer	one computer, one person
Internet–Widespread Distributed Computing	*. . . transition to . . .*
Ubiquitous Computing	many computers share each of us

Phase I—The mainframe era

The first era we call "mainframe," to recall the relationship people had with computers that were mostly run by experts behind closed doors. Anytime a computer is a scarce resource and must be negotiated and shared with others, our relationship is that of the mainframe era. There is mainframe computing today: a shared office PC; and the great physical simulations of everything from weather to virtual reality have in common the sharing of a scarce resource. If lots of people share a computer, it is mainframe computing.

Phase II—The PC era

The second great trend is that of the personal computer. In 1984 the number of people using personal computers surpassed the number of people using shared computers.[7] The personal computing relationship is personal, even intimate. You have *your* computer, it contains your stuff, and you interact directly and deeply with it. When doing personal computing you are occupied, you are not doing something else. Some people name their PC—many people curse or complain to their PC.

The personal computer is most analogous to the automobile—a special, relatively expensive item, that while it may "take you where you want to go," requires considerable attention to operate. And just as one can own several cars, one can own several personal computers: for home, for work, and for the road. Any computer with which you have a special relationship or that fully engages or occupies you when you use it is a personal computer. Most handheld computers, such as the Zaurus, the Newton, or the Pilot, are today still used as personal computers. A $500 network computer is still a personal computer.

Transition—The internet and distributed computing

A lot has been written about the Internet and where it is leading us. We will say only a little. The Internet is deeply influencing the business and practice of

technology. Millions of new people and their information have become interconnected. Late at night, around 6 A.M. while falling asleep after twenty hours
at the keyboard, the sensitive technologist can sometimes hear those thirty-five
million web pages, three hundred thousand hosts, and ninety million users
shouting "pay attention to me!"

Interestingly, the Internet brings together elements of the mainframe era and
the PC era. It is client-server computing on a massive scale, with Web clients the
PCs and Web servers the mainframes (without the MIS department in charge).
Although transitional, the Internet is a massive phenomenon that calls to our
best inventors, our most innovative financiers, and our largest multinational
corporations. Over the next decade the results of the massive interconnection of
personal, business, and government information will create a new field, a new
medium, against which the next great relationship will emerge.

Phase III—The UC era

The third wave of computing is that of ubiquitous computing, whose
crossover point with personal computing will be around 2005–2020.[7] The
"UC" era will have lots of computers sharing each of us. Some of these computers will be the hundreds we may access in the course of a few minutes of Internet browsing. Others will be embedded in walls, chairs, clothing, light
switches, cars—in everything. UC is fundamentally characterized by the connection of things in the world with computation. This will take place at a
many scales, including the microscopic.[4]

There is much talk today about "thin clients," meaning lightweight Internet
access devices costing only a few hundred dollars. But UC will see the creation
of *thin servers,* costing only tens of dollars or less, that put a full Internet server
into every household appliance and piece of office equipment. The next generation Internet protocol, IPv6,[3] can address more than a thousand devices for
every atom on the earth's surface.[1] We will need them all.

The social impact of embedded computers may be analogous to two other
technologies that have become ubiquitous. The first is writing, which is found
everywhere from clothes labels to billboards. The second is electricity, which
surges invisibly through the walls of every home, office, and car. Writing and
electricity become so commonplace, so unremarkable, that we forget their
huge impact on everyday life. So it will be with UC.

Two harbingers of the coming UC era are found in the imbedded microprocessor and the Internet. It is easy to find forty microprocessors in a middle-
class home in the USA today. They can be found in the alarm clocks, the mi-

crowave oven, the TV remote controls, the stereo and TV system, and the kids' toys. These do not yet qualify as UC for two reasons: they are mostly used one at a time, and they are still masquerading as old-style devices like toasters and clocks. But network them together, and they are an enabling technology for UC. Tie them to the Internet, and now you have connected together millions of information sources with hundreds of information delivery systems in your house. Clocks that find out the correct time after a power failure, microwave ovens that download new recipes, kids' toys that are ever refreshed with new software and vocabularies, paint that cleans off dust and notifies you of intruders, and walls that selectively dampen sounds are just a few possibilities.

The UC will bring information technology beyond the big problems like corporate finance and school homework to the little annoyances like, Where are the car-keys, Can I get a parking place, and Is that shirt I saw last week at Macy's still on the rack? Many researchers are working towards this new era— among them our work at Xerox PARC, MIT's AI-oriented "Things That Think" program,[9] the many mobile and wearable computing programs[12] (many funded by ARPA), and the many companies integrating computation into everyday objects, including Mattel and Disney.

What qualifies these as fundamental trends? First, they are about basic human relationships, and so they are trends about what matters to us, what we cannot avoid. Second, they have the property of building upon one another. It is apparent that the mainframe relationship will never die completely away, nor the personal computing relationship. Each is used as a ground for the next trend, confirming its importance in its own mode of decline. Third, they are each bountiful sources of innovation and have required reopening old assumptions and re-appropriating old technology into new contexts.

It has been said many times that PC operating systems are about twenty years behind mainframe operating systems—but this statement misunderstands what happens in technological revolutions. The radically new context of the PC—uncontrolled room, uncontrolled third party software, uncontrolled power, third party hardware components, retail sales, low cost requirements, frequent upgrades—meant that mainframe technologies required considerable adaptation. The era of ubiquitous computing is already starting to see old assumptions questioned top to bottom in computer systems design. For instance, our work on ubiquitous computers required us to introduce new progress metrics such as MIPS/watt and bits/sec/m^3. (After over a decade of stagnation, MIPS/watt has improved over a hundredfold in the past three years.) Research from radios to user interface, from hardware to theory, are impacted by the changed context of ubiquity.[13]

The most potentially interesting, challenging, and profound change implied by the ubiquitous computing era is a focus on *calm*. If computers are everywhere, they had better stay out of the way, and that means designing them so that the people being shared by the computers remain serene and in control. Calmness is a new challenge that UC brings to computing. When computers are used behind closed doors by experts, calmness is relevant to only a few. Computers for personal use have focused on the excitement of interaction. But when computers are all around, so that we want to compute while doing something else and have more time to be more fully human, we must radically rethink the goals, context, and technology of the computer and all the other technology crowding into our lives. Calmness is a fundamental challenge for all technological design of the next fifty years. The rest of this paper opens a dialogue about the design of calm technology.

Calm Technology

Designs that encalm and inform meet two human needs not usually met together. Information technology is more often the enemy of calm. Pagers, cellphones, news services, the World Wide Web, e-mail, TV, and radio bombard us frenetically. Can we really look to technology itself for a solution?

But some technology does lead to true calm and comfort. There is no less technology involved in a comfortable pair of shoes, in a fine writing pen, or in delivery in the *New York Times* on a Sunday morning than in a home PC. Why is one often enraging, the others frequently encalming? We believe the difference is in how they engage our attention. Calm technology engages both the *center* and the *periphery* of our attention and in fact moves back and forth between the two.

The periphery

We use "periphery" to name what we are attuned to without attending to explicitly.[2] Ordinarily, when we are driving our attention is centered on the road, the radio, our passenger, but not the noise of the engine. But an unusual noise is noticed immediately, showing that we were attuned to the noise in the periphery and could come quickly to attend to it.

It should be clear that what we mean by the periphery is anything but on the fringe or unimportant. What is in the periphery at one moment may in the next moment come to be at the center of our attention and so be crucial. The same physical form may even have elements in both the center and periphery. The ink that communicates the central words of a text also peripherally clues us into the genre of the text through choice of font and layout.

A calm technology will move easily from the periphery of our attention, to the center, and back. This is fundamentally encalming, for two reasons.

First, by placing things in the periphery we are able to attune to many more things than we could if everything had to be at the center. Things in the periphery are attuned to by the large portion of our brains devoted to peripheral (sensory) processing. Thus the periphery is informing without overburdening.

Second, by recentering something formerly in the periphery we take control of it. Peripherally, we may become aware that something is not quite right, as when awkward sentences leave a reader tired and discomforted without knowing why. By moving sentence construction from periphery to center we are empowered to act, either by finding better literature or accepting the source of the unease and continuing. Without centering, the periphery might be a source of frantic following of fashion; with centering, the periphery is a fundamental enabler of calm through increased awareness and power.

Not all technology need be calm. A calm videogame would get little use; the point is to be excited. But too much design focuses on the object itself and its surface features without regard for context. We must learn to design for the periphery so that we can most fully command technology without being dominated by it.

Our notion of technology in the periphery is related to the notion of affordances, due to Gibson[6] and applied to technology by Gaver[5] and Norman.[10] An affordance is a relationship between an object in the world and the intentions, perceptions, and capabilities of a person. The side of a door that only pushes out *affords* this action by offering a flat pushplate. The idea of affordance, powerful as it is, tends to describe the surface of a design. For us the term "affordance" does not reach far enough into the periphery, where a design must be attuned to but not attended to.

Three signs of calm technology

Technologies encalm as they empower our periphery. This happens in two ways. First, as already mentioned, a calming technology may be one that easily moves from center to periphery and back. Second, a technology may enhance our *peripheral reach* by bringing more details into the periphery. An example is a video conference, which in comparison to a telephone conference enables us to attune to nuances of body posture and facial expression that would otherwise be inaccessible. This is encalming when the enhanced peripheral reach increases our knowledge and thus our ability to act, without increasing information overload.

The result of calm technology is to put us at home, in a familiar place. When our periphery is functioning well we are tuned into what is happening around us and so also to what is going to happen and what has just happened. This is a key property of information visualization techniques like the cone tree[11] that are filled with detail yet engage our preattentive periphery so we are never surprised. The periphery connects us effortlessly to a myriad of familiar details. This connection to the world we called "locatedness," and it is the fundamental gift that the periphery gives us.

Examples of calm technology

We now consider a few designs in terms of their motion between center and periphery, peripheral reach, and locatedness. Below we consider inner office windows, Internet Multicast, and the Dangling String.

Inner Office Windows

We do not know who invented the concept of glass windows from offices out to hallways. But these inner windows are a beautifully simple design that enhances peripheral reach and locatedness.

The hallway window extends our periphery by creating a two-way channel for clues about the environment. Whether it is motion of other people down the hall (it's time for lunch; the big meeting is starting) or noticing the same person peeking in for the third time while you are on the phone (they really

Figure 6.1.

want to see me; I forgot an appointment), the window connects the person inside to the nearby world.

Inner windows also connect with those who are outside the office. If you see a light shining out into the hall, you know someone is working late. If you see someone tidying up their office, you know this might be a good time for a casual chat. These small clues become part of the periphery of a calm and comfortable workplace.

Office windows illustrate a fundamental property of motion between center and periphery. Contrast them with an open office plan in which desks are separated only by low or no partitions. Open offices force too much to the center. For example, a person hanging out near an open cubicle demands attention by social conventions of privacy and politeness.

There is less opportunity for the subtle clue of peeking through a window without eavesdropping on a conversation. The individual, not the environment, must be in charge of moving things from center to periphery and back.

The inner office window is a metaphor for what is most exciting about the Internet, namely the ability to locate and be located by people passing by on the information highway, while retaining partial control of the context, timing, and use of the information thereby obtained.

Internet Multicast

A technology called Internet Multicast[8] may become the next World Wide Web (WWW) phenomenon. Sometimes called the MBone (for Multicast backBONE), multicasting was invented by a then graduate student at Stanford University, Steve Deering.

Whereas the World Wide Web connects only two computers at a time and then only for the few moments that information is being downloaded, the MBone continuously connects many computers at the same time. To use the familiar highway metaphor, for any one person the WWW lets only one car on the road at a time, and it must travel straight to its destination with no stops or side trips. By contrast, the MBone opens up streams of traffic among multiple people and so enables the flow of activities that constitute a neighborhood. Where a WWW browser ventures timidly to one location at a time before scurrying back home again a few milliseconds later, the MBone sustains ongoing relationships between machines, places, and people.

Multicast is fundamentally about increasing peripheral reach, derived from its ability to cheaply support multiple multimedia (video, audio, etc.) connections all day long. Continuous video from another place is no longer television, and no longer videoconferencing, but more like a window of awareness.

A continuous video stream brings new details into the periphery: the room is cleaned up, something important may be about to happen; everyone got in late today on the East Coast, must be a big snowstorm or traffic tie-up.

Multicast shares with videoconferencing and television an increased opportunity to attune to additional details. Compared to a telephone or fax, the broader channel of full multimedia better projects the person through the wire. The presence is enhanced by the responsiveness that full two-way (or multiway) interaction brings.

Like the inner windows, Multicast enables control of the periphery to remain with the individual, not the environment. A properly designed real-time Multicast tool will offer, but not demand. The MBone provides the necessary partial separation for moving between center and periphery that a high bandwidth world alone does not. Less is more, when less bandwidth provides more calmness.

Multicast at the moment is not an easy technology to use, and only a few applications have been developed by some very smart people. This could also be said of the digital computer in 1945 and of the Internet in 1975. Multicast in our periphery will utterly change our world over the next fifty years.

Dangling String

Bits flowing through the wires of a computer network are ordinarily invisible. But a radically new tool shows those bits through motion, sound, and even touch. It communicates both light and heavy network traffic. Its output is so beautifully integrated with human information processing that one does not even need to be looking at it or be very near to it to take advantage of its peripheral clues. It takes no space on your existing computer screen and in fact does not use or contain a computer at all. It uses no software, only a few dollars in hardware, and can be shared by many people at the same time. It is called the "Dangling String" (Fig. 6.2.).

Created by artist Natalie Jeremijenko, the "Dangling String" is an eight-foot piece of plastic spaghetti that hangs from a small electric motor mounted in the ceiling. The motor is electrically connected to a nearby Ethernet cable, so that each bit of information that goes past causes a tiny twitch of the motor. A very busy network causes a madly whirling string with a characteristic noise; a quiet network causes only a small twitch every few seconds.

Much computer use is dependent on computer networks, but while we can hear the disk whir and the screen flash, we cannot see or hear the bits on the network. Like workers in windowless offices who wonder why the lights go out because they could not hear the thunderstorm, it is difficult for us to tune

Figure 6.2.

into network troubles. The dangling string is a window onto the network. It creates a context for those odd pauses, the slow internet browser, or the size of a network file transfer. The purpose of the string is not to provide any particular information, but to provide a background of *data weather* within which our computer use is better informed and less surprising.

Placed in an unused corner of a hallway, the long string is visible and audible from many offices without being obtrusive. It is fun and useful. At first it creates a new center of attention just by being unique. But this center soon becomes peripheral as the gentle waving of the string moves easily to the background. That the string can be both seen and heard helps by increasing the clues for peripheral attunement.

The dangling string increases our peripheral reach to the formerly inaccessible network traffic. While screen displays of traffic are common, their symbols require interpretation and attention, and do not peripheralize well. The string, in part because it is actually in the physical world, has a better impedance match with our brain's peripheral nerve centers.

In Conclusion

It seems contradictory to say, in the face of frequent complaints about information overload, that more information could be encalming. It seems almost nonsensical to say that the way to become attuned to more information is to attend to it less. It is these apparently bizarre features that may account for why so few designs properly take into account center and periphery to achieve an increased sense of locatedness. But such designs are crucial as we move into the era of ubiquitous computing. As we learn to design calm technology, we will enrich not only our space of artifacts, but also our opportunities for being with other people. When our world is filled with interconnected, imbedded computers, calm technology will play a central role in a more humanly empowered twenty-first century.

References

1. Bolt, S. http://www2.wvitcoe.wvnet.edu/~sbolt/ip-density.html.

2. Brown, J.S. and Duguid, P. "Keeping It Simple: Investigating Resources in the Periphery," in *Solving the Software Puzzle*, ed. T. Winograd, Stanford University.

3. Deering, S. and Hinden, R. "IPv6 Specification." http://ds.internic.net/rfc/rfc1883.txt (December 1995).

4. Gabriel, K. "Engineering Microscopic Machines," *Scientific American* 273, no. 3 (Sept. 1995): 118–121.

5. Gaver, W.W. "Auditory Icons: Using Sound in Computer Interfaces." *J. Human-Computer Interaction* 2, no. 2 (1986): 167–177.

6. Gibson, J. *The Ecological Approach to Visual Perception.* New York: Houghton Mifflin, 1979.

7. IDC. "Transition to the Information Highway Era," in *1995–96 Information Industry and Technology Update*, p. 2.

8. Kumar, V. *MBone: Interactive Multimedia on the Internet.* New York: Macmillan, 1995.

9. MIT Media Lab. "Things That Think." http://ttt.www.media.mit.edu/.

10. Norman, D.A. *The Psychology of Everyday Things.* New York: Basic Books, 1988.

11. Robertson, G.G., MacKinlay, J.D., and Card, S.K. "Cone Trees: Animated 3D Visualizations of Hierarchical Information," *HCI 91* (1991): 189–194.

12. Watson, T. "Mobile and Wireless Computing." http://snapple.cs.washington.edu:600/mobile/mobile_www.html.

13. Weiser, M. "Some Computer Science Problems in Ubiquitous Computing." *Communications of the ACM,* July 1993.

PART II

Computers and Human Identity

As computers work their way ever more deeply into our lives and work, they will become part of our identities. Who we say we are and the way we think will be influenced by our computers. We will become the technology we have created.

As profound as this observation may be, it is an old human trait. Scientific models of the mind mimic the dominant technology of their time. René Descartes's mind-body dualism, for instance, proposed a spirit inhabiting a mechanical device resembling an extraordinarily complicated clock—the "ghost in the machine." Freud's theories of the unconscious implicitly evoked a steam engine: impulses blocked from their natural release would build up pressure in the subconscious mind until they blew out elsewhere, far from their point of origin. In the last half century, our models of the mind have become electrical and computational. Today, neuroscientists routinely talk about "feedback loops" and "brain circuitry." Instinctive behaviors are said to be "programmed" or "wired"; we possess the "software" for certain kinds of mental activity. These usages are not only metaphorical, they are part of everyday practice and conversation. It is entirely respectable for a cognitive scientist in the 1990s to maintain that all cognitive processing, including processing of visual images, takes place via abstract, language-like propositions, which sound a great deal like algorithms.

Unlike earlier technological models of the mind, the algorithmic one is complicated by the reality that we have spent much of the past fifty years trying to make computers that resemble the mind. As the steam engine was an iron horse, the computer has been envisioned as a silicon human. Computer scientists have gone beyond replicating our ability to calculate; they have attacked object recognition, language comprehension, reasoning about the world, playing chess, and much more.

Given this history, it is remarkable that the authors in this section either ignore or disavow the idea that computers can or should mimic human abilities. In so doing, they have given voice to a modern paradox: brains are computers, but computers are not brains. This paradox suggests a complex symbiosis. It is as if a fungus managed to invent its own algae: the resulting lichen has new attributes and extends into new dimensions that neither fungus nor alga would have achieved on its own. Similar to us, yet not quite mirrors, computers are our newfound partners in creating something never before seen on earth. Here are some glimpses of what the first stages of this new, amalgamated metaorganism will be like, and who we will be, cohabiting with them.

In "Growing Up in the Culture of Simulation," Sherry Turkle, a computer media expert, sociologist, and anthropologist, describes the profound and surprising ways in which the children to whom she has listened so carefully think about life-nonlife distinctions. Her eight-, nine-, and ten-year-old subjects, largely innocent of the notions of the precomputer age, show us how the presence of evolving "life-forms" in games like SimLife are training them to be comfortable with fluid, mutually distinct, and sometimes even contradictory ideas of the fundamental properties of life. They are of an age at which one can still learn to speak a foreign language without an accent; an age at which talent may be fostered into virtuosity. These children will ultimately manipulate computers, and the ideas underlying them, with a facility and apparent effortlessness that will leave their elders gaping with awe. If we want to know how people will think about computing in the future, Turkle's subjects are well worth our attention.

Donald Norman, a psychologist who has studied computers and people for many years, compares the thought styles of the two symbiotic partners, human and computer—one unpredictable, robust, relatively error-insensitive, and redundant; the other abstract, linear, consistent, rational, and precise. The increasing complexity of modern life stems in large part from our attempts to accommodate ourselves to a thought style for which we never evolved and which we are not especially good at. Anyone who has had to interact with a mainframe computer, master a command-based operating system like DOS, keep track of a bewildering number of passwords, or even program a VCR knows that it is not an intuitive process. Rather than continually try to adapt to a world in which we feel awkward and ill at ease, we can look for ways to make that world accommodate itself to us. We can leave to computers the things they are good at—calculation, memory, precise and flawless repetition—and reserve for biological humans the pattern-based, language-based, sensory tasks they do best.

In counterpoint to Norman's discussion of why it's good that computers don't work like the brain, David Gelernter might have titled his essay "Why It's Bad That Computers Don't Work Like the Brain." In "The Logic of Dreams," Gelernter, a professor of computer science at Yale, proposes a radical idea that is in its way one of the more conservative ideas in this book. He is still pursuing the goal of a machine made in the mind's image. Not satisfied with distinctions such as Norman has drawn between the natural capacities of computers and humans, and unwilling to throw up his hands and admit defeat in modeling any mental capacity, Gelernter looks at one of the most distinctive of all human attributes, the ability to glean new ideas out of undirected, seemingly random associations—in other words, creativity—and suggests how such a capacity could be modeled in a computer program.

Franz Alt is a founder and past president of the ACM and a pioneer of the computing field. In "End-Running Human Intelligence," he returns us to the dominant strategy for thinking about computing capabilities: how we can take advantage of what computers do well. As if in reply to Gelernter and in support of Norman, Alt writes, "The danger lies in any attempt to let AI imitate the same strategies as are followed by the human mind in solving a problem." He compares such efforts to nineteenth-century attempts to invent a machine that would reproduce human handwriting. Since writing by hand was obviously more efficient than setting lead type, it was clearly the more promising model to follow in trying to produce machine writing. But the machine that ultimately succeeded, the typewriter, employed a mechanical strategy that in no way resembled handwriting. Alt suggests a number of tasks, many of them surprising, where entirely nonhuman strategies could outperform human intelligence: the drawing up of contracts; medical diagnosis; weather forecasting; and conducting public opinion surveys.

From the distribution of abilities comes the distribution of labor. Will computers one day take over every conceivable task, as envisioned by Jack Williamson's 1954 science-fiction story "With Folded Hands"? Paul Abrahams, a programming language expert, software engineer, private consultant, and former ACM president, takes a skeptical look at this suggestion in "The World Without Work." Comparing the prospect with an attempt to build a tower to the moon ("Each year [the builders] point with pride at how much higher the tower is than it was the previous year"), he also asks the very useful question of how far we want to go in this direction.

Finally, in "The Design of Interaction," Terry Winograd examines three current trends in the human-computer symbiosis and speculates on where they're taking us. "Computation to communication" means not only the increasing connectivity of the now worldwide network but also the shift in usage from calculation to communication. "Machinery to habitat" means that what people are most aware of when they interact with a computer has changed over the years from the machine as a piece of hardware, to the operating system, to an application program, to most recently a fully realized virtual world. "Aliens to agents" refers again to this section's dominant theme: the transformation of our vision of computers from incipient beings like ourselves, if only we could manage to give them birth, to helpers with which together we will create an astonishing new world. Winograd predicts that the new approach to design called for is more likely to be taken up by a new field, interaction design, than by computer science. He suspects that the identity of a "soft designer" does not fit with the inclinations of computer scientists to be hard technologists.

Figure 7.1. All the World's a Stage. *Richard Rosenblum, 1993. Iris inkjet print.*

SHERRY TURKLE

Growing Up in the Culture of Simulation

7

In the "Sim" series of computer games (SimCity, SimLife, SimAnt, SimHealth), a player is asked to build a community or an ecosystem or to design a public policy. The goal in each case is to make a successful whole from complex, interrelated parts. Tim is thirteen, and among his friends, the Sim games are the subject of long conversations about what they call "Sim secrets." "Every kid knows," Tim confides, "that hitting Shift-F1 will get you a couple of thousand dollars in SimCity." But Tim knows that the Sim secrets have their limits. They are little tricks, but they are not what the game is about. The game is about making choices and getting feedback. Tim talks easily about the tradeoffs in SimCity between zoning restrictions and economic development, pollution controls and housing starts.

SimLife is Tim's favorite game, because "even though it's not a videogame, you can play it like one." By this he means that as in a videogame, events in the Sim world move things forward. He is able to act on an intuitive sense of what will work even when he doesn't have a verifiable model of the rules underneath the game's behavior. ("My trilobytes went extinct," he says. "They must have run out of algae. I didn't give them algae. I forgot. I think I'll do that now.") When Tim is populating his universe in a biology laboratory scenario, he puts in fifty each of his favorite creatures, trilobytes and sea urchins, but only twenty sharks. ("I don't want fifty of those, I don't want to ruin this.") Tim can keep playing even when he has no very clear idea of what is driving events. For example, when his sea urchins become extinct, I ask him why in a conversation that only I find frustrating:

> Tim: I don't know, it's just something that happens.
> ST: Do you know how to find out why it happened?
> Tim: No.
> ST: Do you mind that you can't tell why?
> Tim: No. I don't let things like that bother me. It's not what's important.

"Your orgot is being eaten up," the game tells us. I ask Tim, "What's an orgot?" He doesn't know. "I just ignore that," he says. "You don't need to know that kind of stuff to play."

I am clearly having a hard time accepting this, because Tim tries to appease me by coming up with a working definition of orgot. "I ignore the word, but I think it is sort of like an organism. I never read that, but just from playing, I would say that's what it is."

The orgot issue will not die. A few minutes later the game informs us, "Your fig orgot moved to another species." This time I say nothing, but Tim reads my mind: "Don't let it bother you if you don't understand. I just say to myself that I probably won't be able to understand the whole game any time soon. So I just play."

As recently as ten to fifteen years ago, it was almost unthinkable to speak of computers as involved with ideas such as those Tim is putting forth—ideas about unstable meanings and emergent, evolving "truths." The computer had a clear intellectual identity as a calculating machine, a machine about certainties. In an introductory programming course I took at Harvard in 1978, the professor introduced the computer to the class by calling it "a giant calculator." Programming, he assured us, was a cut-and-dried technical activity whose rules were crystal clear.

Such reassurances captured the essence of the computer in a culture of calculation. It was an image of the computer that corresponded to the aesthetics of a mechanical age: no matter how complicated a computer might seem, what happened inside it could be mechanically unpacked. Programming was a technical skill that could be done a right way or a wrong way. The right way was dictated by the computer's calculator essence. The right way was linear and logical. This linear, logical model guided thinking not only about technology and programming, but about how computational models might inform economics, psychology, and social life. Computational ideas were one of the great modern meta-narratives, stories of how the world worked, that provided unifying pictures and analyzed complicated things by breaking them down into simpler parts. Computers, it was commonly assumed, would become more powerful, both as tools and as metaphors, by becoming better and faster calculating machines, better and faster analytical engines.

From today's perspective, these fundamental lessons of computing have been called into question. Programming is no longer cut-and-dried. Are you programming when you customize your word-processing software? When you design "organisms" to populate a simulation of Darwinian evolution in a computer simulation game called SimLife? Or when you build a room in an online community so that opening a virtual door will cause the song "Happy Un-Birthday" to ring out on all but one day of the year?

Today, the lessons of computing are not about calculation and rules, but about simulation, navigation, and, as Tim illustrated, the manipulation of "surface." The very image of the computer as a giant calculator has become quaint and dated. Fifteen years ago, most computer users were limited to typing commands. Today they use off-the-shelf products to manipulate simulated desktops, draw with simulated paints and brushes, fly in simulated airplane cockpits, and populate virtual landscapes with evolving orgots.

Today's computational models of the mind often embrace what might be characterized as a postmechanical aesthetic of complexity. Mainstream computer researchers no longer aspire to program intelligence into computers but expect intelligence to emerge from the interactions of communicating subprograms. And as human beings become increasingly intertwined with the technology and with each other via the technology, old distinctions between what is specifically human and specifically technological become more complex. Are we living life on the screen or life in the screen? To what extent have we become cyborgs, transgressive mixtures of biology, technology, and code?

Today, children such as Tim are comfortable with the idea that inanimate objects—the computers and programs that populate their education and play worlds—can both think and have a personality. It was the genius of the child psychologist Jean Piaget, first writing in the late 1920s and early 1930s, to show us the degree to which it is the business of childhood to take the objects in the world and use an understanding of how they "work" to construct theories—of space, time, number, causality, life, and mind. Fifty years ago, a child's world was full of things that could be understood in simple, mechanical ways. A bicycle could be understood in terms of its pedals and gears and a wind-up car in terms of its clockwork springs. Electronic devices such as simple radios could, with some difficulty, be brought into the old system. Since the end of the 1970s, the introduction of "intelligent" electronic toys and games has changed this understanding dramatically. When they were first introduced, some children insisted on trying to understand these intelligent toys in the same ways that they had understood mechanical systems. Some children tried to take off the back cover of an electronic toy or game to see what went on inside. But when they did so, all they could find was a chip or two, some batteries, and some wire. These new objects presented a scintillating surface and exciting, complex behavior. However, they offered no window onto their internal structure as did things with gears, pulleys, levers, or even radio tubes.

Frustrated by this opacity, the first generation of children of the computer culture sought novel ways to overcome it.[6] One way was to try to understand the workings of computational objects by pointing to the largest and most familiar objects they could find within them, the batteries. Ultimately, however, explaining how their toys worked by the code word "batteries" was not satisfying. There was nowhere children could go with it, nothing more they could say about it. The batteries were as opaque as the toy itself. So children turned to a way of understanding where they did have more to say: They turned to a psychological way of understanding.

The psychological qualities attributed to computational objects were important to how children in the first generation of the computer culture looked at the question "What is alive?" In the world of "traditional," that is, noncomputational objects, children classified things that move of their own accord as alive, while things that needed an outside push or pull were not.[3] Gradually, "moving of one's own accord" was refined to mean the "life motions" of breathing and metabolism. But from children's earliest encounters with computational toys and games, it was clear that whether or not they thought these objects were alive, children were absolutely sure that how the toys *moved* could not help them answer the question. Children discussed the computer's life in terms of the computer's apparent psychology.

Children appropriated computers by thinking of them as psychological machines. One nine-year-old, Tessa, made this point very succinctly in a comment about the chips she had seen when her computer was being serviced: "It's very small, but that doesn't matter. It doesn't matter how little it is, it only matters how much it can remember." The physical object was dismissed. The psychological object became the center of attention.

The development of a psychological language about computers began with children even younger than Tessa. In the late 1970s, a group of children at the seaside became deeply engrossed in the question of whether the computer toy Merlin could cheat at tick-tack-toe, and, if so, whether this meant it was alive. The children came up with such formulations as, "Yes, it's alive, it cheats," "Yes, it's alive, it cheats, but it doesn't know it's cheating," and "No, it's not alive, knowing is part of cheating." Four children, ages six to eight, played in the surf amid their shoreline sand castles and argued the moral and metaphysical status of a machine on the basis of traits normally reserved for people and animals: Did the machine know what it was doing? Did it have intentions, consciousness, feelings?

In the 1980s, the Aristotelian definition of man as a "rational animal" (powerful even for children when it defined people in contrast to their nearest neighbors, the animals) gave way to a different distinction. People were still defined in contrast to their neighbors. But now, children saw people as special because they could "feel." Instead of being rational animals, people were emotional machines. One twelve-year-old, David, put it this way: "When there are computers who are just as smart as people, the computer will do a lot of the jobs, but there will still be things for the people to do. They will run the restaurants, taste the food, and they will be the ones who will love each other, have families and love each other. I guess they'll still be the ones who will go to church." Like him, many children responded to the computer presence by erecting a higher wall between the cognitive and affective, the psychology of thought and the psychology of feeling. Computers thought; people felt. Or, people were distinguished from the machines by a "spark," a mysterious element of human genius.

By the early 1990s, things had changed: Children had strikingly different responses to the computer presence. Questions of whether computers were alive still provoked animated discussion, but by this time many children knew how to dispose of these questions. Many had absorbed a ready-made, culture-made response, which was, "Computers are not alive. They are just machines."[5] On one level, what had seemed problematic for children a decade earlier no longer seemed to cause such a stir. But there was something deceptive about this return to a seemingly peaceful border between the human and the technological. Although the boundary between people and machines was intact, what children saw across that boundary had changed dramatically. Children were no longer concerned with the question of whether computers were alive. They knew they were not. The issue of aliveness had moved into the background as though it was settled. But the notion of "the machine" had been expanded to include having a psychology. Children retained a psychological language as the dominant way of talking about computers: "It's talking, it's thinking, it's deciding, its brain is too tired to give another answer," they say. In this choice of language, children allowed computational machines to retain an animistic trace, a mark of having passed through a stage where the issue of the computer's aliveness was a focus of intense consideration. Children tuck computers into the "machine" category, but even as they do, they attribute certain properties to "made" objects that were previously reserved to natural ones. "Knowing, thinking, and having memories" no longer seem to transgress the boundaries between machines and people, because being a machine has come to include the capacity to do all of these things. A generation ago, the idea of a "psychological machine" seemed a contradiction in terms. This is no longer the case.

The most recent generation of children is willing to grant psychological status to not-alive machines because it has become accustomed to objects that are both interactive and opaque. These children have learned what to expect of computational objects and how to discriminate between them and what is alive. But even as children make these discriminations, they also grant new capacities and privileges to the machine world on the basis of its animation if not its life. They endow the category of artificial objects with properties, such as having intentions and ideas, previously reserved for living beings. They come up with a new category, "sort of alive," for describing life on the screen.

Tim says, "You get to mutate plants and animals into different species. . . . You are part of something important. You are part of artificial life." As for the Sim creatures, Tim thinks that the "animals that grow in the computer could be alive," although he adds, "This is kind of spooky." Laurence, a more blasé fifteen-year-old, doesn't think the idea of life on the screen is spooky at all. "The *whole point* of this game," he tells me,

> is to show that you could get things that are alive in the computer. We get energy from the sun. The organisms in a computer get energy from the plug in the wall. I know that more people will agree with me when they make a SimLife where the creatures are smart enough to communicate. You are not going to feel comfortable if a creature that can talk to you goes extinct.

Trisha, a ten-year-old who has been given a modem for her birthday, puts the emphasis not on communication but on mobility when she considers whether the creatures she has evolved on SimLife are alive:

> I think they are a little alive in the game, but you can turn it off and you can also not "save" your game so that all the creatures you have evolved go away. But if they could figure out how to get rid of that part of the program so that you would *have* to save the game and if your modem were on, then they could get out of your computer and go to America Online.

Sean, thirteen, who has never used a modem, comes up with a variant on Robbie's ideas about Sim creatures and their Internet travel: "The [Sim] creatures could be more alive if they could get into DOS. If they were in DOS, they would be like a computer virus and they could get onto all of your disks and if you loaned your disks to friends, it would be like they were traveling."

In Piaget's classical studies of the 1920s, the central variable in how children thought about what was alive was motion. Simply put, children took up the question of an object's "life status" by asking themselves whether the object could move of its own accord. Now, in children's comments about the creatures that exist on simulation games, in talk about "travel," via circulating disks or over modems, in talk of viruses and networks, movement is resurfacing in a new guise, now bound up in the idea of communication. *Significantly, the resurfacing of movement is also bound up with notions of presumed psychology: it is universally assumed that the creatures on Sim games have a desire to "get out" of the system into a wider computational world.*

The creatures that exist in simulation space challenge children to find a new language for talking about their status as alive or not alive, as do mobile robots who wander about making their "own decisions" as they go. When the computer scientist Rodney Brooks asked his young daughter whether his "mobots" (small, mobile robots that demonstrate some degree of "emergent" intelligence) were alive, she said: "No, they just have control." At the end of the 1992 Artificial Life Conference, I sat next to eleven-year-old Holly as we watched a group of robots with distinctly different "personalities" compete in a special "Robot Olympics." Holly's father had an entry, but since his turn would not come for quite some time, Holly was happy to have company. Our conversation turned to robots and life, and Holly became quite thoughtful. Then she said unexpectedly, "It's like Pinocchio."

> First Pinocchio was just a puppet. He was not alive at all. Then he was an alive puppet. Then he was an alive boy. A real boy. But he was alive even before he was a real boy. So I think the robots are like that. They are alive like Pinocchio [the puppet], but not "real boys."

Holly used the fairy tale to support a classification that separated the merely-animated puppet from biological life. When boundaries are challenged we look for ways to support them. Holly called upon Pinocchio for support as she watched robots that pretended to a kind of life. Her reaction to the boundary-transgressing robots recalled the science fiction story by Philip K. Dick, "Do Androids Dream of Electric Sheep?"—the story on which the film *Blade Runner* was based. When a devastating war destroys most biological life, highly sophisticated androids do much of the work, and the society's police are occupied with preserving the boundary between "real" and "artificial" life. A "real" insect or frog or fish is a valuable and cherished pet. In our own culture, we are in a complex position in our attitudes towards biological life. There is a new preoccupation with tracing one's biological parents, a new preoccupation with genetics as a predictor of life's successes and difficulties. Genetic essentialism puts computational objects on the "other side" of the line. But the computational enterprise of artificial life—trying to create machines that manifest emergent properties of evolution and natural selection—challenges the line itself. At the same time as we cultivate a new genetic essentialism, computational objects are challenging our ideas about the uniqueness of biological life. We live in a time of making boundaries and relaxing them in a complex double movement.

Among the children I have studied most recently, there is a significant diversity of opinion about the parameters of life. Faced with the Robot Olympics in 1992, Holly drew a line; in my 1994 study of children and the game of SimLife, my young informants were willing to be more inclusive. They spoke easily about a list of things that encourage them to see the "stuff" of computers as the same "stuff" of which life is made. The list is led by "shape shifting" and "morphing." Shape shifting is the technique used by the evil android in the popular film *Terminator II* to turn into the form of anything he touched—including people. A nine-year-old showed an alchemist's sensibility when he explained how this occurs: "It is very simple. In the universe, anything can turn to anything else when you have the right formula. So you can be a person one minute and a machine the next minute." For children, morphing has become a general term that covers changes in form, including changes across the animate/inanimate barrier. Different children expand on it in somewhat different ways. For a thirteen-year-old girl, it is a photographic technique, much used in advertising and now available at home: "You can do morphing at home with software that you can buy for less than a hundred dollars; my friend has it, I know." A ten-year-old boy has a lot to say about morphing, all of it associated with the adventures of "The Mighty Morphin Power Rangers," a group of action heroes who, as he explains, "turn from teenagers to androidal/mechanical dinozords and megazords and back." He patiently elaborates, "Well, the dinozords are alive; the Power Rangers are alive, but not all the parts of the dinozords are alive, but all the parts of the Power Rangers are alive. The Power Rangers become the dinozords." And of course, there are the omnipresent "transformer toys" that shift from being machines to being robots to being animals (and sometimes people). Children play with these plastic and metal objects, and in the process, they learn about the fluid boundaries between mechanism and flesh.

It is Spring, 1994, and a group of seven-year-olds is playing with a set of plastic transformer toys that can take the shape of armored tanks, robots, or people. The transformers can also be put into intermediate states so that a "robot" arm can protrude from a human form, or a human leg from a mechanical tank. Two of the children are playing with the toys in these intermediate states (that is, in their intermediate states somewhere between being people, machines, and robots). A third child insists that this is not right. The toys, he says, should not be placed in hybrid states. "You should play them as all tank or all people." He is getting upset because the other two children are making a point of ignoring him. An eight-year-old girl comforts the upset child. "It's okay to play them when they are in between. It's all the same stuff," she said, "just yucky computer 'cy-dough-plasm.'"

I have said that when Piaget interviewed children in the 1920s and 1930s about which objects were alive and which were not, he found that children honed their definition of life by developing increasingly sophisticated notions about motion, the world of *physics,* whereas when I studied the nascent computer culture in the early 1980s, children argued about whether a computer was alive through discussions about its *psychology.* Did the computer "know things" on its own or did it have to be programmed? Did it have intentions, consciousness, feelings? Did it "cheat"? Did it "know" it was cheating?

My work on children and computers in the 1980s was separated from Piaget's by a half century. In that time there had been a radical change in the kinds of objects in the world offered to children. The presence of computational objects disrupted the coherency of an older story about life and motion that children had told for generations because psychology had entered the picture. But even with this big change, Piaget's findings and my own had something crucial in common: they both told a story of children seeking and finding consistency. By the mid 1980s, faced with "intelligent" machines, children took a new world of objects and imposed a new world order.

In the past ten years, that order has been strained to the breaking point. In the mid 1990s, children will talk about computers as "just machines" but describe them as sentient and intentional. The very notion of a machine has been reconfigured to include an object with a psychology. Faced with the objects of the culture of simulation, children still try to impose order, but they do so in the manner of theoretical bricoleurs, "making do" with whatever materials are at hand, "making do" with whatever theory can fit a prevailing circumstance. Different children comfortably hold different theories, and individual children are able to cycle through different theories at a rapid pace.

My current collection of comments about life by children who have played with computational objects that exhibit some "evolutionary" properties (programmable robots, the Sim creatures, programs called "The Blind Watchmaker" and "Tierra") includes, The robots are in control but not alive, would be alive if they had bodies, are alive because they have bodies, would be alive if they had feelings, are alive the way insects are alive but not the way people are alive; the Tierrans are not alive because they are just in the computer, could be alive if they got out of the computer, are alive until you turn off the computer and then they're dead, are not alive because nothing in the computer is real; the Sim creatures are not alive but almost alive, they would be alive if they spoke, they would be alive if they traveled, they're alive but not "real," they're not alive because they don't have bodies, they are alive because they can have babies, and finally, for an eleven-year-old who is relatively new to SimLife, they're not alive because these babies don't have parents. She says, "They show the creatures, and the game tells you that they have mothers and fathers but I don't believe it. It's just numbers, it's not really a mother and a father." There is a striking heterogeneity of theory here, and children cycle through different theories.

The MIT computer scientist Mitchel Resnick reported on a striking example of theoretical cycling-through in a fifth grader named Sara. She jumped back and forth from a psychological to a mechanical language as she talked about the creatures she had built from a construction kit of Lego construction blocks controllable with the Logo programming language. Sara was considering whether her Lego-Logo robot would sound a signal when its "touch sensor" was pushed, and she said, "It depends on whether the machine wants to tell . . . if we want the machine to tell us . . . if we tell the machine to tell us"[4] (p. 402). Resnick commented that within a span of ten seconds, "Sara had described the session in three different ways. First she viewed the machine on a psychological level, focusing on what the machine 'wants.' Then she shifted intentionality to the programmer, and viewed the programmer on a psychological level. Finally, she shifted to a mechanistic explanation, in which the programmer explicitly told the machine what to do."

Within less than ten seconds, Sara "cycled through" three perspectives on her creature (as psychological being, as intentional self, as instrument of its programmer's intentions). These perspectives are equally present for her at all times. For some purposes, she finds one or another of them more useful.

In the short history of how the computer has changed the way we think, it has often been children who have led the way. In the early 1980s, children, prompted by computer toys that spoke, did math, and played tick-tack-toe, dissociated ideas about consciousness from ideas about life, something that historically had not been the case. These children were able to contemplate sentient computers that were not alive, a position which I find in grownups now, a decade later. Today, children are pointing the way towards a radical heterogeneity of theory in the presence of computational artifacts that evoke evolutionary processes.

In his history of artificial life, Steven Levy[2] suggested that one way to look at where artificial life can "fit in" to our way of thinking about life is to envisage a continuum in which the Sim creatures, for example, would be more alive than a car, but less alive than a bacterium. My observations of how children are dealing with artificial life's objects suggests that they are not constructing hierarchies but are heading toward parallel definitions that they alternate in a way that recalls Sara's rapid cycling.

In this style of thinking, children are not alone. Adults, too, are exhibiting the same sort of behavior. A compelling example of what this style of thinking looks like in adults is powerfully captured in *Listening to Prozac*, a book by the psychiatrist Peter Kramer[1] that describes a series of personal experiences that led Kramer to call into question his basic preconceptions about people. In one, Kramer prescribed an antidepressant medication for a college student. The young man took Kramer's prescription and thanked him. At the next therapy session the patient appeared with symptoms of anxiety. Kramer was not concerned. It is not unusual for patients to respond with jitters to the early stages of treatment with antidepressants. Sometimes the sensation disappears by itself, sometimes the prescribing physician changes the antidepressant, or adds a second, sedating medication at bedtime. Kramer says:

> I considered these alternatives and began to discuss them with the young man when he interrupted to correct my misapprehension: He had not taken the antidepressant. He was anxious because he feared my response when I learned he had "disobeyed" me.
>
> As my patient spoke, I was struck by the sudden change in my experience of his anxiety. One moment, the anxiety was a collection of meaningless physical symptoms, of interest only because they had to be suppressed, by other biological means, in order for the treatment to continue. At the next, the anxiety was rich in overtones . . . emotion a psychoanalyst might call Oedipal, anxiety over retribution by the exigent father. The

> two anxieties were utterly different: the one a simple out-
> pouring of brain chemicals, calling for a scientific response,
> however diplomatically communicated; the other worthy of
> empathic exploration of the most delicate sort. (173)

Kramer experienced this "alternation" of perspective because his patient did not take his medication. Other people experience such "alternations" when they *do* take medication. It is commonplace for people to have moments when they equate their personality with their chemistry, just as women who feel the effects of their hormones on their states of mind during their monthly cycle and even more so during pregnancy may also go in and out of a sense that chemistry is in control. The experience of taking a pill and observing a change in one's "self" challenges any simple notions of a psychological self as mind divorced from chemistry, but people typically do not abandon a sense of themselves as psychology and spirit. Rather, they *cycle through:* "I am my chemicals" to "I am my history" to "I am my genes."

It may in fact be in the area of genetics that we have become most accustomed to cycling through. In *Listening to Prozac,* Kramer follows his story about the antidepressant and his alternating notions of anxiety with a story about genetics and alternating views of personal identity. About to admire his friends' two children for qualities in which they "took after" their parents with a comment like, "Don't the genes breed true?" Kramer stopped himself when he remembered that both children were adopted. "Since when had I—I, who make my living through the presumption that people are shaped by love and loss, and above all by their early family life—begun to assume that personality traits are genetically determined?" (p. 174) In fact, Kramer hadn't begun to assume this, he just *sometimes* did. "Cycling through" alternative theories has become how we think about our minds. In the culture of simulation it is coming to be the way we think about life itself. And it is our children who are leading us.

References

1. Kramer, P. *Listening to Prozac: A Psychiatrist Explores Antidepressant Drugs and the Remaking of the Self.* New York: Viking, 1993.

2. Levy, S. *Artificial Life: A Report from the Frontier Where Computers Meet Biology.* New York: Vintage Books, 1993.

3. Piaget, J. *The Child's Conception of the World,* translated by J. Tomlinson and A. Tomlinson. Totowa, NJ: Littlefield, Adams, 1960.

4. Resnick, M. "Lego, Logo, and Life," in Langton, C. *Artificial Life: I.* Redwood City, CA: Addison-Wesley, 1989.

5. Turkle, S. *Life on the Screen: Identity in the Age of the Internet.* New York: Simon and Schuster, 1995.

6. Turkle, S. *The Second Self: Computers and the Human Spirit.* New York: Simon and Schuster, 1984.

DONALD A.
NORMAN

Why It's Good That Computers Don't Work Like the Brain

8 A common prediction among technologists—and a common fear among the general population—is that computers and robots will come to mimic and even surpass people. No way. Computers and people work according to very different principles. One is discrete, obeying Boolean logic; and deterministic, yielding precise, repeatable results. The other is nondiscrete, following a complex, history-dependent mode of operation, yielding approximate, variable results. One is carefully designed according to well-determined goals and following systematic principles. The other evolves through a unique process that is affected by a wide range of variables, severely path dependent, fundamentally kludgy, difficult to predict, and difficult to emulate. The result—biological computation—is complex, parallel, multimodal (e.g., ionic, electrical, and chemical).

People are mobile, social, cooperative, and competitive agents, with a rich biological, evolutionary, and cultural heritage that has taken tens of thousands of years to develop and that is implicit in the structures and patterns of the world, human artifacts, and patterns of interactions. People are very good at some things (such as walking and seeing), very bad at others (such as arithmetic). The differences between humans and machines make for excellent complements, even while they also make for remarkably poor interaction.

It's good that computers don't work like the brain. The reason I like my electronic calculator is because it is accurate: it doesn't make errors. If it were like my brain, it wouldn't always get the right answer. The very difference is what makes the device so valuable: I think about the problems and the method of attack. It does the dull, dreary details of arithmetic—or in more advanced machines, of algebraic manipulations and integration. Together, we are a more powerful team than either of us alone.

The same principle applies to all our machines: the difference is what is so powerful, for together, we complement one another. However, this is useful only if the machine adapts itself to human requirements. Alas, most of today's machines, especially the computer, force people to use them on their terms, terms that are antithetical to the way people work and think. The result is frustration, an increase in the rate of error (usually blamed on the user—human error—instead of on faulty design), and a general turning away from technology.

Will the interactions between people and machines be done correctly in fifty years? Might schools of computer science start teaching the human-centered approach that is necessary to reverse the trend? Are you an optimist or a pessimist?

The ever-increasing complexity of everyday life

One thing seems clear about the technology of the future: it will get more complex. We will have to rethink a number of our basic assumptions. The ever-connected world provides unheralded advantages, but also the potential for large-scale disruptions in basic functions. The need for security and safety provides conflicts with the need for ease of use and personal privacy.

Think of all those interconnecting systems. Think of everyone always being connected to a worldwide system of information servers and other people. Privacy goes away, or at least is much modified. The ability to work with others improves: the ability to enjoy quiet and solitude declines. All of these problems are known: much has been written about them. But one inherent problem has been little remarked upon—the ever-increasing complexity of everyday life.

Technology provides more and more functions essential to our life. Many of the new technologies involve communication networks that interconnect large numbers of systems. These lead to an increase in the complexity of social interactions and the sheer number of contacts among people. As a result, the number of potential weak points increases and thereby the dangers. As we become ever more dependent upon technology, any failure causes increasing disruption of business, education, and everyday life. True, the systems are often designed to minimize disruption, but the result is that although failures are not common, when they do occur, they have the potential to disrupt large geographic regions.

The United States has already seen large-scale disruptions: unusual combinations of loads have caused electrical power to fail over a number of states for tens of hours. Accidental severance of telephone cables has brought down the air traffic control for the country. A simple programming error has caused havoc to a large region of telephone switching offices. A failure of an online computer system deprived businesses and individuals across the country of essential e-mail services for a day—even longer when some of the messages could not be recovered. Each of these occurrences is always accompanied by assurances that they are unique events that will not happen again. The assurances are correct: the very same event will indeed not reoccur. Instead, some new situation will arise that causes an even larger failure to cascade across the multiple, interconnected systems, to create heretofore unpredicted circumstances in a unique, never-again-to-be-repeated problem.

The ever increasing amount of interactions among people, institutions, and governments presents ever more opportunities for disaster. Many entrepreneurs marvel at and revel in the complexity, which offers bountiful business opportunities. The natural tendency of governments and institutions is to tackle each known problem by formulating new rules, regulations, and laws to control the abuses. But these (usually) well-intentioned efforts simply proliferate, adding yet more complexity to our lives.

A critical question is whether our governmental and legal societies are up to the challenge. Rule-based systems are a standard area of concern to computer scientists. Within this discipline, the difficulties of working with a large body of unstructured, unsystematic rules are well known. But government and organizations do not appear to have the same degree of understanding. Society is governed by the laws and rules of institutions and governments that have been designed by many groups of people over decades—centuries—of time. The result is inconsistent, vague, and ambiguous rules that interact in unplanned ways. Some might have been clear and precise in the era in which they were developed, but they have become outmoded or imprecise with the passage of time and the invention of new technologies. The results are unstable, unpredictable systems.

Even my own home grows rapidly in complexity. Eight remote control devices to operate my home television. An ever increasing set of manuals for the ever increasing number of home appliances. A dozen or so electric clocks to be reset when power fails and during the biannual time switchover. Items to be lubricated, adjusted, dusted, tested. Batteries to be checked and replaced. Security precautions increase in the home, the office, and in public buildings and transportation centers. We need to carry multiple keys, identification cards and badges, and other security aids. And each of these aids has to be protected against unauthorized duplication.

The need for protection has given rise to an increase in the number of different passwords individuals are required to use for everything from computer accounts, telephone and bank services, entry to restricted areas, and an increasing number of Internet services. The demands upon security of these passwords are exactly counter to human abilities. People are best at remembering meaningful information, but these are the easiest keys for others to discover. The security requirements drive us toward the use of nonsense—randomly generated symbol strings—different for each application, each to be changed at frequent intervals.

Experimental psychologists will quickly point out that the requirements for increased security go exactly counter to ease of memory: the most secure strings are exactly those that are most difficult to remember. People rebel, with the usual solution either to disregard the rules and select a simple password, the same for all applications, or to write them all down.

What will the solution be? Probably reliance upon physical or biometric devices. The former is simply a modern, electronic expansion of the mechanical key: a physical device that must be inserted into the system before one is allowed access. But because this can possibly be counterfeited or stolen, it will have to be accompanied by some personal identification. Today this is the much-abused memorized password, but it will most likely migrate to biometric data: face recognition, voice recognition, thermal fingerprints, retinal scans, DNA analysis, and so on.

The demands for more security go counter to the demands for privacy. This is simply an extension of the existing conflict between law-enforcement agencies that would like the ability to discover illegal activities and individuals and institutions that wish to keep their activities private. The same forces that require better identification of individuals before they can access locations or services also give rise to the potential for severe privacy violations. The traditional tension between freedom and security will increase.

The question is, Are there alternatives, or are we doomed to ever increasing complexity, ever increasing loss of privacy and freedom?

Humans versus computers

The ever increasing complexity of everyday life brings with it both great opportunities and major challenges. One of the challenges, that the brain does not work at all like a computer, also provides us with an opportunity: the possibility of new modes of interaction that allow us to take advantage of the complementary talents of humans and machines.

The modern era of information technology has been with us but a short time. Electronic computers are less than half a century old. The technology has been constructed deliberately to produce mechanical systems that operate reliably, algorithmically, and consistently. Their bases are mathematics, or more precisely arithmetic in the case of the first computing devices and logic in the case of the more modern devices. Even analog computers followed similar guidelines, the design was algorithmic and precise: repeatable, understandable operation was the goal.

Contrast this with the human brain. Human beings are the results of millions of years of evolution, where the guiding principle was survival of the species, not efficient, algorithmic computation. Robustness in the face of unexpected circumstances plays a major role in the evolutionary process. Human intelligence has coevolved with social interaction, cooperation and rivalry, and communication. The ability to learn from experience and to communicate and thereby coordinate with others has provided powerful adaptations for changing, complex environmental forces. Interestingly enough, the ability to deceive seems to have been one driving force. Only the most intelligent of animals is able to employ a sophisticated level of intentional, purposeful deception. Only the most sophisticated animal is capable of seeing through the deceit. Sure, nature also practices deception through camouflage and mimicry, but this isn't willful and intentional. Primates are the most skilled at intentional, willful deception, and the most sophisticated primate—the human—is the most sophisticated deceiver of all.

Note that some deception is essential for the smooth pursuit of social interaction: the "white lie" smoothes over many otherwise discomforting social clashes. It is not best to tell the truth when someone asks how we like their appearance or their presentation or the gift they have just given us. One could argue that computers won't be truly intelligent or social until they too are able to deceive.

We humans have learned to control the environment. We are the master at creating artifacts. Physical artifacts make us stronger, faster, and more comfortable. Cognitive artifacts make us smarter. Among the cognitive artifacts are the invention of writing and other notational systems, such as mathematics, dance, and musical notation. The result of these inventions is that our knowledge is now cumulative: each generation grows upon the heritage left behind by previous generations. This is the good news. The bad news is that the amount to be learned about the history, culture, and the techniques of modern life increases with time. It now takes several decades to become a truly well-educated citizen. How much time will be required in fifty years? In one hundred years?

Biological brain computation is very different from the precise, logic-driven systems that constitute current computers. The differences are dramatic. Computers are constructed from a large number of fast, simple devices, each following binary logic and working reliably and consistently. Errors in the operation of any of the underlying components are not tolerated, and they are avoided either by careful design to minimize failure rates or through error-correcting coding in critical areas. The resulting power of the computer is a result of the high speed of relatively simple computing devices.

Biological computation is performed by a very large number of slow, complex devices—neurons—each doing considerable computation and operating through electrical-chemical interactions. The power of the computation is a result of its highly parallel nature and the complex computations done by each of the billions of neural cells. Moreover, these cells are bathed in fluids whose chemistry can change rapidly, providing a means for rapid deployment of hormones and other signals to the entire system, chemicals that are site-specific. Think of it as a packet-switching deployment of chemical agents. The result is that the computational basis is dynamic, capable of rapid, fundamental change. Affect, emotion, and mood all play a powerful—and as yet non-understood—role in human cognition. Certainly, all of us have experienced the tension when logic dictates one course of action but mood or emotion another: more often than not, we follow mood or emotion.

Whatever the mode of computation—and the full story is not yet known—it is certainly not binary logic. Each individual biological element is neither reliable nor consistent. Errors are frequent—whole cells may die—and reliability is maintained through massive redundancy as well as through the inherently error-tolerant nature of the computational process and, for that matter, the relatively high error-tolerance of the resulting behavior.

These last points cannot be overemphasized. The body, the brain, and human social interaction have all coevolved to tolerate large variations in performance under a wide-ranging set of environmental conditions. It is a remarkably error-tolerant system. It uses both electrical and chemical systems of communication and processing. Conscious and subconscious processing probably use different computational mechanisms, and the role of emotions and affect is not yet understood.

Human language serves as a good example of the evolution of a robust, redundant, and relatively noise-insensitive means of social communication. Errors are corrected so effortlessly that often neither party is aware of the error or the correction. The communication relies heavily upon a shared knowledge base, intentions, and goals: people with different cultural backgrounds often clash, even though they speak the same language. The result is a marvelously complex structure for social interaction and communication. Language is learned effortlessly by all humans yet still defies complete scientific understanding.

Human error

Machines, including computers, don't err, in the sense that they are fully deterministic, always returning the same value for the same inputs and operations. Someday we may have stochastic and/or quantum computation, but even then, we will expect those computers to follow precise laws of operation. When computers do err, it is either because a part has failed or because of human error, either in design specification, programming, or faulty construction. People are not fully deterministic: ask a person to repeat an operation, and it is subject to numerous variations.

People do err, but primarily because they are asked to perform unnatural acts: to do detailed arithmetic calculations, to remember details of some lengthy sequence or statement, or to perform precise repetitions of actions. In the natural world, no such acts would be required: all are a result of the artificial nature of manufactured and invented artifacts. Perhaps the best example of the arbitrary and inelegant fit of human cognition to artificial demands contrasted with a natural fit to natural demands is to contrast people's ability to communicate with programming languages versus human language.

Programming languages are difficult to learn, and a large proportion of the population is incapable of learning them. Moreover, even the most skilled programmers make errors, and error finding and correction occupy a significant amount of a programming team's time and effort. Moreover, programming errors are serious. In the best circumstances, they lead to inoperable systems. In the worst, they lead to systems that appear to work but produce erroneous results.

A person's first human language is so natural to learn that it is done without any formal instruction: people must suffer severe brain impairment to be incapable of learning language. Note that "natural" does not mean "easy": it takes over a decade to master one's native language. Second-language learning can be excruciatingly difficult.

Natural language, unlike programming language, is flexible, ambiguous, and heavily dependent on shared understanding, a shared knowledge base, and shared cultural experiences. Errors in speech are seldom important: Utterances can be interrupted, restarted, even contradicted, with little difficulty in understanding. The system makes natural-language communication extremely robust.

Human error matters primarily because we followed a technology-centered approach in which it matters. A human-centered approach would make the technology robust, compliant, and flexible. The technology should conform to people, not people to the technology.

Today, when faced with human error, the traditional response is to blame the human and institute a new training procedure; blame and train. But when the vast majority of industrial accidents are attributed to human error, it indicates that something is wrong with the system, not the people. Consider how we would approach a system failure due to a noisy environment: we wouldn't blame the noise, but we would instead design a system that was robust in the face of noise.

This is exactly the approach that should be taken in response to human error: redesign the system to fit the people who must use it. This means to avoid the incompatibilities between human and machine that generate error, to make it so that errors can be rapidly detected and corrected, and to be tolerant of error. Blame and train does not solve the problem.

Humans and computers as cooperating systems

Because humans and computers are such different kinds of systems, it should be possible to develop a symbiotic, complementary strategy for cooperative interaction. Alas, today's approaches are wrong. One major theme is to make computers more like humans. This is the original dream behind classical artificial intelligence: simulate human intelligence. Another theme is to make people more like computers. This is how technology is designed today: the designers determine the needs of the technology and then ask people to conform to those needs. The result is an ever increasing difficulty in learning the technology, and an ever increasing error rate. It is no wonder that society exhibits an ever increasing frustration with technology.

Consider the following attributes of humans and machines taken from today's machine-centered point of view:[1]

The Machine-Centered View

People	Machines
Vague	Precise
Disorganized	Orderly
Distractible	Undistractible
Emotional	Unemotional
Illogical	Logical

Note how the humans lose; all the attributes associated with people are negative, all those associated with machines are positive. But now consider attributes of humans and machines taken from a human-centered point of view:

The Human-Centered View

People	Machines
Creative	Dumb
Compliant	Rigid
Attentive to change	Insensitive to change
Resourceful	Unimaginative

Now note how machines lose: all the attributes associated with people are positive, all the ones associated with machines are negative.

The basic point is that the two different viewpoints are complementary. People excel at qualitative considerations, machines at quantitative ones. As a result, for people, decisions are flexible because they follow qualitative as well as quantitative assessment, modified by special circumstances and context. For the machine, decisions are consistent, based upon quantitative evaluation of numerically specified, context-free variables. Which is to be preferred? Neither: we need both.

As stated earlier in this chapter, it's good that computers don't work like the brain. An electronic calculator is accurate: it doesn't make errors. If it were like a brain, it wouldn't always get the right answer. The very difference is what makes the device so valuable. This is the approach we should follow in all of our systems: exploit the differences.

The power of representation

Human beings have evolved over time to perform in the world through a variety of mechanisms. One is symbolic representation, supplemented by a rational processing system. Another is the use of perceptual representations. A third is a form of distributed processing, in which the world itself and other humans are part of the computational and representational process.

In general, humans can be characterized as pattern-recognizing, meaning-finding systems, excellent at interpreting information, finding meaning, and explaining phenomena rapidly and efficiently. Humans usually go beyond the information available, relying heavily upon a large body of prior experience. Humans excel at pattern recognition, especially context-dependent recognition: people are very good at integrating meaning and context into a task. Usually this is very good, but it occasionally leads to unfortunate decision biases and perceptual narrowing that exclude alternative interpretations. When we are good, we are very very good, and when we are bad, we are awful.

In general, perceptual processes are performed rapidly and efficiently with specialized, parallel processes.

Human symbolic processes are slow, serial, and limited in power. Here there are severe limits on the size of working memory. People are excellent at determining meaning and maintaining the spirit of the content. They are poor at maintaining high accuracy, at integrating large quantities of symbolic information, and at detecting patterns in symbolically displayed information.

Representation is the key to human cognition. Examine tick-tack-toe, the children's game, contrasted with the game of "15": Tick-tack-toe is represented perceptually, the goal being to form a straight line of three of your pieces before your opponent does. The Game of "15" is symbolic: given the digits 1 through 9, the game is played by the two opponents alternately selecting digits until one person has succeeded in accumulating three digits whose sum is 15.

The game of "15" is completely isomorphic to tick-tack-toe, which means that the two are logically equivalent, but people find the game of "15" difficult and tick-tack-toe simple. The difference is in the form of representation. People play tick-tack-toe perceptually: a glance at the board shows which pieces form a straight line, which do not. Computers lack this kind of perceptual system, so it would be difficult to program a computer to play tick-tack-toe by performing a perceptual analysis for lines and other geometric patterns among the pieces. Of course, tick-tack-toe doesn't present much of a challenge for computers, but this is because they are usually programmed so that the representation used for tick-tack-toe is very similar to that used for the game of "15," and even the most brute-force search through the tree of possible moves doesn't present much of a computational challenge.

There are several lessons to be learned from the above comments:

- If we want to empower people, we must translate symbolic problems and data collections into perceptual ones. Human working memory for symbolic information is limited: provide rich external sources of information. Exploit human sensory capabilities, which are extremely powerful and robust.
- Rely on people for rapid assessment and analysis. Use people for strategic overviews. Let people interpret and provide meaning to information.
- Do not rely on people for accurate or reliable responses or for precise information (e.g., numerical values, names, or positioning control). Instead, treat any such information as an approximation. Ideally, machines should take over the requirement for accuracy and reliability, letting people provide high-level guidance and interpretation.

The development of modern computers and their associated fast, real-time, interactive display systems makes it possible to translate otherwise symbolic information into a format that fits human cognition. Usually this means perceptual information rather than symbolic or numeric. But it also means eliminating or minimizing the need for the person to provide precise numerical information. In this way, people can be freed to do higher-level evaluation, to state intentions, to make mid-course corrections and reformulations of the problem.

Biological computation

The differences between people and machines result from the form of logic and electronic circuits used by today's machines. Suppose we were able to grow biological circuits? Fifty years ago, nobody predicted the transistor, let alone integrated circuits and very large scale integration. Perhaps within the next fifty years we can do biological computation.

"Biological computation" means a system of neurons, grown biologically in an appropriate nutrient substrate, shaped for the computing requirements of the system under construction. I don't mean neural networks, which are computer simulations of abstract neurons. Nor do I mean DNA computation in which the chemistry of DNA molecules is exploited to solve complex problems. I mean artificially grown neurons doing biologically real, brain-like operations.

The human brain is unexcelled at tasks such as pattern recognition, natural language, and control of locomotion. The sensory system is unmatched in the sheer number and density of its powerful receptors for touch, temperature, taste, spatial orientation, and of course, sight and sound. Why build artificial logic circuits when we could use the already existing ones: biological cells?

Will there be other advances in computation? Very likely. Moreover, conventional computing will not go away. Today's computers are superior to biological computers in accuracy, precision, and repeatability. I expect the two to merge, with biological computers excelling at the pattern-recognition, pattern-driven aspects of computing, and logic computers excelling at numerical computation and anything that requires precision and repeatability. The result can be a true complement of action, a true symbiosis of people and machines.

Reference

Norman, D.A. *Things That Make Us Smart*. Reading, MA: Addison-Wesley, 1993.

The Logic
of Dreams

9

We understand half the mind fairly well and the other half barely at all—which is surprising given the suggestive facts that are all around us, scattered like shells on the beach at low tide, so plentiful it is hard to avoid crunching them underfoot. Most cognitive scientists do largely succeed, though, in proposing theories that simply ignore the nonanalytic, non-problem-solving, non–goal-directed aspect of thought. It would be absurd for me to claim that my work (or that of the small number of others who are interested in these problems) accounts for all the neglected facts. It doesn't, but at least it acknowledges that they exist and need explaining.

Although you rarely hear the term "thought style," no variable is more important if you are trying to understand human beings. It refers to the way a person strings thoughts together (like beads on a necklace) into a thought stream, or "train of thought," or "stream of consciousness." Thinking is the process of successively choosing, on purpose or subliminally, a next thought to follow your current one. The first fact you might casually pick up off the beach, a fact everyone knows but most cognitive scientists ignore, is that a person's thought style tends to change in broadly predictable ways over a day and a lifetime. Most adults, furthermore, have a characteristic thought-style, the one in which they are most comfortable, a "cognitive gait"—and different people have different gaits. One person notices a loose bolt on the driveway and thinks, "I'll bet that's why the lawnmower's handle looks askew"; another sees the same bolt and thinks about the glint of morning sun on shiny metal and a certain pond at sunrise. How do we account for these differences and what do they mean? How do we account for the variations in cognitive gait over a day and a lifetime?

For concreteness, here are two sample thought streams in different styles. "Tide's coming in . . . space between water and sea wall disappearing . . . trek down the beach into town to buy hamburgers likely to work going, fail coming home . . . go later? Drive instead?" versus, "Tide's coming in . . . waves smashing and churning . . . colonial village butter churn . . . second grade, grind of the school buses. . . . " Each is sensible, neither is random, but they accomplish different things. We understand thought streams of the first type (often called "analytic" or "logical" or "abstract") fairly well. We barely understand the second style (which I will call "low focus"; the other is "high focus") at all.

Let's grab a few more facts off the beach. In the limit, "low-focus" thought turns into the item psychoanalysts call "free association." There is a continuum of styles between maximum focus (strictly goal-directed) and minimum focus (pure free association). As you slide down the continuum, your mental focus has an increasing propensity to wander away from the problem at hand or the scene before you. Ultimately, when you are free-associating, it wanders all over the mental landscape and never returns anywhere except by accident. One thing everyone knows about the spectrum is that the low end is associated with relaxation or tiredness. Your thoughts are more likely to drift when you are tired or relaxed; you are most apt to stay focused when you are wide-awake and alert. As you fall asleep, your thinking turns into free-associating. (Sleep-lab studies of "sleep-onset mentation" confirm this.) Psychoanalysts are famous for promoting free association by inviting their patients to take a load off, lie down, and relax.

Merely by picking up facts on the beach you might guess, then, that the cognitive spectrum is connected in some way to your physical state. Low-focus thought has to do with sleepiness, but isn't restricted to the moments before you fall asleep; the body cycles through alert and tired states throughout the day, and you might hypothesize that your mental gait cycles too.

But why should it? What good is low-focus thought? Is it mere mental junk—the absence of real thought? Many cognitive psychologists seem to think so. When a distinguished psychologist like Robert Sternberg writes that "reasoning, problem solving, and intelligence are so closely interrelated that it is often difficult to tell them apart,"[11] the message is that "intelligent thought" and "problem solving" are essentially the same thing—which defines low-focus thought out of existence.

Yet to define thought as "problem solving" is obviously wrong; when you lean back, gaze out the window, and let your mind wander, you are solving no problem, but plainly you *are* thinking. What good is low-focus thought? For one, it is the indispensable precursor to sleep. We tend to assume that the body chooses some state and thought follows—you lie down on the psychoanalyst's couch and relax, then start to free-associate; you fall asleep and then start to dream; some Asian meditation methods use physical relaxation to bring about low-focus mental states. But the actual relationship between mental and physical states is more complicated: sleep-onset experiments have shown that you start to dream (you experience brief hallucinations) *before* you fall asleep.[12] Low-focus thought almost certainly plays a role in *creating* physical relaxation.

But there is far more to the low-focus story—including parts that are of more interest to computer scientists, who have never been terribly interested in putting their machines to sleep.

Here is an interesting pair of hinged-together beach facts. However hard you try, you cannot make yourself fall asleep. Sleep is not a thing that can be accomplished by effort or concentration; it can only be accomplished by *un*concentrating. Exactly the same holds for creative insight: you cannot accomplish it by effort or concentration; it can only be accomplished by *un*concentrating. Most people know this from first-hand experience. It is a hard thing to establish objectively, but some fascinating and ingenious experiments[7] tend to confirm it. There is also a large anecdotal literature of first-person introspective reports, often by scientists, about the "creative moment" at which insight hits. (Some of the most interesting stories are summarized in Penrose's *The Emperor's New Mind*.[9]) The anecdotes tend to confirm what we know, that creative insights are associated not with concentration but with unconcentration.

(Many cognitive scientists dismiss such anecdotes as "unscientific," "mere introspection." They are indeed unscientific and mere introspection, yet it strikes me as the height of arrogance to ignore them. Suppose the anecdote-reporting scientists are wrong in their beliefs about creativity's psychological profile. Suppose their best insights really *did* hit them in moments of hard concentration or methodological thought. But if that's so, exactly what cognitive phenomenon caused all these thoughtful people to be deluded in exactly the same way? Accept their stories at face value or reject them; you owe us an explanation either way. Dismissing them as "unscientific" misses the point.)

It is natural to ask, then, whether creativity might not be associated with low-focus thought. The one thing most psychologists accept about creativity is that it is based on the discovery of new analogies: on the sticking-together of thoughts (say "high tide" and "butter churn") that don't usually go together but do somehow make sense together. Analogies lead, if you are lucky, to the "restructuring" of a problem and the discovery of a creative solution, or to random creative insights. "Eureka!" you might shout, "I'll bet I could churn butter by anchoring a sealed container of cream near the sea wall at high tide!" It won't make you rich and could possibly get you committed, but it's something.

Low-focus thought is the kind in which thoughts are linked up in a "free-wheeling" way. It makes sense to guess, then, that low-focus thought is the context in which analogies are formed and creative insights come to you. That doesn't explain how analogies are discovered in the first place (doesn't explain *why* you happened to think of "butter churn" after you had contemplated the sea beating the wall at high tide), but it does put the analogy-finding process in context and suggests something important about the cognitive spectrum. Roughly speaking, you need the upper end for analytic problem-solving, the middle for creativity, the bottom for sleep. (If your focus is *too* low, you can't be creative—if you stumble across a new and suggestive connection, you will merely stumble onward. Creativity requires a focus level that is low enough to reveal connections but high enough so that you notice when something interesting has happened, and thereupon "tighten up your focus" and figure out where you stand and what you've got.)

A coherent picture starts to emerge, then, on the basis of a few fascinating research papers and (mainly) putting two plus two together. Everyone has a continuum of thought styles available to him; high-focus thought is analytical, problem-solving thought; as you slide down the spectrum, analogies and metaphors are more apt to emerge, and you pass through a region in which creativity occurs; as you slide further downward you wander off into free-association and eventually fall asleep.

Such a spectrum would be important to computer science because it would suggest that no machine stands any chance of simulating human thought unless it simulates the cognitive spectrum first.

We can flesh out the spectrum a bit by noting that if sleep onset or sleep thought itself represents the bottom edge, the most striking fact about this type of thinking is that it is hallucinatory. Which prompts us to ask, Does thought grow "more hallucinatory" as you slide down the spectrum? Do your thoughts grow more vivid, in other words, until they occupy you completely and shut off your access to external reality altogether? The fascinating phenomenon of "involuntary childhood memories" (discussed by Salaman[10]) involves adults remembering childhood incidents with near-hallucinatory intensity; such memories crop up in low-focus, mind-wandering mental states. These are topics I will not get into here, but childhood thought and premodern thought (as captured for example in ancient literature) both seem to be richer in low-focus states than typical modern adult thought—and they are both associated, also, with thoughts that occasionally reach near-hallucinatory intensity. (I discuss these topics and the cognitive spectrum in general in my book *The Muse in The Machine*.[6])

But if the spectrum is going to serve any practical purpose in computer science, there is a big question we have yet to touch upon. Granted that low-focus thought is free-flowing and sometimes makes connections between thoughts that are superficially distant or wholly unrelated and that such connections can serve as the bases for new analogies and, in turn, for creative insights—where do the connections come from? How do we know when two "unrelated" thoughts go together?

Analogy formation is the biggest open question in cognitive science. Most researchers acknowledge that in the end, we simply don't understand how it happens. The philosopher Jerry Fodor[3] writes, "It is striking that, while everybody thinks analogical reasoning is an important ingredient in all sorts of cognitive achievements that we prize, nobody knows anything about how it works." Nevertheless, many cognitive scientists lean toward a "spreading activation" view of analogy-finding inspired by computer science: a given memory "activates" other memories with which it shares attributes; the newly-activated memories activate more memories, and so forth. Of the many theories of analogy in circulation, almost all have this "spreading activation" flavor at least in part: the bay at high tide makes you think of a butter churn because a particular aspect of the bay (the motion of its surface) happens also to be an aspect of churning cream.

Analogy-finding probably does depend in part on something like spreading activation. Yet spreading activation alone is a screamingly inadequate explanation. It cannot possibly be the whole story. Imagine someone writing (in a blaze of inspiration) "my love is like a red, red rose." It used to be that poets routinely compared women to flowers, and yet it is hard to think of two objects that are more dissimilar—in size, shape, color, texture, and habits, to name only a few of the more important departments. The similarities (such as they are) are intensely abstract. And yet this analogy is one of the most hackneyed and obvious ones around. It was hackneyed in the seventeenth century and was well known to Biblical authors thousands of years ago. What makes this seemingly nonobvious analogy so blazingly obvious in fact?

I will summon one poet and one psychologist to explain. Samuel Taylor Coleridge wrote in a remarkable letter to the poet Robert Southey,

> I hold, that association depends in a much greater degree on the recurrence of resembling states of Feeling, than on Trains of Ideas. . . . I almost think, that Ideas *never* recall Ideas, as far as they are Ideas—any more than Leaves in a forest create each other's motion—The Breeze it is that runs through them; it is the Soul, the state of Feeling—(in Willey,[13] p. 96.)

Metaphor is driven, the psychologist C.E. Osood claimed in 1963, by the fact that "such diverse sensory experiences as a *white* circle (rather than black), a *straight* line (rather than crooked), a *rising* melody (rather than a falling one), a *sweet* taste (rather than a sour one), a *caressing* touch (rather than an irritating scratch) . . . can share a common affective meaning" (cited in Paivio[8] p. 159)

Here is the obvious guess: the poet's rose and his girlfriend make him *feel* the same way. They occasion similar emotions.

Computer science gives us better words to describe this phenomenon than does psychology or poetry. "Emotion" is a remarkably powerful cognitive phenomenon because it is a many-to-one mapping: a *function* that, when presented with a large bunch of separate values, yields *one particular* value in return. When confronted with a complex scene or picture or memory you feel *some* particular way. The crowded beach at high tide in midsummer, the empty beach on a raw day in midwinter are each complex scenes with many attributes; each scene incorporates the look, sound, smell, and feel of many separate elements. But for all its complexity, the scene before you makes you feel some particular way.

And that fact, that emotion is a single-valued function of many arguments—that it captures a complex scene in a single characteristic value—is obviously relevant to the unsolved problem of analogy. The analogy problem is exactly this: given two complex thoughts or memories that share few attributes or none, how does your brain manage to plunk them down next to each other in a low-focus thought stream? The "emotion function" is an obvious solution: if (while gazing idly out the window) you happen to invent a brand-new analogy between "hippopotamus" and "Land Rover," it needn't be because hippos and Land rovers *look* or *sound* or *are built* the same way; it can happen because they make you *feel* the same way.

For computer science, the implications are obvious and immediate. Let's say you are writing a program that has managed to capture in a database a large number of scenes or events or cases or records or simulated memories. You want to discover analogies among the elements of your database. How do you do it? This way: you code a function called emotion(). Your emotion function accepts one database record (with its many elements) and yields an "emotion code"—the emotion code is represented, let's say, as a real number. To find candidate analogies, you compute emotion(R) for each record R in your database; if the values yielded by emotion(R1) and emotion(R2) are close, there may be a valid analogy between R1 and R2 (however superficially dissimilar they appear; even if they are as far apart as a woman and a rose).

If you wanted to simulate not merely analogy-finding but the cognitive spectrum itself, you'd build a "focus" variable into your system and have the software build thought streams: repeatedly fetch a record from the database, examine it, and fetch another. The way it would "fetch another" would depend on the current value of focus. When focus is relatively high, your system would insist on a high degree of overlap between successive thoughts: they would have to be *about* more or less the same things. As the value of focus dropped, your program would show an increasing propensity to place two records next to each other in the stream for no better reason than that they engender similar emotions.

How would you carry this trick off? How would you build your emotion function? Your one alternative is to try stealing one from a human being (or from a group of humans averaged together). You would attempt to ascertain how records like the ones in your database make some actual person feel; you would wire that information into the system and try to get the software to ape human performance as you feed it fresh records.

We are working along these lines in an ongoing research project called the "FGP Machine"—a piece of software (a "virtual machine") centering on three operations called "Fetch," "Generalize," and "Project." Our intention at first was to build on the cognitive spectrum idea to build an expert database. When you described an "event" or "scene" or "case" to the system (for example a chest x-ray to be diagnosed, a flower to be identified), it used a database of previous cases to propose values for unknown attributes of the new case. In the process of doing so, it fetched from the database and presented for the user's consideration exactly those previous cases that seemed most "relevant" to the new one—on the basis not of simple keyword matching but of "deep similarity."

Once the system was capable of doing these pragmatic tasks convincingly, we set out to add simulated emotion in an attempt to support lower-focus "thought" chaining. (The "thoughts" are nothing like real thoughts, of course; each "thought" is simply a database record—an immensely crude approximation of a real thought or memory.) In the early stages of this work, we've proceeded like this: we built a database of anecdotes—a collection of microstories, each a few paragraphs long. The microstories are variations on a common narrative theme; but each story has different details and outcomes, and so they each have a different tone and feel. We wanted the system to be capable of computing an "emotion value" for each story, where an emotion value consists of ratings on each of thirteen separate "emotion axes." (The stories and rating scale were borrowed from cognitive psychologists.) If the system succeeded in computing plausible emotion values, those values could be used in turn to drive lower-focus thought chaining. The system could fetch a story and then, depending on its focus level, fetch another that was either "rationally" (in higher-focus modes) or "emotionally" (when focus was lower) related to the first.

The system would base its computation of emotion values on a database of ratings reported by human subjects. Just as it is capable of proposing a diagnosis of "fibroadenoma" for an undiagnosed breast lesion based on a database of related cases, it can propose an emotion rating for a story based on ratings generated by human subjects for related stories. (In no sense does it "understand" these stories; it views each one as a clump of meaningless features.)

Results are encouraging but are too preliminary to report. (This phase of the project is joint research with Yale student Matt Feizli; the software was built by Scott Fertig of Yale, and earlier phases are described in such papers as Fertig and Gelernter 1991[2]; Fertig and Gelernter, 1993[1]; and the *Muse* book.[6])

If we succeed in adding a primitive kind of simulated emotion to the FGP system, we will still be miles from even a preliminary simulation of the cognitive spectrum. We believe, nevertheless, that we are ambling slowly but surely in the right direction. Fellow researchers see in our work a project that is dramatically at odds with the field's current heading and its best wisdom, but as far as we are concerned, we are merely picking facts off the beach and putting them together in the obvious way. It is good for the field, we believe, to have a range of projects underway, some mainstream and some (like ours) eccentric. Beachcombing is unfashionable at the moment, but it's always possible that the fashion will change.

What are the implications of this research effort for computer science—particularly in the long term, not over the next five months but the next fifty years? The question may sound presumptuous; a research effort as risky and unorthodox as the one I've described could sink without a trace at any time and have no long-term implications for anything. If it has prospered and generated fruitful results so far, it has yet to tackle the (in engineering versus intellectual terms) hardest parts of the job. But a researcher with a radical program assumes ipso facto a responsibility to think big and damn the funding cuts, torpedoes, etc. This work has long-term practical implications and long-term theoretical ones.

Our secondary goal in practical terms is to produce software that is capable of bringing experience to bear on hard problems—broadly speaking, hard problems of the fill-in-the-blank, complete-the-picture type. Our software, even if it were fully developed, would never rock the intellectual boat—would not be capable of announcing, "Never mind what kind of heart disease this patient has, we are actually seeing an entirely new type of disease process based not on bacteria or viruses but on Third Rate Palooka-cells. And the only treatment is two weeks in Acapulo." But our system *would* be capable of pointing to the right diagnosis on a list of choices, and capable of explaining its "thinking" not on the basis of abstract disease models (it knows nothing about disease) but on experience: consider case x, case y, case z; note that this case resembles x in the following ways, suggesting the following conclusions; resembles y in the following ways, and so forth. Interestingly, expert clinicians often do talk this way. Experience carries a lot of weight; in most areas it is the only real basis of expertise.

The system could perform "diagnosis" in any domain where the basic objects or events could be captured electronically. It could propose business or financial strategies or legal precedents, predict legal outcomes, diagnose broken machinery or broken processes.

But its most important implications in practical terms have to do with knowledge management. We are faced repeatedly nowadays with situations in which we would like to tell the computer "show me data that is relevant to. . . . " This would, often, be the desirable way of using a huge news database like Nexis: not "find me every story that uses these keywords," but "what have you got on zeppelins?" Our system is capable of detecting the "word cloud" that hovers around zeppelins—of noticing that "rigid airships" is essentially determining for zeppelins, that "airships" and "blimps" are related, that "helium" or "hydrogen" or "Blaugas" or "Eckener" or "Hindenburg" might be telltales of a zeppelin-related case.

The biggest problem computer science faces over the next fifty years is this: how do we handle too much data? Our data-collecting and data-storage capabilities are gigantic and growing fast. How do we convert these untold trillions of bytes into information? How do we get value out of this mass of data instead of getting buried under it? I discussed this problem in relation to the FGP system in a 1989 general-audience piece[4] and a 1991 book (*Mirror Worlds*[5]). I believe that the problem continues to pick up steam today and that our research project will play a valuable role in solving it.

There are implications here also for the future of AI. AI in its first incarnation tended to see thought as the mere working out of theories. Since the early 1980s a second phase has set in, where experience and common sense are understood as the driving forces in almost all thought processes outside of highly specialized and unusual ones. It's a healthy trend. But it has produced little of value because of the painfully shallow view its exponents tend to have of human thought; their views are virtually always less nuanced, less comprehensive, and less sophisticated than those Wordsworth or Coleridge entertained around two centuries ago. AI's most important discovery over the next half century might turn out to be humility.

References

1. Fertig, S. and Gelernter, D. "Is connectionism necessary?" in *Proc. Bar Ilan Symp. on Foundations of Artificial Intelligence:* 1993.

2. Fertig, S. and Gelernter, D. "A Software Architecture for Acquiring Knowledge from Cases," in *Proc. of the International Joint Conference on Artificial Intelligence:* 1991.

3. Fodor, J. *The Modularity of Mind: An Essay on Faculty Psychology.* Cambridge, Mass.: MIT Press, 1983.

4. Gelernter, D. "The metamorphosis of information management." *Scientific American* (Aug. 1989).

5. Gelernter, D. *Mirror Worlds.* New York: Free Press, 1991.

6. Gelernter, D. *The Muse in the Machine.* New York: Free Press, 1994.

7. Metcalfe, J., and Weibe, D. "Intuition in Insight and Nonsight." *Memory and Cognition* 15(1987):238–246.

8. Paivio, A. "Psychological Processes in the Comprehension of Metaphor," in *Metaphor and Thought,* ed. A. Ortony. New York: Cambridge University Press, 1979.

9. Penrose, R. *The Emperor's New Mind: Concerning Computers, Minds and the Laws of Physics.* Oxford and New York: Oxford Univ Press, 1989.

10. Salaman, E. *A Collection of Moments: A Study of Involuntary Memories.* London: Longman, 1970.

11. Sternberg, R.J. "Reasoning, Problem Solving, and Intelligence," in *Handbook of Human Intelligence,* ed. R.J. Sternberg. New York: Cambridge University Press, 1982.

12. Vogel, G.W. "Sleep-onset Mentation," in *Mind in Sleep: Psychology and Psychophysiology,* eds. S.J. Ellman and J.S. Antrobus. New York: John Wiley, 1991.

13. Willey, B. *Samuel Taylor Coleridge.* New York: W.W. Norton, 1973.

FRANZ L. ALT

End-Running Human Intelligence

10

1.

In the context of mapping out the directions in which "computing" may be advancing in the next several decades, it may be useful to think about some tempting approaches that should *not* be followed.

It seems to me that we are in danger of falling into a trap in some of our efforts to solve problems by means of "artificial intelligence." Specifically, the danger lies in any attempt to let AI imitate the same strategies as are followed by the human mind in solving a problem. Artificial intelligence is different from human intelligence, and it should exploit the difference.

In the following we shall consider several problem areas in which future progress is less likely to be achieved by AI programs imitating human behavior than by AI approaches making use of the computer's strengths. In these problem areas a computer-germane approach is likely to outperform humans.

An example from a different field of human endeavor may help to illustrate a reason for this caution. It seems that at some time in the nineteenth century a great deal of effort was put into inventing a "writing machine" that would trace in ink on paper a semblance of human handwriting. This was before the existence of practical typewriters. Since it was then obvious that handwriting was easier and faster than printing—the latter requiring cumbersome assembly of movable type—it is understandable that some inventors should have directed their efforts at mechanization of the former.

These efforts turned out to be a blind alley once typewriters had become available. Not only were typewriters faster and more efficient than mechanized handwriting machines could have been, but they turned out to be more useful as well—easier-to-read and more presentable. Nowadays it is fairly straightforward to produce software for simulating handwriting, but its usefulness is quite limited.

Why were the efforts at a handwriting machine misdirected? Because they adopted a strategy suggested by the preexisting state of the art, rather than one appropriate to new technology.

What turns out to be successful in the end is to follow the path of least resistance—to let a new technology do what comes easiest to it and let it find its own niche.

Imitating the human mind by computer programs is only one of many possible strategies for AI. It is a most worthwhile endeavor in its own right, if only because of what it teaches us about human thinking, and even more because it is a problem that wants to be solved—in Edmund Hillary's words, "because it is there." It should not be misused for solving other problems when other AI strategies are more computer-germane.

2.

For an example of an efficient way of using AI, turn to recent software for playing chess. The difference between the computer's strategy and a human's was succinctly expressed by world master Gary Kasparov after losing the first game, trying the second one, and winning the remaining games of the tournament. The strength of the computer program was in evaluating all possible outcomes of the next half dozen or more moves ahead, far more than the human player can keep in his head. The human is more likely to select a move on the basis of similar situations in past games. He is also trying to get a feel for his opponent's strategy—which improves his play in the later games of the series.

In other words, current programs for playing chess, paradigms of AI, are efficient because they do not imitate the human mind. They do, of course, contain other features besides following possible sequences of future moves, but these are not likely to be their strongest points.

One would like to see a master player *assisted by* a computer, an unbeatable combination. A tournament between two human masters, each with a different computer and program at his fingertips, would test the man-machine combination, just as a horse race tests the combination of a jockey and his steed.

In theory, a chess computer could map an unbeatable strategy at the first move by following all possible sequences of moves to the end. The number of possible sequences of moves is, however, so astronomically large that no computer is likely to be up to it even fifty years from now. On the other hand, the computer is even now so closely matched to the human player's capacity that far from needing fifty years, it may well be a clear winner after the next round of improvements.

3.

Let us now look for other problems that might be attacked by AI, and where the computer might outrun the human mind by using different strategies.

A lawyer drafting a contract between two corporations has to consider a number of different circumstances that might arise in the future—changing economic conditions, for instance, or the outcomes of future business decisions, third-party actions, patent suits, or whatnot—and make sure that the interests of his client are safeguarded.

The number of possible combinations of circumstances may well be too large for human contemplation. Each requires calculating the "payoff" for the client. As an oversimplified example, suppose the only circumstances that need to be considered are the prices of four commodities, each of which might take one of ten possible values—a total of ten thousand possible situations.

A mere listing of all possible situations, though helpful, may be unwieldy. A more useful computer program would divide the situations into classes such that the same contract provisions are required for all situations within a class.

In one sense these applications in the field of law are analogous to chess playing, namely, in that a large number of possible situations has to be considered. In the case of chess, however, that number is potentially so large that it is limited by the capacity of the computer, and substantially improved performance will result from hardware development. Legal applications, on the other hand, can probably be greatly expanded even with today's hardware; only new software is needed.

What is important in both fields is that the large amount of data is generated by the computer itself from a limited number of rules: for chess, the rules governing the permissible moves for each piece; for the simplified legal case we have described, merely a four-dimensional grid of numbers. In contrast, the human player has to spend the greatest mental effort in selecting a small number of likely outcomes, a strategy that is difficult to imitate by AI and less effective than the brute-force approach of the computer.

Today's computer applications in the field of law consist mainly of data banks of past court decisions, and they use the methods of AI at most in a limited way.

4.

Now let us turn to another field of professional work, that of medicine.

In a pipe dream that could be reality in fifty years, a patient is so wired up that all his or her body functions are monitored continually and the results automatically recorded in a computer. Abnormal levels (syndromes) are noted and diagnoses obtained by the computer program from the simultaneous presence of certain sets of syndromes, using a large data bank of syndromes.

The procedure differs from the one followed by a human physician. When confronted with a patient's complaint (headache!), the physician will search for other complaints that from experience frequently occur at the same time (fever? eye strain? mental stress? bruise or other injury to the head?) and perform or request a small number of lab tests (blood pressure, urine analysis, chest x-ray). This may suggest one or more possible diagnoses, or none. Depending on the outcome, the process may be repeated step by step.

To consider and evaluate all possible tests simultaneously would be beyond the mental capacity of the physician, but it is a simple and straightforward task for the computer. An AI program that imitates the human physician's process, on the other hand, would be long and cumbersome. Even so, the outcome of this process is less dependable than that of the data bank we are envisaging.

Since we mentioned experience, let it be remarked that AI "learning programs" for the most part do not imitate the learning processes of the human brain but follow simpler and more computer-germane strategies.

5.

Weather forecasting, strange as it sounds, has characteristics analogous to those of medicine. We may envisage a future in which a very large number of densely spaced stations record the current weather and read the data automatically into a large central computer, or network of computers, that calculates the forecasts from the mathematical equations governing air flow.

By contrast, human weather forecasters do not integrate the differential equations of air flow, nor could they do so in the future if confronted with a wealth of data from weather stations. What they do is to look at a weather map the way a hiker looks at a topographical map, observing the shape and spacing of contour lines (of elevation for the hiker, of air pressure for the meteorologist) and draw conclusions based on past experience, obtaining approximate averages of temperature and precipitation.

It would be possible to write AI programs following the human train of thought, but the computer-germane approach of routinely integrating the equations would most likely be both faster and more accurate.

What weather prediction and medical diagnosis have in common is that both will require large amounts of data to be automatically recorded in a computer—an economic problem more than a technological one.

6.

Public opinion surveys! We are approaching the point where virtually everybody will have access to the Internet, or perhaps a part of it, or perhaps something else to replace it, especially if or when this is done free of charge, the cost being borne perhaps by advertisers. At that stage every holder of, or candidate for, elected office can have up-to-date information about how his or her constituents feel about a range of current issues.

Ultimately, the whole population becomes one virtual town meeting. We no longer need senators or representatives, the people can vote directly on every proposed bill. But for now, let us leave this horrifying thought aside and consider how, say, a candidate can use such data.

One problem to be faced is the correlation, if any, between different issues. On many issues respondents will simply line up, for example left to right or liberal vs. conservative; thus, we may expect a high degree of correlation between respondents' reactions on human rights, civil liberties, and poverty. We might think of every respondent as being placed at some point on a straight line. If we ask questions about additional issues of this kind, we get little additional information.

But attitudes on other issues—say abortion—cut across this simple lineup. We now must mentally place respondents on a two-dimensional scheme. And if we add issues that correlate with neither of these—importance of lowering taxes? of reducing the budget deficit, or the national debt?—we need more dimensions. Potentially, there could be as many dimensions as there are separate issues; that is, if there is no correlation between any two of them.

It is of practical importance to find the minimum number of dimensions that we can get away with, and which issues best represent these. In our two-party, winner-take-all system a one-dimensional lineup, or an approximation to it, will suggest an optimal campaign strategy. (The situation would be different with, for example, proportional representation.)

A human investigator will get a solution to this problem by intuition from a small sample of answers. A computer would be hard put to imitate this approach but would find a better solution by straightforward computation. The mathematics for this is well known and need not be detailed here.

7.

We have considered five examples of problem areas in which future progress may be expected: chess playing, legal problems, medical diagnosis, weather prediction, and public opinion surveys. One thing they all have in common is that progress can be made by handling large amounts of data, larger than can conveniently be examined by humans. In chess playing and legal problems these data are developed by the computer itself; in the other three cases they are automatically recorded on input devices using mostly existing technologies, but on a large scale.

Chess playing will require greater computing speed and perhaps greater storage capacity. The same may be true in weather forecasting, though less crucially. Otherwise, no new technology is needed, though of course whatever comes along will help. In legal problems existing hardware seems quite adequate, though radically new software would have to be created.

In every case the computer will compete with human professionals (if we take the liberty to call chess playing a professional activity). The introduction of such methods may therefore encounter political resistance, which could be harder to overcome than either technical or economic obstacles.

How will professional people be affected? Consider two scenarios:

(a) The equipment is so expensive that only big firms can afford it. Thus professional activities would become big business, with sufficient political clout to establish themselves. Independent professionals would disappear.

(b) As has happened in the past, the price of the equipment comes down enough to make it widely available (perhaps by time-sharing). Independent professionals remain and are forced by competition to use the most powerful equipment available. The services they render, through man-machine cooperation, are enormously superior to those available at present.

Finally: Our reason for considering these examples is that they show how artificial intelligence can *surpass* human intelligence by not imitating the strategies used in human thinking but by adopting strategies better adapted to computers.

8.

A few words about the oldest application of computers, numerical calculation. Customarily, this is not considered as an instance of artificial intelligence. For the most part the programs follow faithfully the path of human thinking. There are some examples, however, of numerical calculation supplanting other mathematical approaches employed by humans.

The compilation of mathematical tables was a very active undertaking just before the advent of electronic computers. The New York Mathematical Tables Project produced, in the late 1930s and early 1940s, a succession of volumes of tables of mathematical functions of unsurpassed accuracy. Started as a WPA project under the direction of Arnold Lowan, the MTP was used for computations for the military during World War II; it subsequently moved to Washington D.C. and was incorporated into the National Bureau of Standards.

At Harvard University an IBM-built large automatic (but nonelectronic) computer produced, under the direction of Howard Aiken, a series of volumes of values of Bessel functions. And there were other groups engaged in the production of mathematical tables.

The usefulness of such tables was greatly impaired by the availability of electronic computers. Their main use had been for scientists and engineers to look up numbers needed as input to computations; once such computations were done on computers, it was easier to write subroutines ("macros" in today's terminology) to produce these input values as needed.

Another example of a mathematical activity being supplanted by numerical calculation was the solution of differential equations. Some types of differential equations can be solved explicitly by formulas, and it used to be that mathematicians used great effort and ingenuity to find such formulas. When they were unable to do this, they regretfully had recourse to step-by-step numerical integration. But with electronic computers numerical integration became so effortless that it was often used even when formulas might have been available. *Sic transit gloria mundi.*

9.

We now turn to one field that may possibly serve as a counterexample to the ideas expressed earlier in this paper: the understanding of natural language. It is not implausible to assume that this problem can best be attacked by imitating human thinking.

(We are not referring to the problem of recognition of *spoken* words, another worthwhile and difficult problem. Rather we are dealing with a case where sentences formulated in unrestricted natural language have already been introduced into the computer.)

What is the computer to do with such an expression? How is it to be used? Speaking simply: If it is a command, carry it out. If it is a question, answer it. If it is a statement of fact or a conjecture, store it in such a way that it can be retrieved and used later.

Stating it so simply in a way begs the question. To do anything like what we have demanded will in almost every case require that the computer, before dealing with one expression, must already have dealt with many others, which it must have organized into a system.

Why do I say that just possibly this problem can best be attacked by imitating human thinking? Perhaps only because I personally cannot think of any other way to approach it. More deeply, perhaps because human language is so closely related to thought. By some schools it is a chicken-and-egg question whether all thinking presupposes the existence of language. Do we have a thought first and then translate it into words? Or is the thought itself, as soon as it occurs to us, already formulated in words?

I propose to leave such questions open. The purpose of this article was merely to show that in many mundane cases end runs around the strategies of human thinking are more powerful than these strategies by themselves.

PAUL W. ABRAHAMS

A World Without Work

11

Imagine a world where smart machines do all the work—a world in which man no longer lives by the sweat of his brow. Intelligent robots, freely available to all, provide all the economic benefits of slavery without any of its moral and ethical drawbacks. Want a new home? Just ask a robotic architect to design your dream house, a crew of construction robots to build it. Want to travel to a faraway place? A robot taxi can take you to the airport, where a robotically piloted aircraft can whisk you to your destination. Ready for dinner? A few words to your robotic chef and the food will be prepared just as you wish, with inventive touches ensuring that no meal is just like a previous one—unless you want it that way, of course.

Looking for diversion? An authorial robot can create a new, unique entertainment for you in any medium, be it a simulated football game, a rock video, a baroque cantata, or an oil painting. Want to play tennis or chess? A perfectly matched robotic opponent awaits you.

Are you physically ill? A robotic physician, possessing all the medical knowledge known to civilization and the dexterity of the perfect surgeon, will see to your cure. And despite your life of comfort and luxury, are you sick at heart? Talk as long as you wish to a robotic therapist—ever patient, never judgmental, always wise and insightful.

I was a graduate student at MIT in the late 1950s and early 1960s when the field of artificial intelligence, fathered by my advisor Marvin Minsky, was just getting started. In those heady times, machines that could think seemed to be no more than a couple of decades away. The General Problem Solver program of Newell, Simon, and Shaw appeared to offer deep insight into how the human mind worked and the prospect of being able to simulate it on a computer. Their paper on the General Problem Solver Self-Applied proposed an exciting model of how computers could program *themselves* to be intelligent. The model ran into a few programming difficulties, but we all thought that those difficulties would not be hard to overcome. Experience showed otherwise: the General Problem Solver Self-Applied was never successfully implemented.

In the hubris of those days, I thought a lot about what people would do when intelligent machines did all the work. I imagined the computer of the future as an intelligent, capable slave, offering the promise of the benefits of slavery without any of its moral and ethical drawbacks. I contemplated how people would spend their time in the "world without work" and how people would respond to computer-created art or how well they could be helped by computerized psychiatrists.

More than thirty years later, despite extraordinary progress in computer technology, the promises of artificial intelligence remain unfulfilled. It's as though a group of people had proposed to build a tower to the moon. Each year they point with pride at how much higher the tower is than it was the previous year. The only trouble is that the moon isn't getting much closer.

Hubris about what computers can do has been with us since the early days of computing. About the time that ACM was created fifty years ago, one of its founders, Edmund Berkeley, was publishing the magazine *Computers and Automation*, which often described "giant brains" in glowing terms. We can see the same kind of hubris today in the bright portraits of the Information Superhighway painted by publications such as *Wired* magazine. To be sure, other fields of science and technology share that hubris—think of the world of nearly free electricity that nuclear power was once supposed to bring us via the Atoms for Peace program or the ambitious plans for space exploration that captured the imagination of Americans in the Sixties.

An instructive example of the unfulfilled promises of artificial intelligence is the fate of the Fifth Generation Computer Project, sponsored by the Japanese Ministry of International Trade and Industry in the 1980s. Edward Feigenbaum (himself an AI pioneer) and Pamela McCorduck described it in their book *The Fifth Generation: Artificial Intelligence and Japan's Computer Challenge to the World.*[1] In 1983 they wrote:

> The vehicles of revolution are to be known as knowledge information processing systems. . . . The Japanese expect these new computers, which users will be able to speak with in everyday conversational language . . . to penetrate every level of society. . . . They will not even require the user to be very specific about his needs, because they will have reasoning power and will be able to tease out from the user, by questioning and by suggestions, just exactly what it is the user wants to do or know. . . . The Japanese expect these computers to be the core computers—that is, the computers most generally in use worldwide—by the 1990s.

Although the Fifth Generation Project may have accomplished a great deal, these 1983 predictions (by Americans, it must be said, not the Japanese) have little connection to where we are in 1996.

The world without work seemed both plausible and appealing when I contemplated it in my graduate student days. Now, several decades later, I've come to reexamine that world. Is it technically feasible? Assuming it's technically feasible, can society make the transition to a world without work? What are the limits in principle on what machines can do in the world without work? And how much better is a world without work than the world we live in now?

The prospects aren't very bright that we'll soon be able to build the marvelous robots that make the world without work possible. Most of the amenities of the world without work require not just raw artificial intelligence but also robotics—using sensors and actuators so that the computer can analyze and act on its environment. Simulating the behavior of human sensory organs is a particularly difficult task for computers, at least given what we know so far about how to do it.

Not all the work to be done in a robot-served world requires sensory input. Some tasks only require the computer to analyze and react to data presented in textual form. Yet even these tasks are often far beyond what current software can do. For instance, there are many programs now on the market that check text for errors in spelling, grammar, and usage, but these programs do a pitiful job indeed compared with what a human proofreader does.

A good example of a difficult task for computers is the task of answering the telephone at a large company. Switchboard operators at those companies have largely been replaced by automated response systems, which callers almost invariably dislike. But imagine a computer that could do what a human operator does: interpret what a caller is saying (and not just by limiting the caller to a restricted vocabulary), ask whatever questions are necessary, and either answer the caller's question or dispatch the call to the appropriate person. This task, which is not difficult for a human being with a modicum of intelligence, calls for freeform speech recognition and interpretation as well as a lot of commonsense reasoning. These capabilities are well beyond the state of the art in artificial intelligence.

Here's another example: building a robotic taxi for New York City that can understand the passenger's instructions and carry the passenger safely to the destination. Among other things, this task calls for real-time visual analysis of complex street scenes, understanding freeform speech from many speakers (as in the switchboard example), and a good deal of rather complex reasoning about the best way to get from one place to another under widely varying traffic, obstructions, and other conditions. And to really perform this task with style, the taxi-robot would have to be able to entertain the passenger with jokes when it gets stuck in traffic.

Coming back to tasks that don't require sensory input, consider what it would take to produce a faithful translation of a literary work into a foreign language. A literal, word-for-word translation will hardly do. The computer needs to understand both languages, of course. But more than that, it needs to understand what the book is about. It needs to capture and translate the author's style, rendering the allusions, idioms, and metaphors in a way that is true to their intent. And it needs to perceive and preserve the multiple levels of meaning inherent in the text. Providing such a deep understanding of natural language, even in its written form, is far beyond anything we know how to do today.

In my idealized portrait of the world without work, I brought up the notion of a robotic chef. Collecting recipes and measuring ingredients would be easy enough—but how about tasting the ragout to correct the seasoning? There's a long way to go from chemical analyses to a simulation of our senses of taste and smell, and a long way from a simple simulation to a program that could capture the aesthetics of cuisine.

Then there are all the low-paid, physically or psychologically stressful jobs that so many people perform out of necessity: fruit and vegetable harvesting, garment manufacturing, carpet weaving, cleaning and janitorial work, food service, and so forth. These jobs have resisted full automation because they call for complex pattern recognition and flexibility, even though they can be performed by people with no formal education. It's one thing to design a robot that can navigate around a room without bumping into things, quite another to design a robot that can harvest the fruit from an apple orchard. Picking an apple requires locating the apple within the surrounding leaves and branches, assessing its ripeness, maneuvering around obstacles to grasp it without bruising it, and detaching it from the tree with just the right amount of force. These are easy tasks for a person, very difficult ones for today's computers.

In a remarkable irony, computerization itself has created a major automation-resistant job: data entry. Computerized databases have a voracious appetite for information, and it takes an army of typists at computer screens to feed it. While some printed information can be processed using optical scanners, human beings still have to check the results for accuracy and correct the inevitable errors.

It will be hard enough to create smart machines that can perform tasks like these. But that won't suffice for tasks where the machine must interact with people. If machines are to serve us well, they have to perform those tasks in a human-sensitive way. In his book *Things That Make Us Smart*,[3] the cognitive scientist Donald Norman notes how often computer-based systems force people to conform to the attributes of the machine and therefore don't work very well. Automated-response telephone systems are a good example. These computer-based systems may save money for the companies that use them, but only by shifting work to the callers. To make matters worse, their design is often user-hostile. They compel you to listen to a sequence of alternatives before you get to the one you want—if it's there at all. And if you don't realize which alternatives you need until you've heard the entire list, you have to go back and listen to it all over again. It's no wonder that people almost always prefer to talk to a human being.

There's yet another technological problem in building the machines of the world without work. It's not enough to make our machines work; we have to make them work reliably, or at least control what happens when they don't work as they're supposed to. We've learned from sad experience that computer systems have failure modes as novel as computers themselves were when they were first built, and that the consequences of computer failures are often strange, unexpected, and far-reaching. The more we invent, the more failure modes we discover. Reliability engineering is an important subdiscipline of software engineering, but its record of success is spotty at best. A solid theory of how to build reliable systems continues to elude us.

For many years the noted software engineer Peter Neumann has been running a Risks Forum, reporting on the failures of various partially or fully automated systems and their consequences to the public. Less than a year after California's Pelican Bay State Prison was opened, the inmates figured out how to pop open the supposedly escape-proof pneumatic cell doors. The San Francisco Muni Metro was long plagued by a ghosting problem in which the signalling system insisted that a nonexistent train was blocking a switch. A Northwest Airlines DC-9 crashed over Detroit in 1987 because the flaps and the thrust computer indicator had not been set properly before takeoff.

All kinds of engineering artifacts have failure modes, not just computers. Computer scientists often cite civil engineering as an example of a discipline that knows how to build reliable structures, yet bridges and buildings do collapse now and then. The failures of computer systems have a particularly exotic quality to them, however; computer systems rarely fail in mundane ways.

Murphy's Law—that almost anything that can fail will fail—bedevils nearly every effort we make to better our lives by modifying our environment, and not only when it comes to computer-related technology. The gypsy moth caterpillar, once thought to be a superior silkworm, escapes confinement and ravages the deciduous trees of the northeastern United States. The zebra mussel escapes from the ballast water of oceangoing ships and clogs intake pipes throughout the Great Lakes region. Chlorofluorocarbons chew holes in the ozone layer. Miracle pharmaceuticals lead to new mutations of viruses and microbes, creating ever more drug-resistant infections. If we can't prevent the side effects of our wondrous machines from causing these sorts of disasters, those machines will not have bettered our lives.

So, technological challenges exist on several levels. First, there are specific tasks that computer technology, and artificial intelligence in particular, is far from mastering. Next is the challenge of getting machines to behave in a human-sensitive say, well beyond the current art of user-interface design. After that, we must deal in a systematic way with the problem of unreliability and its sometimes catastrophic consequences.

One tempting response to these challenges is that we might eventually be able to build computer programs in the spirit of the General Problem Solver Self-Applied—programs that not only design the technologies we need but also figure out how to deal with whatever unfavorable consequences those technologies might bring. That kind of symbolic task is actually easier for computers than tasks where they have to sense and manipulate their physical environment directly. However, the thought of such powerful thinking machines raises the scary issue of whether we would have enough foresight to control their path of development. Were we to fail in that, we could well find our lives controlled by machines in ways we never intended.

None of these challenges are anywhere near to being met, and the prospect that all of them will be met within the next half century is slight indeed. A technological optimist would say that it's just a matter of time; a technological pessimist would doubt it. History may be full of pessimists who were proven wrong, but lots of optimists have been proven wrong when they were foolhardy enough to attach dates to their predictions. The optimists may argue that if something hasn't yet happened, we only have to wait a while longer. But will we have to wait forever?

There's a story about a traveler in Vermont who lost his way while driving through the countryside. Seeing a grizzled old farmer working near the side of the road, he stopped to ask directions to Rutland. "Rutland, eh?" said the farmer. "Oh, you can't get there from here." Let's assume that the technological optimists are right—that within the next half century, we will indeed invent the smart machines that will finally enable artificial intelligence to fulfill its extravagant promises. We then run up against the second difficulty with the world where no one has to work: can we really get there from here, given the obstacles our economy and culture places in the way of the transition?

In a recent article in the *New York Times Magazine,* the economics writer Peter Passell asked the question, Why doesn't the best always win? Why doesn't the best technology survive the rough-and-tumble of the free market? In answer, he described the phenomenon of path dependence—the way that small, random events at critical moments can determine whether or not a useful or superior technology is actually deployed. Once those events have occurred, their outcome is extremely difficult and expensive to change.

The classic example of path dependence is the QWERTY typewriter keyboard, so named because QWERTY is the sequence of keys on the left side of the top row. This example was examined by Paul David, an economic historian at Stanford, in a 1985 article called "Clio and the Economics of QWERTY." Originally designed so as to prevent early mechanical typewriters from jamming when common sequences of keys were struck too rapidly in succession, the QWERTY keyboard became effectively locked in. People use it because it is universally available and standardized; it is universally available because people demand it. Other keyboard layouts that enable people to type more rapidly and less stressfully have been designed, most notably the Dvorak keyboard, but they've made little headway against QWERTY. The force of the standards and practices of a very large community is simply too powerful to overcome.

Another of Passell's examples is the adoption of Matsushita's VHS standard for videocassette recorder over Sony's technically superior Betamax system. The original Betamax machines were limited to one-hour tapes, too short to play an entire movie. Although this was not a fundamental limitation—Sony could have produced longer tapes but was rushing to get the product out the door—it provided the market opening that Matsushita was able to exploit. The Betamax system was never able to overcome the rapid penetration of VHS into the marketplace.

Although path dependence has been thought of mainly in terms of its effects on the adaptation of specific technologies, it also describes quite well the way the work ethic would make it very difficult for a society such as ours to adapt to and accept the world without work. The work ethic, which is deeply embedded in nearly all Western societies and appears in various forms in other societies as well, has two aspects: first, the belief that work is virtuous and godly; second, the insistence that those who are able to work ought to work.

We probably could design an economic system in which the existence of free, plentiful, and intelligent labor would be turned to the advantage of all. But it almost certainly would have to be a system in which people were neither expected nor asked to work for a living, since there simply would not be enough useful, let alone necessary, work to go around. And for a society that believes in the work ethic, such a system would be very hard for most people to accept.

To understand this obstacle to achieving the world without work, think about how difficult it is for a highly developed nation to utilize cheap overseas or immigrant labor without severe damage to its social fabric. Businesses, of course, have historically used overseas or immigrant labor to lower their costs and often (but not always) have passed on the savings to consumers. You'd think that cheap labor would obviously be beneficial to society because it makes goods and services easier to obtain (the moral issues created by the laborers' working conditions aside). But since cheap labor by foreigners usually depresses the wages of native workers and often abolishes their jobs altogether, native workers have fought it fiercely. This struggle has taken place not just in the United States but in several European countries, notably France and Germany, as well.

Smart machines are, of course, the ultimate form of cheap labor, and the harshness of their working conditions is not a moral issue. But workers respond to automation much as they do to competition from cheap labor. Adam Smith once pointed out that candlemakers were in competition with the sun, and that a world of darkness would improve their prospects enormously. Most workers respond like Adam Smith's candlemakers to the thought of their jobs being automated out of existence, even if the net economic effect of automation might be beneficial (for example, creating new jobs for a different class of workers). And without the total restructuring of society that abandoning the work ethic would imply, who can blame them?

So even if we could solve all the technological problems of constructing smart machines that would do nearly all of humankind's work, we would still have to face the problem of how to introduce those machines into our socio-economic systems without rending the fabric of our society. It isn't enough to plan a world in which the work ethic no longer governs our social structures; we need a way to get there. And getting there would be far more difficult than getting to a world in which keyboards followed the Dvorak layout and video-cassette recorders followed the Betamax standard. The work ethic is likely to prove to be the QWERTY keyboard of the world of smart machines.

But suppose, despite all the difficulties, we could build truly smart machines and create the technology to support the world without work. Suppose in addition that we could somehow overcome or bypass the obstacles the work ethic poses to their effective and universal deployment. Daunting as these technical and societal obstacles are, I know of no convincing argument in principle that says they can never be overcome. But having overcome them, we would still have to face the most fundamental difficulties with that idealized world in which no one need work and all can prosper: the limits in principle on what smart machines—robots, that is—can do. These limits dictate the answers to the two questions that really matter: To what extent can robots replace people? And can robots make the world a much better place in which to live?

No matter what we can achieve technically, there will always be a distinction between machines and people. That distinction is a critical one because so much of our response to other creatures, be they humans, animals, or machines, is deeply rooted in our instincts. We respond to people in a certain way precisely because they *are* people. A machine can never meet those human needs where humanness matters.

It's doubtful, for instance, that you could ever feel the same kind of love for a robot you can feel for a person, or even the same quality of sexual attraction. Bisexuals aside, it's rare enough for a heterosexual to be sexually attracted to a member of the same sex or a homosexual to a member of the opposite sex. If people of the "wrong" sex cannot tap into our libidos, it's unlikely a robot ever could. True, people can be sexually aroused by photographs and drawings—

but beneath that arousal lies the knowledge that there's at least an imaginary human being behind the picture. And when people become aroused by what's often called cybersex, they are well aware that there's a real person at the other end of the conversation.

In a similar vein, it's hard to see how a machine could inspire or lead. Leadership and charisma are inherently human qualities. We respond to a Winston Churchill or a Mother Theresa not only because of what that person says and does, but because of who that person is. Leadership is rooted in courage, and courage is meaningful only for a creature that cares about its own survival in a way no computer ever could. And though I can imagine a computer preaching a sermon, I can't imagine the congregation shouting "Amen, brother" in response.

The thought of a robotic psychiatrist raises some related questions. According to orthodox Freudian and other psychoanalytic theory, an essential part of the analytic process is transference and countertransference—basically, the subconscious projection of feelings by the patient onto the therapist or vice versa. What sort of transference is possible when the therapist is not a human being? What does the notion of countertransference even mean for a robotic psychiatrist that has no subconscious and no way of "listening with the third ear"? And does the lack of transference and countertransference seriously compromise the possibility of effective therapy (assuming, of course, that these phenomena are as essential as the Freudians assume they are)?

How we respond to people affects how we respond to the artifacts they produce. Take art, for example. We respond to it not only because of its physical manifestation but also because of its provenance. What's on the canvas isn't all that matters; we also care who painted it, how, and why. Otherwise, why would we value originals over forgeries? A skillful forgery may appear to be just as beautiful as the original, but we value it far less or not at all once its origin has been exposed. Were a computer to produce magnificent sculptures as judged by the usual criteria of the fine arts, we might find those sculptures interesting—but our emotional, intuitive response to them would inevitably be muted by their lack of human provenance.

Some of those most skeptical of using computers to replace people are themselves computer experts. Clifford Stoll, an astronomer and authority on computer security, is one of them. In his book *Silicon Snake Oil*,[4] Stoll questions the nature of the interaction between people and computers. He observes that computers substitute mediated experience for direct experience and points out what is lost in the transition. "No computer can teach what a walk through a pine forest feels like," says Stoll. "Sensation has no substitute."

Stoll catalogues a variety of computer-human interactions in which mediated experience is replacing immediate experience, leaving us worse off. Face-
to-face conversation gives way to "net chat." Computer-based instruction replaces the inspiring teacher. Online library catalogs replace helpful librarians.
A human quality is lost, and even the cleverest and best-designed of computer
systems cannot replace it.

As these examples show, some of the qualities that make people irreplaceable have little to do with how cleverly we can program our computers—or
even how cleverly they can program themselves. Making smart machines more
humanoid won't change this. After all, how human-like could a robot ever be?
Could it eat? Bleed? Die? Procreate? Take pleasure or feel sorrow? If, through
some almost unimaginable miracle of technology, we somehow managed to
build humanoid robots, would we feel that those creatures were truly human?
Would we consider them to be subject to the same moral imperatives as are the
children of humans? Could we without compunction treat them as slaves?
And if not, then what, other than intellectual curiosity or a desire for power,
would be the point of building them—since humans can create other humans
easily (and pleasurably) enough?

If we think of the world without work more narrowly, attempting only to
free ourselves from tasks where the humanness of the worker isn't essential,
the world without work becomes possible in principle. And we're probably
better off that way; though the necessities of life would be free in such a world,
the luxuries—namely, those services that only humans could render—would
not be. You could get a machine to rub your back tirelessly for hours on end—
but if you wanted a massage from a person, you'd have to pay for it.

I now turn to the other basic question: Can smart machines make the
world a much better place to live? In particular, how much can smart machines
do to put an end to human misery?

When you're selling hammers, all the world's a nail. All too often, people
who tout technology talk about what the technology can achieve without
much reference to what for most people is actually most critical to leading a
happy and satisfying life. Take, for instance, the recent enthusiasm for the
World Wide Web. The Web provides novel and powerful ways to retrieve information—but retrieving the kinds of information available over the Web, or
any information at all for that matter, plays a limited part in most people's
lives. Indeed, the Web offers not the slightest benefit to the majority of the
earth's population. It's not merely a coincidence that a typical portrayal of the
wonders of the Web invokes as its example a high-school research project—
preferably one involving either dolphins or Shakespeare. These examples, the

kind that often appear in books and articles on how to use the Web, create a warm and fuzzy image for certain middle- and upper-class populations, but they're utterly irrelevant to most of humanity.

When we look at the sources of human misery, conflict ranks high among them. It may take the form of an interpersonal vendetta or an intense ethnic feud enduring for centuries. Many conflicts have their roots in poverty, something that computers might help us overcome, but not all conflicts do. The families of millionaires are beset by quarrels and hatred; rich nations still war with each other. The bitterness between Hindu and Muslim, Serb and Croat, Arab and Jew, or Hutu and Tutsi often is rooted in a struggle over ancestral land, a struggle in which one side or the other is bound to lose because both sides can't exclusively own and occupy the land simultaneously. These conflicts are zero-sum games; what one side wins, the other must lose. No amount of machine intelligence or computer-induced abundance can resolve them amicably.

Nor are computers of much help in resolving the moral controversies that stem from different views of how we ought to lead our lives. For those who view homosexuality as an utter abomination, no amount of earthly riches nor any rational argument can persuade them to tolerate it. Those devout Muslims who view the writer Salman Rushdie as a blasphemer deserving to be put to death cannot be reconciled with those who believe in untrammeled literary expression. Supporters of reproductive freedom for women battle with those who believe in the absolute sanctity and personhood of the fetus. Technology stands powerless in the face of these bitter disputes, disputes that make lives miserable when people act on their beliefs.

There's another aspect of the world without work that would disturb many people: it would take a powerful, socialistic government to support it and make it possible. Someone or something has to ensure that all those free goods are manufactured and distributed and all those free services are provided. Yet this government could well accommodate a degree of personal freedom we're not accustomed to, since it would not need to regulate individual behavior in order to perform its functions. There's much irony in that, since socialism and individual freedom are usually thought of as incompatible values. To be sure, the regents might be computers rather than people, but that's not likely to be thought of as an improvement.

There also remains the question of whether people could lead satisfying lives in the world without work. Retired people on generous pensions often find themselves at loose ends, not knowing what to do with their time. Many wealthy people work tirelessly even though they could afford not to. Is it just the work ethic in effect here, or do people have some more fundamental, instinctual need to feel that they're productive members of society?

I do believe that the world without work, if we could ever achieve it, would be a better place to live. Even partial progress towards the world without work would be beneficial. Machines (not just computers) have made our lives easier and have immensely amplified our physical and mental abilities, and that's on the whole a positive contribution to human welfare. And to the extent that we can substitute computational effort for the consumption of natural resources, computers can help solve an array of environmental problems.

The earth's resources and carrying capacity are finite, but through the clever use of computers we may be able to stretch them. For example, smart machines might enable us to exploit low-grade ores that are not now economical to mine and to scrupulously repair the earth after the ores have been extracted. They might be able to sort trash so that we could recycle almost all of it with no human effort at all.

There's also the tantalizing prospect that smart machines might someday be able to advise us on how to improve our lives and our society—and also know how to get us to take their advice. It may be that humans just aren't smart enough to figure out how to deal effectively with their own problems. If computers can ever do that for us through advances in artificial intelligence, they will truly have become the most important artifacts humanity has ever conceived.

References

1. Feigenbaum, E. A. and McCorduck, P. *The Fifth Generation: Artificial Intelligence and Japan's Computer Challenge to the World*. Reading, Mass.: Addison-Wesley, 1983.

2. Neumann, P. G. *Computer-Related Risks*. Reading, Mass.: Addison-Wesley, 1995.

3. Norman, D. A. *Things That Make Us Smart: Defending Human Attributes in the Age of the Machine*. Reading, Mass.: Addison-Wesley, 1993.

4. Stoll, C. *Silicon Snake Oil: Second Thoughts on the Information Highway*. New York, N.Y.: Doubleday/Anchor, 1995.

The Design
of Interaction

12

When asked to project fifty years ahead, a scientist is in a bit of a quandary. It is easy to indulge in wishful thinking or promote favorite current projects and proposals, but it is a daunting task to anticipate what will actually come to pass in a time span that is eons long in our modern, accelerated age. If fifty years ago, when the ACM was founded, biologists had been asked to predict the next fifty years of biology, it would have taken amazing prescience to anticipate the science of molecular biology. Or for that matter, only a few years before the initiation of the ACM even those with the most insight about computing would have been completely unable to foresee today's world of pervasive workstations, mobile communicators, and gigabit networking.

1. Directions of change

In order to get some grip on the future we need to take advantage of the past and the present: to identify some trajectories that are already in swing, and to look at some further points towards which they are headed. The method isn't foolproof—we can always be surprised. But at least it gives us some starting points. So we will begin by examining three trends whose directions are already visible and then project an image of where they may lead in the coming half century. For convenience, let us label these trajectories:

1. Computation to communication;
2. Machinery to habitat;
3. Aliens to agents.

From computation to communication

When digital computers first appeared a half century ago, they were straightforwardly viewed as "machinery for computing." A computer could make short work tasks such as calculating ballistics trajectories or breaking codes, which previously required vast amounts of computation done by teams of human "computers." Even a quarter century later, when the Internet was created, the network was seen primarily as a tool for facilitating remote computation (for a history of the Internet, see the article by Hafner[6]). On the net, a computing task could be carried out using a computer that was physically removed from the person who needed the work done and who controlled its activity.

With the recent—and quite sudden—emergence of mass-appeal Internet-centered applications, it has become glaringly obvious that the computer is not a machine whose main purpose is to get a computing task done. The computer, with its attendant peripherals and networks, is a machine that provides new ways for people to communicate with other people. The excitement that infuses computing today comes from the exploration of new capacities to manipulate and communicate all kinds of information in all kinds of media, reaching new audiences in ways that would have been unthinkable before the computer.

In retrospect, it didn't take the World Wide Web to show us the centrality of communication. There are many earlier points in the development of computers that dramatically revealed the precedence of communication over computation. One obvious clue could be seen in the pattern of adoption of the Internet itself. Instead of using the net for remote computing, as in the original proposals, the vast majority of people with Internet connections have used it to communicate with each other: through e-mail, newsgroups, and real-time "talk," for example. Whole new families of communication-centered applications have appeared, from "groupware" to MUDs and MOOs.

The story is the same for the "personal" computer. The suites of applications that dominate the office market today consist primarily of communication tools: word processors, presentation programs, e-mail, file sharing, and contact managers. Even the one apparent exception—the spreadsheet—is used more prominently for communicating results than for calculating them.

In one sense this should be no surprise, given what we can observe about human nature. People are primarily interested in other people and are highly motivated to interact with them in whatever media are available.

New technologies, from the telegraph to the World Wide Web, have expanded our ability to communicate widely, flexibly, and efficiently. This urge to communicate will continue to drive the expanding technology with the advent of widespread two-way video, wireless connectivity, and high-bandwidth audio, video, 3-D imaging, and more yet to be imagined.

Within the computing industry we are now seeing a new emphasis on communication, reflected in a concern for "content." The companies that can put extensive resources into computing-system development are shifting their gaze away from what the machine "does" towards what it "communicates." As an illustrative series of points along our trajectory, consider the history of Microsoft, which began with operating systems, then expanded into the world of software applications, and now is actively moving into the content arena with a joint TV effort with NBC, an online magazine, and major acquisitions of visual materials. The latter may not be under the Microsoft banner, but new companies by the founders Bill Gates (Orbis, a graphical image library) and Paul Allen (Starwave, an online information and entertainment service) give a sense of where the big money is heading. This shift towards content extends beyond the software companies, such as Microsoft, reaching to those that have been primarily hardware companies. Workstation maker Silicon Graphics is moving into the entertainment business, and chip maker Intel has recently opened a new research laboratory with an interest in high-level questions about human communication and uses for computers in the home.

There will always be a need for machinery and a need for software that runs the machinery, but as the industry matures, these dimensions will take on the character of commodities, while the industry-creating innovations will be in what the hardware and software allow us to communicate.

From machinery to habitat

In the early days of computing, the focus of computer scientists was—as the original name of the ACM implies—on the "machinery." In order to use a computer, one needed to understand how to give it instructions. As the field matured, the details of the physical machinery were gradually submerged beneath the surface of the software: the higher-level expressions of the computations to be performed, separated from the details of how an electronic device would operate to carry out such computations. Most people who use computers today (with the obvious exception of computer scientists) do not know or care much about the details of the processor, its architecture, or the ways in which it operates. If you ask people what computer they use, they will often say "Windows." Going one step further, many people will say that the computer they use is "Microsoft Word" or "Netscape" without even distinguishing among the operating-system platforms on which the software is executing.

It is easy for experts to sneer at this kind of technical inaccuracy as a symptom of ignorance or misunderstanding. But in fact, it is quite logical and appropriate for many kinds of computer users. I could ask a relatively sophisticated computer user whether he or she has a computer with NMOS or CMOS transistors and draw a complete blank. For the chip manufacturer, this is an important distinction, but for the average user (even the average computer professional), the distinction only matters because it is reflected in performance parameters: How fast is the machine? How much electric power does it require? The domain in which NMOS and CMOS are distinguished isn't the domain in which the computer user experiences its activity. In just that same manner, whether a machine is PowerPC or Wintel, whether it runs Windows95 or MacOS, isn't in the domain in which the average user is coming to experience the computer. Differences at this level can have an impact in terms of speed, cost, the availability of new software, and the like, but they are only of relevance in this indirect way.

With the Web we are seeing the distancing from the machine taken yet a step further. In spite of tremendous efforts by Netscape and Microsoft to differentiate their browsers, users of the Web will end up caring only indirectly about what software is running on their machines at all. Their experience isn't of a machine, or a program, but of entering into the reaches of a cyberspace populated with text, graphics, video, and animations, or even more to the point, consisting of catalogs, advertisements, animated stories, and personal picture galleries.

The word "cyberspace" is often bandied about as a symbol of the new computing, and it has become a trendy cliché. But it has a more significant meaning than that. The fact that cyberspace is termed a "space" reflects a deep metaphor, of the kind that Lakoff and Johnson say we "live by."[7] A space is not just a set of objects or activities but a medium in which a person experiences, acts, and lives. The ultimate extension of cyberspace is depicted in "cyberpunk" science fiction works such as William Gibson's *Neuromancer*[5] and Neal Stephenson's *Snowcrash*.[10] In these bleak visions of the future, technologies of virtual reality enable the protagonists to live in a virtual world that is in many ways more real than the physical world from which they are "jacked in." For the voyager in this cyberspace there are no computers, no software in sight— just the "metaverse," which is experienced through the operation of necessary but ultimately invisible computing machinery.

In spite of all the popular excitement about virtual reality, an immersive high-fidelity 3-D display with gloves and goggles isn't a necessary (or even a major) component of creating a captivating virtual space. Over the past decade a menagerie of virtual worlds have evolved that offer their denizens nothing more than plain text, typed and read on a standard display. In these MUDs, MOOs, and IRC (Internet Relay Chat), people carry on their professional, recreational, and private lives in a way that challenges our basic notions about what is "real." As one of her informants said to Sherry Turkle, author of *Life on the Screen*, "real life is just one more window".[11]

Turkle's informant may be extreme, as are some of the others she interviewed who spend most of their waking hours online, meeting and falling in love with people, having fights and sex and generally doing all of the things that make up our everyday lives. But anyone who uses computers extensively is aware of the feeling that when we are online we are located in cyberspace as surely as we are located in physical space. When I carry my laptop computer with me on a trip and connect to the network from a hotel room, I feel very much that I am at my office. But if I am physically in my office and the computer is down, I feel that I am not at my normal workplace. In a very real sense, the "webhead" who spends the night surfing from site to site has been traveling in cyberspace, not sitting in a chair in her dorm room or computer laboratory.

The traditional idea of "interface" implies that we are focusing on two entities, the person and the machine, and on the space that lies between them. But beyond the interface, we operate in an "interspace" that is inhabited by multiple people, workstations, servers, and other devices in a complex web of interactions. In designing new systems and applications, we are not simply providing better tools for working with objects in a previously existing world. We are creating new worlds. Computer systems and software are becoming media for the creation of virtualities: the worlds in which users of the software perceive, act, and respond to experiences.

Aliens to agents

The cyberpunk novels that glorify life in cyberspace offer an interesting contrast to an older and still prevalent vision of the computer future, one in which computing machines come to be independent, alien beings in the world. From ancient tales of the golem to Arthur Clarke's *2001*[2] and Isaac Asimov's robots[1] people have been fascinated by the prospect of sharing our physical and mental worlds with a new species of beings that we ourselves have created. The field of artificial intelligence (AI) was born from this vision, and its founding leaders made bold predictions of "ultra-intelligent machines" and the inevitability of building computers that would soon duplicate and then surpass the human intellect.

From the vantage point of AI researchers of twenty-five years ago, it would have been ludicrous to predict that as we approached the year 2001, almost all of the companies devoted to AI technologies would have faded from existence, while the hot new mega-company that shattered Wall Street records was Netscape, a producer of better network terminals (as browsers would have been called in those days). And right behind it were companies such as Yahoo, whose only product is an index of things to be found on the net. What happened to the intelligent computers?

In the early days of artificial intelligence, researchers' vision was focused on quasi-intelligent beings that would duplicate a broad range of human mental capacities. Even such apparently simple mental feats such as walking, seeing what is around us, and employing common sense turned out to be surprisingly hard. As the field matured into the engineering of "expert systems" in the 1980s, the focus shifted from "intelligence" to "knowledge." The large investments and research projects shifted to creating large knowledge bases that would encode human expert knowledge for computers to serve as skilled, narrow, and presumably submissive experts in practical areas of commerce and science. When the promises of massively increased productivity through knowledge engineering[4] didn't come true, expert systems joined ultra-intelligent machines in the category of "not practical with today's technology." Expectations gradually became more modest, concentrating on the development of "intelligent agents," which apply AI technologies in limited ways to help people interact with computer systems.

Today's popular press plays up efforts like those of Pattie Maes and her research group at the MIT Media Laboratory, where they have produced agents to help people browse the web, choose music, and filter e-mail. In fact, a notable indicator of the current trajectory is the ascendancy of MIT's Media Lab, with its explicit focus on media and communication, over the AI Laboratory, which in earlier days was MIT's headline computing organization, one of the world centers of the original AI research.

With hindsight, of course, it is easy to fault early predictions and quixotic enterprises, such as Lenat's attempt[8] to produce common sense in computers by encoding millions of mundane facts in a quasi-logical formalism. But we can sympathize with the optimistic naiveté of those whose predictions of future computing abilities were based on projecting the jump that led us from almost nothing to striking demonstrations of artificial intelligence in the first twenty-five years of computing. A straightforward projection of the rate of advance seemed that it would lead within another few decades to fully intelligent machines.

But there is something more to be learned here than the general lesson that curves don't always continue going up exponentially (a lesson that the computing field in general has yet to grapple with). The problem with artificial intelligence wasn't that we reached a plateau in our ability to perform millions of LIPS (logical inferences per second) or to invent new algorithms. The problem was in the foundations on which the people in the field conceived of intelligence.

As was pointed out from early in the history of computers by philosophers such as Hubert Dreyfus,[3] the mainstream AI effort rested on a view of human intelligence and action that implicitly assumed that all of intelligence could be produced by mechanisms that were inherently like the conscious logical manipulation of facts represented in language. This chapter is not the appropriate place to present the detailed arguments (see Winograd and Flores, *Understanding Computers and Cognition*[13] for an extended discussion). What is relevant to our analysis here is that what appeared to be inevitable trends were based on misconceptions about intellectual foundations. Although philosophically based critiques were considered imprecise and irrelevant by most people in computing, the passage of time has made them seem more revealing and predictive than the more obvious technical indicators that were visible at the time.

These critiques focused on the central body of technological development that is sometimes referred to as "Good Old Fashioned AI (GOFAI)". What about neural nets, genetic programming, self-organizing systems, and other nontraditional approaches to producing intelligent computers? Although the practical results from these efforts are as of yet rather meager, their proponents reflect an attitude that is at the center of technological progress. The biggest advances will come not from doing more and bigger and faster of what we are already doing, but from finding new metaphors, new starting points. Of course, most of these will fail, and we cannot tell in advance which ones will lead to surprising success or how long it will be until something good shows up. But there are ways to open up a clearing in which new possibilities can be glimpsed, even if their full potential cannot be known. The message from the history of AI is that we need to be prepared to reexamine our foundational assumptions and start from new footings.

The ascendancy (and independence) of interaction design

Among the many possibilities suggested by these three trajectories, one seems particularly relevant to the ACM and its role in the next fifty years of computing. In a way the following prediction is paradoxical—the computing field will become larger, and at the same time the computing profession will become narrower.

In the next fifty years, the increasing importance of designing spaces for human communication and interaction will lead to expansion in those aspects of computing that are focused on people, rather than machinery. The methods, skills, and techniques concerning these human aspects are generally foreign to those of mainstream computer science, and it is likely that they will detach (at least partially) from their historical roots to create a new field of "interaction design."

The shifting boundaries

As the trajectories depicted here continue along their current courses, the computing industry will continue to broaden its boundaries—from machinery to software to communication to content. The companies that drive innovation will not be those that focus narrowly on technical innovation but those that deal with the larger context in which the technologies are deployed.

As the focus of commercial and practical interest continues to shift, so will the character of the people who will be engaged in the work. Much of the most exciting new research and development in computing will not be in traditional areas of hardware and software but will be aimed at enhancing our ability to understand, analyze, and create interaction spaces. The work will be rooted in disciplines that focus on people and communication, such as psychology, communications, graphic design, and linguistics, as well as in the disciplines that support computing and communications technologies.

As computing becomes broader as a social and commercial enterprise, what will happen to computer science as a professional discipline? Will it extend outward to include graphic design, linguistics, and psychology? What would it even mean to have a science of that breadth?

It is more realistic to imagine that computer science will not expand its boundaries, but will in fact contract them while deepening its roots. Much of the commercial success of computing-related industries will be driven by considerations outside of the technical scope of computer science as we know it today, but there will always be new theories, discoveries, and technological advances in the hardware and software areas that make up the core of the traditional discipline.

As an analogy, consider the role of mechanical engineering and thermodynamic theory in the world of the automobile (or, more broadly, transportation vehicles). It is clear that success in today's automotive market is determined by many factors that have little to do with science and engineering. They range from the positioning of a vehicle in the market (consider the rise of four-wheel drive sports vehicles) to the ability to associate it with an appealing emotional image through styling, furnishing, and advertising. Engineering is still important and relevant, but it isn't the largest factor for success, and it isn't the dominating force in the automobile industry.

We can expect the same kind of decoupling in the computer world. The flashy and immensely lucrative new startup companies will depend less on new technical developments and more on the kinds of concerns that drive the film industry or the automobile industry. The computing industry will come to encompass work from many different professions, one of which will be the computer science profession, which will continue to focus on the computing aspects that can be best approached through its formal theories and engineering methods. As the center of action shifts, computer science may lose some of its current highly favorable funding position, but it will gain in its intellectual coherence and depth. To put it simply, it will become easier in the future to see the difference between a significant scientific insight and a hot new product—a distinction that is blurred in today's world of proliferating technology startups and product-driven research funding.

The emergence of interaction design

In portraying the broadening scope of computing, I have alluded to many existing disciplines, ranging from linguistics and psychology to graphic and industrial design. Human-computer interaction is by necessity a field with interdisciplinary concerns, since its essence is interaction that includes people and machines, virtual worlds and computer networks, and a diverse array of objects and behaviors.

In the midst of this interdisciplinary collision, we can see the beginnings of a new profession, which might be called "interaction design." While drawing from many of the older disciplines, it has a distinct set of concerns and methods. It draws on elements of graphic design, information design, and concepts of human-computer interaction as a basis for designing interaction with (and habitation within) computer-based systems. Although computers are at the center of interaction design, it is not a subfield of computer science.

As a simple analogy, consider the division of concerns between a civil engineer and an architect as they approach the problem of building a house or an office building. The architect focuses on people and their interactions with and within the space being created. Is it cozy or expansive? Does it provide the kind of spaces that fit the living style of the family or business for whom it is being designed? What is the flow of work within the office, and what kinds of communication paths does that flow depend on? How will people be led to behave in a space that looks like the one being designed? Will the common areas be ignored, or will they lead to increased informal discussion? What are the key differences between designing a bank and a barbershop, a cathedral and a cafe?

The engineer, on the other hand, is concerned with issues such as structural soundness, construction methods, cost, and durability. The training of architects and engineers is correspondingly different. Architects go through an education in a studio environment that emphasizes the creation and critique of suitable designs. Engineering emphasizes the ability to apply the accumulated formal knowledge of the field to predict and calculate the technical possibilities and resource tradeoffs that go into deciding what can be constructed.

As with a house or an office building, software is not just a device with which the user interacts; it is also the generator of a space in which the user lives. Interaction design is related to software engineering in the same way architecture is related to civil engineering.

Although there is no clear boundary between design and engineering, there is a critical difference in perspective (see Terry Winograd, *Bringing Design to Software*[12]). All engineering and design activities call for the management of tradeoffs. In classical engineering disciplines, the tradeoffs can often be quantified: material strength, construction costs, rate of wear, and the like. In design disciplines, the tradeoffs are more difficult to identify and measure because they rest on human needs, desires, and values. The designer stands with one foot in technology and one foot in the domain of human concerns, and these two worlds are not easily commensurable.

As well as being distinct from engineering, interaction design does not fit into any of the existing design fields. If software were something that the computer user just looked at, rather than operated, traditional visual design would be at the center of software design. If the spaces were actually physical, rather than virtual, then traditional product and architectural design would suffice.

But computers have created a new medium—one that is both active and virtual. Designers in the new medium need to develop principles and practices that are unique to the computer's scope and fluidity of interactivity.

Architecture as we know it can be said to have started when building technologies, such as stone cutting, made possible a new kind of building. Graphic design emerged as a distinct art when the printing press made possible the mass production of visual materials. Product design grew out of the development, in the twentieth century, of physical materials such as plastics, which allowed designers to effectively create a vastly increased variety of forms for consumer objects. In a similar way, the computer has created a new domain of possibilities for creating spaces and interactions with unprecedented flexibility and immediacy. We have begun to explore this domain and to design many intriguing objects and spaces, from video games and word processors to virtual reality simulations of molecules. But we are far from understanding this new field of interaction design.

A striking example at the time of this writing is the chaotic state of "web page design." The very name is misleading, in that it suggests that the World Wide Web is a collection of "pages," and therefore that the relevant expertise is that of the graphic designer or information designer. But the "page" today is often much less like a printed page than a graphic user interface—not something to look at, but something to interact with. The page designer needs to be a programmer with a mastery of computing techniques and programming languages such as Java. Yet, something more is missing in the gap between people trained in graphic arts and people trained in programming. Neither group is really trained in understanding interaction as a core phenomenon. They know how to build programs and they know how to lay out text and graphics, but there is not yet a professional body of knowledge that underlies the design of effective interactions between people and machines and among people using machines. With the emergence of interaction design in the coming decades, we will provide the foundation for the "page designers" of the future to master the principles and complexities of interaction and interactive spaces.

The mastery we can expect is, of course, incomplete. Taking seriously that the design role is the construction of the "interspace" in which people live, rather than an "interface" with which they interact, the interaction designer needs to take a broad view that includes understanding how people and societies adapt to new technologies. To continue with our automotive analogy, imagine that on the fiftieth anniversary of the "Association for Automotive Machinery" a group of experts had been asked to speculate on the "the next fifty years of driving." They might well have envisioned new kinds of engines, automatic braking, and active suspension systems. But what about interstate freeways, drive-in movies, and the decline of the inner city? These are not exactly changes in "driving," but in the end they are the most significant consequences of automotive technology.

Successful interaction design requires a shift from seeing the machinery to seeing the lives of the people using it. In this human dimension, the relevant factors become hard to quantify, hard even to identify. This difficulty is magnified when we try to look at social consequences. Will the computer lead to a world in which our concept of individual privacy is challenged or changed? Will online addiction become a social problem to rival drug use? Will political power gravitate towards people or institutions that have the most powerful communications technologies or who aggregate control over media? Will there be a general turning away from computing technologies in a "back-to-nature" movement that reemphasizes our physical embodiment in the world?

All of these and many more futures are possible, and they are not strictly determined by technological choices. There is a complex interplay among technology, individual psychology, and social communication, all mixed in an intricate, chaotic system. Details that seem insignificant today may grow into major causal factors over the next fifty years. Trends that seem obvious and inevitable may be derailed for what currently appear to be insignificant reasons.

As with technological predictions, we need to accept the unpredictability of changes in the social dimension without abandoning our attempts to see, and guide, where things are going. Perhaps fifty years is too long a span across which to see clearly, and would more profitably ask what is happening in the next ten of twenty years, or even this year or this month. Many of the concerns that are dimly visible in the future have concrete reflections in today's society. Many of them are more highly visible to those who have an understanding of the theoretical and practical potentials of new computing technologies, and therefore we as professionals with relevant areas of expertise have a special responsibility to point out both the possibilities and the dangers.

Interaction design in the coming fifty years will have an ideal to follow that combines the concerns and benefits of its many intellectual predecessors. Like the engineering disciplines, it needs to be practical and rigorous. Like the design disciplines, it needs to place human concerns and needs at the center of design; and like the social disciplines, it needs to take a broad view of social possibilities and responsibilities. The challenge is large, as are the benefits. Given the record of how much computing has achieved in the last fifty years, we have every reason to expect this much of the future.

References

1. Asimov, I. *I, Robot*. New York: New American Library Of World Lit., 1950; *The Foundation Trilogy*. Garden City, N.Y.,: Doubleday [1951–1953]; *The Complete Robot*. Garden City, N.Y.: Doubleday, 1982; *Robots, Machines In Man's Image*. New York: Harmony Books, 1985.

2. Clarke, A. 2001: *A Space Odyssey*, London: Hutchinson/Star, 1968.

3. Dreyfus, H. L. *What Computers Can't Do*. (1st ed.). New York, Harper & Row, 1972.

4. Feigenbaum, E. A. and P. McCorduck. *The Fifth Generation*. Reading, MA: Addison-Wesley. 1983.

5. Gibson, W. *Neuromancer*. New York: Ace Science Fiction Books, 1984.

6. Hafner, K. and M. Lyon. *Where Wizards Stay Up Late: The Origins of the Internet*, New York: Simon and Schuster Macmillan, 1996.

7. Lakoff, G. and M. Johnson. *Metaphors We Live By*, Chicago: University of Chicago Press, 1980.

8. Lenat, D. B. *Building Large Knowledge-Based Systems*. Reading, MA: Addison-Wesley, 1990.

9. Maes, P. *Designing Autonomous Agents*. Cambridge, MA: MIT Press, 1990.

10. Stephenson, N. *Snow Crash*. New York: Bantam, 1993.

11. Turkle, S. *Life on the Screen: Identity in the Age of the Internet*. New York: Simon and Schuster, 1995.

12. Winograd, T., with J. Bennett, L. De Young, and Bradley Hartfield (eds.). *Bringing Design to Software*, Reading, MA: Addison-Wesley, 1996.

13. Winograd, T. and F. Flores. *Understanding Computers and Cognition: A New Foundation for Design*. Norwood, NJ: Ablex, 1986. Paperback issued by Addison-Wesley, 1987.

14. Winograd, T. "Thinking machines: Can there be? Are We?," in J. Sheehan and M. Sosna, eds., *The Boundaries of Humanity: Humans, Animals, Machines*, Berkeley: University of California Press, 1991, pp. 198–223.

PART III

Business and Innovation

Samuel Morse invented the telegraph in 1837, and the world changed. Within a decade, it became possible to communicate in seconds with thousands of people who were previously reachable only in days or weeks. A young man in Los Angeles could send a birthday greeting to his mother in Atlanta. A merchant in Philadelphia no longer had to travel to Boston to close a deal on imported coffee, tea, and spice. The sheriff in El Paso could alert the marshal in Flagstaff that Billy the Kid was heading his way. The ticker tape enabled the New York, Chicago, and San Francisco stock exchanges to operate at the same time. And the Pony Express disappeared because it could not compete with the telegraph for speed of communication or with the railroad for movement of goods.

A similar phenomenon is happening today on account of the silicon chip and the glass fiber. Anyone can open a storefront on the Web and sell to anyone in the world who is lucky enough to find the storefront. E-mail and fax know no national boundaries and are beyond the control of governments. Time zones and national borders are no longer barriers to business. Some professions are becoming obsolete—for example, the telephone operator, the clerk typist, and the mainframe computer salesman. New professions undreamt-of in 1990 are now hiring voraciously—jobs with names like Internet service provider, Internet identity designer, Web page creator, or network engineer. Many people are uneasy. Not only do the changes come ever more rapidly, many come as surprises. The anxious look to the sages for explanations of what is happening and where things are moving, and to education to keep them up to date. The authors of the eight essays of this section offer some glimpses of the changes in store for business, leadership, security, innovation, work, and education.

Bob Evans was an executive with IBM when IBM began to find itself in decline. The personal computer, commodity software, open systems, and the Internet had completely changed what people sought from computer companies. IBM's overall approach to its markets, products, and customers, which had served it well since 1950, had lost much of its appeal. Evans gives an eyewitness account of IBM's struggles to change itself to fit the new world, and how it seemed to fall back two steps for every one forward. It is an instructive case study of how a major computer company can inexplicably find itself facing extinction, a problem that all the computer companies must face daily.

Fernando Flores picks up where Evans leaves off and paints a vivid picture of leadership, which is not the formation of vision statements, strategies, and management structures, but the continuing invention of beguiling new worlds for customers and employees. This type of leader is fairly common in entrepreneurial companies, but the skills and practices of those leaders are poorly understood because they cannot be described in the favored paradigm of "information." Until these skills are understood, they cannot be taught or learned by novices. Flores calls the patterns of action engaged in by these consummate leaders "recurrences" and suggests that only a few dozen such patterns exist; the complexity of real organizations comes from the myriad combinations of simple recurrent patterns. A knowledge of the recurrent patterns will enable new tools to support leadership to be designed in the years ahead. Flores knows whereof he speaks. He has himself been an industrial engineer, a philosopher, a cabinet minister, and a founder of software, education, and business consulting companies. Today he works with top executives of major companies to teach them and their companies how to become the leaders of the future.

Larry Druffel, formerly the director of the Software Engineering Institute at Carnegie-Mellon University, formerly an Air Force officer, and today an entrepreneur, directs our attention to the major threats faced by business and commerce from intruders, viruses, criminals, and terrorists. Once an arcane branch of military science, information warfare has become a buzzword of the nineties as network engineers, software designers, and business leaders seek defenses against the economic devastation that could be wrought by attacks on the information infrastructure. The security of the information infrastructure will be ever more important in the decades ahead. We can think of it as analogous to the immune system of a living organism: we cannot guarantee that the organism will not be attacked, but we can give it defenses that will limit damage and speed recovery.

Abbe Mowshowitz, a professor of computer science at the City University of New York, paints a picture of a dysfunctional world toward which we could be drifting. In this world, large corporations defy governments by moving capital and information around in the network, across borders and beyond jurisdictions, hidden behind cryptographic cloaks. Individuals are forced to declare their loyalties to an organization, which can provide them with asset protection and physical security that declining, cash-starved governments cannot offer. Mowshowitz's worry resembles the one expressed by William Manchester, who wrote in *A World Lit Only by Fire* (Little Brown, 1992) that the tendency to kill off people who don't think like us are is as strong today as in the Dark Ages. Not all the futures made possible by the silicon chip and glass fiber are bright.

Donald Chamberlin has been a manager of system products at IBM for many years. Here he argues, following a line of reasoning underlying many of the papers in the previous section, that computer programs can be thought of in the same terms as life—as expressions of an information-carrying medium similar to DNA. Like the biosphere, the "bitsphere" began with very primitive organisms, shows an evolutionary trend toward increasing complexity and diversity, and is governed by natural selection. Chamberlin then asks, What is the nature of the selective forces on electronic species? Far from being competitive with humans, he argues, electronic species are deeply symbiotic to the point of complete dependence on us. All of the selective forces are human-mediated. The electronic ecology has less in common with a rainforest or a swamp than it does with a farm.

William Mitchell is the Dean of the School of Architecture and Planning at MIT. Oliver Strimpel is executive director of the Computer Museum, in Cambridge, Massachusetts. They have combined their talents to address telepresence, one of the great promises for the future Internet. Telepresence is eventually supposed to reduce the need for commuting to work (thereby relieving traffic jams), enable shopping without going to the store, enable dangerous work by remote-controlled robots, and enable meetings and other collaborative work. How many of these promises should we believe? Mitchell and Strimpel bring the perspective of architecture to this question. The distinctions between local and remote and between simultaneous and delayed action are not new. Some of the combinations do not make economic or esthetic sense and will not be realized in electronic media. Others do; that is where technological development can most profitably be directed.

Wilhelm von Humboldt, the founder of the University of Berlin, in 1809, did more than anyone else to establish the modern research university. He believed that research was essential to the dynamics and intellectual ferment of the university. His model was immensely successful and spread throughout the world. In recent years, the reputation of university research has waned; politicians and business leaders appear more interested in spending their money on other, immediate-payoff projects. Interestingly, the next successful model of research may already have been invented by another German institution, GMD, the German national research laboratory for information technology. Its chairman, Dennis Tsichritzis, claims that the ultimate value of research lies not in the discovery of information but in the innovations that result. He proposes three basic processes for innovation—new ideas, education, and product design—and suggests that they can become the basis for a new social contract between government, industry, and academia to meet the long-range research needs in the years ahead. It works. He's done it at GMD.

Peter Denning was one of the founders of the young discipline of computer science in the 1960s; he has contributed new core curricula and has proposed reforms that would keep engineering schools from being put out of business by Internet-based competitors. He suggests that the universities will overcome the travails they experience today as they transform their understanding of knowledge to include not only information but also the capacity for action. They will become more sensitive to their customers (students, parents, employers, and research program managers); they will create engineering schools whose graduates are both educated generalists and trained specialists; they will adopt the Tsichritzis paradigm for research; they will offer continuing, competence-based professional education in a big way; and they will transform teaching. Although he does not believe that all universities will rescue themselves from oblivion, he is optimistic that the majority will. Everyone will benefit.

The Stumbling Titan

13

With personal computers essentially ubiquitous, an emerging broadband WWW, the $500 Internet interface, DRAM selling for less than 50 microcents per bit, 300 mm wafer silicon heading to 0.1 micron and smaller, virtual reality moving in all directions, and other such levers, the computer industry is changing more swiftly at this time than ever before. Indeed, the key players have changed at a dizzying pace.

Consider the 1950s with Engineering Research Associates, Philco, IBM, and a few others.

Consider the 1960s with Control Data, Burroughs, Univac, RCA, NCR, Honeywell, General Electric, IBM, and some others.

Consider the 1970s with Digital, Siemens, CalComp, Data General, Prime Computer, Amdahl, Nixdorf, Olivetti, ICL, Wang, Groupe Bull, IBM, Univac, NCR, Burroughs, and several others.

Consider the 1980s with Apple, HP, Digital, Fujitsu, AT&T, Storage Technology, Computer Sciences, Hitachi, NEC, Amdahl, Oki, Radio Shack, Tandem, Unisys, Olivetti, Groupe Bull, IBM, Mips, and many others.

Consider the 1990s with Compac, Apple, HP, 3COM, Adobe, Bay Networks, Dell, Toshiba, Acer, Intel, Computer Associates, Computer Sciences, EDS, Zenith, EMC, Intergraph, Novel, Sybase, Informix, Microsoft, IBM, Oracle, Silicon Graphics, Group Bull, IBM, Netscape, Sun Microsystems, Cisco, and hundred of others.

Not only is the landscape changing ever so swiftly, so are the principals as time and again, normally stalwart names drop by the wayside in baths of red ink, doomed by bad management decisions while bright new visionaries smile as they revel in their new fortunes measured in the tens of millions and even billions of dollars!

One might say that a more durable company has been IBM since it took an early lead, had the joy of commanding world success, then fell into deep difficulty. However, while still a very large company, IBM is now a question mark as to the long-term future and certainly has lost its dominance.

There are glaring lessons in every one of the failures and the successes. A central question is, Which companies will survive and lead the computer industry in the twenty-first century? If past is prologue, the names will continue to change as current heroes splatter and new heroes emerge. One would believe that the lessons of the past could moderate the failures in the future. Thus, this chapter is devoted to describing the pivotal events at one company, IBM, in the conviction that lessons learned can be important to the computer industry's future. In wonderful hindsight there are multiple lessons that can be learned from errors in structure, errors in strategy, and errors in execution.

In studying the history of IBM, its rise to great success and the troubles that eventually removed it from its lofty peak, it is worthy of note that IBM was only a moderately successful company in the industry until it undertook a very bold strategy. By the early 1960s, IBM's product line had grown to seven different, incompatible families. The consequences to its customers were severe, as most were unsophisticated and dependent upon whatever software the systems manufacturer provided or that they could develop themselves, since there was no meaningful software industry providing alternatives. Moreover, with seven product families to maintain and evolve, IBM's R & D resources were embargoed just to keep the processors moving; minimal resources were available to develop peripherals, communications, software and new applications. Moreover, new peripherals such as disk products were suboptimized as they were applied to the different product families—from parallel architectures for scientific applications to serial architectures used in business applications. Software was minimal, generally limited to a few utilities and rudimentary operating systems. In 1964 IBM led the computer world in a dramatic move that obsoleted every one of their multiple product lines, replaced by a new, unified architecture—an upward- and downward-compatible set of systems implemented in an advanced microminiature technology. The product line, System 360, provided each customer with both scientific and business processing, allowed easy migration up and down as the user's needs dictated, allowed IBM to focus on only a few operating systems, and freed substantial R & D resources to permit IBM to move more swiftly into peripherals, new software, communications, and new applications. System 360 led IBM to extraordinary financial success and was followed by System 370, System 370 Advanced Function, and later by the 303X, 43XX, 9370, 308X, 309X, and ES9000 series. Uncannily, the basic architecture has lasted more than thirty years!

However, at the apogee of its success around 1969, behind the scenes were deliberations at IBM that were to sow the seeds for significant change in IBM's strategy and eventually induce stresses that are likely still not over. The catalyst was the brooding concern of over having put "all the eggs in one basket" that lurked in the back of senior management's minds even as System 360 was enjoying its first success. Indeed, during the development of System 360, some financial and technical voices whispered in senior management's ears that rather than betting on the System 360 family, two or even three product lines would be substantially better than the existing seven product lines and would moderate the company's risk. However, Tom Watson Jr.'s IBM drove on, fully committed to System 360. Nonetheless, even with System 360's success assured, in the front of corporate management's mind was the question of whether the risk taken had been unwise. A new rationale came into view that, despite being erroneous, influenced the strategic decisions of the early 1970s. This rationalization was that the power and flexibility of new software and new design tools would allow IBM to turn its strategy around one hundred eighty degrees and customize future systems to users' individual needs.

One result of this thinking was that the General Systems Division was created in 1970 to produce entry-level systems for small businesses, deemed to be a huge new market, and one where System 360 had been unable to achieve sufficiently low costs to enter. However, instead of moving into the $500–$2500 computer price range, GSD drove promptly into the midrange with several product lines: the Series 1, Systems 32, 34, 36, and 38, on top of which, another division added the 8100 to the central System 370 product family. As a result, IBM was all too swiftly back in the product mess where it had found itself in the early 1960s. This variety of incompatible products set IBM up to be pummeled at most every point in the midrange market with no compelling reasons for customers to buy IBM, as IBM's hodgepodge of systems were too frequently judged inadequate in terms of peripheral support, programming, and communications when compared to the more orderly offerings of DEC, HP, and Data General. By 1980 IBM's midrange share had plummeted from more than fifty percent to under twenty percent! This was a severe blow to IBM, as not only were midrange revenues reduced, the midrange to mainframe migration was tempered. In retrospect, it is certainly a valid argument that IBM's strategy for success in System 360 and its follow-ons should have been the core strategy that could have been improved upon in both technology and architecture. Instead, IBM did just the opposite; it retreated to the past and in the process, shot itself in the foot with a strategy that undermined its midrange and had far-reaching impact into other business areas.

Additionally, in 1972, searching for a formula to manage the rapidly expanding enterprise that was then continuing to ride the crest of the System 360 wave, IBM's new senior management made a significant error by electing to break "the system" into divisions—disks, tapes, and database software in one division, mainframes and operating systems in another, midrange systems and operating systems in two other divisions, and terminals and communications hardware and software in yet another division. Programming and architecture support was assigned separately to each division so they could better optimize their respective businesses. In the process, IBM's systems products, once on a unified path, diverged into incompatibility and because of differing interpretations of architecture, into an inability to communicate between most systems. For this, IBM paid a dear price as customers flocked to its competitors.

In the early 1970s there was an attempt to produce a new, unified complex instruction set [CISC] architecture, the Future System [FS] product line. I share part of the blame for FS's failure, although there were many reasons that doomed that endeavor, particularly rapidly diverging product divisions.

There is another critical key to IBM's fall from invincibility. In 1980, CEO Frank Cary sensed the importance of the PC and ahead of the operating divisions and staffs personally commissioned a project that delivered a product to market in 1981, a substantial feat, especially for IBM. Unhappily, at the time, IBM's vast component operations did not have competitive microprocessors, and thus the startlingly successful IBM PC was driven by a non-IBM microprocessor. In that one move IBM lost control of the architecture and made Intel a worldwide success story while simultaneously losing the opportunity to benefit financially in the inevitable plug compatible industry where IBM semiconductor operations could today be selling IBM engines to the world.

Today, IBM has little control of its computers' architectures as Intel moves ahead with its X86s, Pentiums, and P-6 products.

An egregious mistake came later when IBM lost control of its PC operating system, MS/DOS. That IBM, with its software depth and prowess, was unable to develop its own product was a serious blunder, and that its relationship with Microsoft turned adversarial is another.

The most pivotal error was IBM's failure to produce a broad PC product line based on IBM's own invention of Reduced Instruction Set Computers [RISC]. Some professionals still argue the merits of CISC architecture vs. RISC and other alternatives such as "long word" designs. However, it is generally true that for a specific circuit and packaging technology, in most general-purpose computational applications, RISC is meaningfully faster and meaningfully less expensive than CISC, in addition to the simplification of software in RISC structures coupled with several more subtle advantages including power required, amount of and complexity of engineering changes, and design upgrades. While it is probably an oversimplification to reduce success and failure to a single reason, HP's imaginative moves into a broad family of RISC architecture systems and IBM's repeated failure to do anything other than RISC point products such as the RT and RS 6000 explains much of IBM's troubles and HP's successes.

With respect to the plug compatible industry, an inevitable follow-on to any great product success, the IBM PC's explosive success blindsided the company. In the early 1980s, internal studies convinced some senior executives that IBM's volume would be so large that IBM could afford expansive automation that would make IBM the low-cost producer. That was an ill-conceived position because Taiwanese entrepreneurs soon outstripped IBM in cost, and IBM was amazed as to how quickly competitors were legitimately able to produce their own versions of BIOS, the microcode heart of IBM's PC. By 1985 IBM saw their share of their own PC design fall to low levels, an abyss from which they have been unable to escape.

In sum, instead of building on and improving a strategy for success via unified systems, IBM abandoned the strategy. Instead of capitalizing on their own RISC architecture, they left it by the wayside and in the process lost control of the architecture and eventually the operating system. And structurally, they organized themselves to defeat any hope of a unified systems family. Each of these is a blunder; in total these errors seriously harmed IBM and changed its position as industry leader, probably forever.

While I have spoken to specific management mistakes in strategy, structure, and execution, there is a generic reason for the world's leading computer company to have gone sour so rapidly. What underlies these errors is that IBM changed from a company whose leaders took bold risks to a company stifled by divisional divergence without a unifying strategy and too frequently further choked by "analysis paralysis." The lessons for the aspirants, including IBM, are bountiful. Today, the new industry leaders such as Microsoft and Intel, ironically endowed by IBM's mistakes, have avoided the traps that curbed IBM's leadership. Will these and other leaders in the new century be able to take the requisite risks to maintain their position, follow a cohesive strategy, avoid the deadly bureaucracy, maintain their inertia, and retain their key intellectuals?

The next decade will be fascinating!

FERNANDO
FLORES

The Leaders of the Future

14 | Introduction

Everyone in my office uses a computer. I never travel without one, and my three- and five-year-old grandchildren can play games for hours on their parents' laptops. Not only do many people have access to computers, but given the Internet, we now have access to millions of people to whom we did not have access before. Fifty years ago, we could not have predicted this. I am therefore hesitant even to speculate about *specific* information-technology (IT) products and services that will be invented throughout the next fifty years. In this paper, however, I will discuss some things I am confident will be central in the *direction of computer and software design* over the next fifty years. This confidence comes from an observation about the history and evolution of disciplines and industries dominant today. If we look at the history of many disciplines, we can distinguish certain crucial moments in which the uncovering of a set of simple, *stable recurrences* opens the door to a sudden rush of innovation, providing orientation to the field for some time to come. Perhaps the most obvious example is the field of chemistry. Here, the articulation of atomic structure and the creation of the periodic table created the foundation of our modern discipline, which has consequently led to the rise of several of our most powerful industries. None of these resulting events could have been predicted in detail or with complete accuracy. But once the periodic table existed, it was clear that it would be a secure foundation for design and fruitful exploration for many years to come. Another example is the field of genetics. Certain aspects of heredity were well understood long before DNA was identified as the source of genetic inheritance and its chemical structure determined. But once Watson and Crick discovered the simple, recurrent structure of base pairs and their helical arrangement, suddenly all the variations of species could be understood in terms of the myriad combinations of this simple set of elements. And with the more recent development of chemical means for manipulating DNA, the biotechnology industry has emerged. Again, none of this could have been envisioned clearly at the time the structure of DNA was discovered. But it was clear that for anyone interested in heredity and genetics, DNA was the only game in town and that it is likely to stay that way for some time to come.

I am convinced that at this moment, we are standing at the intersection of three eras of our understanding of computers. The first era, which is rapidly closing, is the use and interpretation of computers as information processing machines. This is rapidly being superceded by another view of computers as communications devices. E-mail, which was a marginal practice until recently, is now finding its way into people's homes. Banking and logistics are being revolutionized by the fusing of computing and telecommunications technologies. While the principles of design of computers and software for information processing have been well understood for some time, the solid grounding for design in this second era has only recently emerged.

Over the past fifteen years or so, my colleagues and I have argued that computers could play an important role in communication because communication is not chaotic or haphazard. There is a set of fundamental, stable recurrences of operational coordination.* We have developed a discipline for process and software design rooted in the claim that an enterprise is a network of commitments. Although we will say more about this discipline in the following section of this paper, for now suffice it to say that we are confident that

---

*See, e.g., Winograd and Flores. *Understanding Computers and Cognition: A New Foundation for Design.* Addison-Wesley Publishing Company, 1986.

computer tools can be designed to support people in the coordination of action and in the management of their commitments. The computer industry has been moving in this direction, and we expect that it will continue to do so in the decades to come.

Beyond operational coordination, business leaders are facing another crucial concern: the velocity of change is increasing exponentially. In response, business leaders must now engage continuously in activities that used to be done only once a generation. They must define, redefine, and project to the widest possible range of stakeholders the identity, or rather the continually changing identity, of their businesses. And at the same moment, we are entering a third age, where computers will increasingly be the medium in which companies and individuals articulate and shift their identities. The Web and the Internet are only the beginnings. As yet, we have a great deal of difficulty understanding what they are bringing us. As before, my colleagues and I are beginning to identify certain stable recurrences in this defining activity of leadership. We offer a first hypothesis in the second section of this paper. These recurrences can serve as a framework of design that will enable the computer industry to build tools to support the continuous reinvention of corporate identities.

Recurrences of operational coordination

Over the course of three decades, computers and information technology have become increasingly important to the everyday operations of business. As new technologies have evolved and been applied to different business concerns, our understanding of what computers are and their role in supporting business has evolved as well. One of the most important shifts of these three decades is the transformation of our understanding of computers from calculators and storage devices to a new medium of communication.

At first, computers were used in business for data calculation, tabulation, printing, and storage in key corporate processes such as accounting and payroll processing. From this era, we inherit our understanding of computers as information processors. Up to today, this continues to be the dominant understanding of computers in the industry. But in the early eighties, with the advent of personal computers, we began to see computers in other roles— such as document preparation, illustration, and desktop publishing. For the people who were using computers in these ways, the machines began to appear not as calculators, but as tools that supplement a person's own creativity. Over last decade, with the advent of networking technologies, the capacity to connect people has led us to see the most important function of computers as devices that expand our capacity for communication.

As I mentioned earlier, practices and applications that were once on the margins of the IT community, such as e-mail and especially the Internet, have become central. As more and more media turn digital, and industries consolidate and blur together, computers and networks are becoming another medium of mass communication. For many new consumers and users, the computer is primarily a communications tool that can also help balance a checkbook.

And yet, these technologies are not always simplifying our lives in the ways that we had hoped. On the contrary, often they are bringing us new kinds of confusion, anxiety, and alienation. Hopelessly overloaded e-mail "in" boxes have become a status symbol, right up there with frequent flyer miles. Searching for relevant information on the Internet is time consuming, baffling, and for many, unproductive. The much-hyped media convergence has yet to show a compelling commercial application. And despite the ink devoted to the development of new on line communities, people who go on line frequently find themselves surfing alone and simply lost at sea.

Communication is about concerns and commitments

The IT industry has made tremendous progress in creating tools that increase people's access to information resources, and the speed and accuracy of transmission. But these very accomplishments are producing different difficulties for people. Not only are many overwhelmed by the amount of information that is flooding in on them, but they are also having difficulty picking out what is most relevant in the constant flow of information. And yet, they feel that if they don't at least try to take it all in, they will be missing something important.

These difficulties arise largely because the IT community has been laboring under a mistaken view of communication. Distinctions of access, accuracy, and transmission miss completely for people what is at the heart of communication: commitment and action that we produce in conversation with others. When people communicate, they don't simply pass information back and forth. They *get things done,* sharing interpretations and making commitments that change the status of their work, their world, their future expectations and possibilities. In this information plays a role, but it is a secondary, supporting role. In the end, people aren't really interested simply in transmitting information to each other. They have concerns that prompt them to reach out and build relationships with others to take care of those concerns.

The mainstream of the IT community has been missing a set of distinctions that allow people to observe these phenomena. As a result, enhancing people's capacity to share their concerns and manage their commitments to each other has not been a serious subject of design. However, a new understanding of communication has been evolving over the last twenty to thirty years. We can see plainly that the fundamental unit of communication is not the particular words or propositions, but the underlying commitment expressed by them.

Take for example the phenomenon of a marketplace. Despite vast differences of language and culture, which would take whole books to describe, there is always a simple way for someone to make an offer to you, or for you to make a request. There are many different kinds of markets, in which people conduct many different kinds of transactions. The one thing that is common to all markets, though, is that any transaction is a mutual exchange of commitments. One person promises to provide a service, the other promises to pay for it. It is this regularity, transcending local culture and language, that allows us to invent systems, such as teller machines, that will make as much sense to people in China just as easily as in Iowa.

The fundamental recurrences of operational coordination

During the course of my work with business leaders and academics, my colleagues and I have developed a framework that reconstructs the enterprise as a network of commitments. From this framework, we have built a discipline for process and software design. The core of this work is a small, finite set of speech acts (see Figure 14.1: "Overview of speech acts"). This provides a "periodic table" of the elements of coordination that is a generic and powerful foundation for design, providing rigor and simplicity even though the particular information employed in a business process may be highly local and appear to have infinite variety.

In observing how people coordinate their actions in the operation of a business, we have also identified certain regular structures in which people make and manage commitments. One basic "business molecule" is the *conversation for action* shown in Figure 14.2 below. (We refer to this diagram as a "workflow" for the purposes of process and systems design.) Each individual workflow is a structure of commitments that constitute a transaction between two people (a "customer" and a "performer") to accomplish something of concern to the customer.

In each phase, people engage in other conversations and activities that culminate in a speech act made by one of the parties, driving the workflow forward to completion:

- *Preparation:* in the first phase of the workflow, the customer makes certain assessments about his concerns and what needs to get done, leading

Speech acts	What is the action?	For example . . .	What does it produce?
Declare	A speaker *declares* a new world of possibilities for action in a community.	"We are founding a new company called IBM that will provide . . . to customers." "We are going to cut out costs by 10%." "An enterprise is a network of commitments."	Leadership and a new context for action for taking care of the concerns of the community that listens to the declaration and makes it effective.
Request	A speaker *asks* a listener to take care of something that the speaker is concerned about.	"Can you get me on a flight to Boston in time for my meeting?" "Why did the power go off?" (Questions are requests for language-action) An application for a mortgage conveys a request.	Commitment to action.
Offer/Promise	A speaker *offers* or *promises* to take care of something that a listener is concerned about.	"Would you like some coffee or dessert?" "I propose we meet and discuss that." "I'll prepare a report on that by Wednesday." Goods displayed in store windows are implicit offers.	Commitment to action.

Figure 14.1. Overview of speech acts

Speech acts	What is the action?	For example . . .	What does it produce?
Assess	A speaker *assesses* how some action or thing relates to specific concerns or commitments.	"We are in a mature industry." "Our customers are happy." "Joe is an arrogant fool." "Computers are revolutionizing our work." "Our costs are increasing."	Preparation for action: orientations, interpretations, and attitudes towards actions or situations.
Assert	A speaker *asserts* (i.e., reports) facts pertinent to the concerns at hand.	It is 4 p.m. PST. The drawer is open. The board is white. That is wood. It is a robin. The gauge reads 200 psi. Our sales were $4.2 million in the quarter. The stock fell by $7/8$.	Confidence that we share a reliable and observable basis for our interpretation of the situation.

Figure 14.1. Continued.

up to a *request* to the performer. (Alternatively, the performer notices some breakdown the customer has in caring for his concerns and makes an *offer*.)

- *Negotiation:* after the request or offer is made, the customer and performer discuss the customer's *conditions of satisfaction* for taking care of the concerns. These conditions include what the performer can deliver and when. The negotiation phase ends with the *promise* of the performer to deliver the conditions of satisfaction agreed upon.
- *Execution:* the performer engages in the production of the customer's conditions of satisfaction, after which he *declares completion*.
- *Completion:* the customer assesses what the performer delivered and how well his concerns have been taken care of. If satisfied, the customer *declares satisfaction* and the workflow is completed.

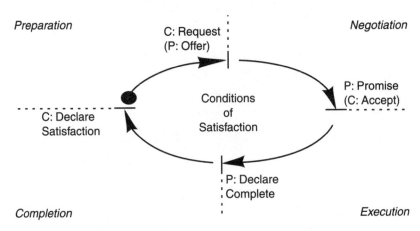

The Conversation for Action

(Basic Action Workflow)

Preparation

C: Request
(P: Offer)

Negotiation

P: Promise
(C: Accept)

Conditions
of
Satisfaction

C: Declare
Satisfaction

P: Declare
Complete

Completion

Execution

Figure 14.2. The conversation for action

Mortgage Lending: Commitment Process

Loan Exec
Loan Officer

Complete
Application

Loan Officer
Appraiser

Appraisal

Loan Officer
Title Search Firm

Title

Loan Officer
Loan Committee

Approve
Credit

Loan Officer
Credit Bureau

Credit
History

**Client
Bank**

**Mortgage
Loan**

Client
Loan Officer

Closing

Loan Officer
Staff

Prepare
Closing

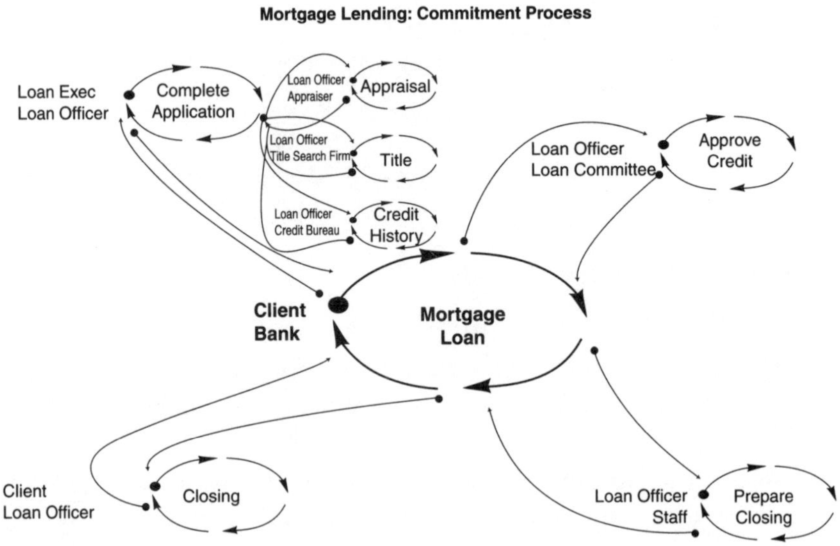

Figure 14.3. The commitment process

This simple structure of transaction is a building block. The structure of commitments of any process within a company can be observed and designed as a collection of interconnected workflows. For example, consider the process of obtaining a mortgage from a bank. This process obviously does not take place in one simple conversation like the one diagrammed above. It involves a whole structure of operational coordination within the bank, which can be mapped and understood as collections of workflow "loops." We call these structures *commitment processes* to distinguish them from more traditional interpretations of business processes as flows of information, materials, and tasks. A commitment process is a network of individual workflows configured to fulfill one of the recurrent commitments or objectives of an enterprise, such as developing and marketing new offers, delivering offers to customers, or conducting preventive maintenance.

Coordination as the foundation for systems design

Over the last fifteen years, my colleagues at Action Technologies and I have embodied these generic structures of commitment in software tools designed to help people manage their commitments more effectively. These range from e-mail applications that embody structures of commitment to large-scale systems that allow the participants in business processes to design and coordinate their actions over corporate networks and the Internet. Fifteen years ago, these tools were considered ahead of the market, and my colleagues and I fought an uphill battle communicating to potential customers that these tools were important for them. Today, as connectivity and access to information is taken for granted, people are demanding tools that will help them work better together. As such, we are seeing the central importance of coordination reflected not only in our own tools, but also in the design of a generation of strategic applications of IT to business problems today. For example:

- FedEx's package tracking system, which allows customers to ask about the status of their delivery request at any moment;
- American Airlines's SABRE reservation system, which helps the airline manage its promises by allowing them to precisely tune the size and availability of planes based on the requests they receive from customers;
- banking, EDI, and other online transaction processing systems that manage high volumes of recurrent requests and promises between companies.

If we were to look at each of these systems based on the logic of information, they would look like very different kinds of applications. But seen through the lens of the distinctions presented above, they are very similar. Each one is a system in which customers and performers make and manage commitments with each other. While we assume that none of these applications were created with these distinctions explicitly in mind, we expect that attention to the recurrent structures of coordination and demand for tools that enable people to work better together will make such applications commonplace in the future. Not only will these systems enhance people's ability to work together, but their structure allows architects to build systems more flexibly and more quickly, and at a greatly reduced cost. As such, we anticipate that the design of systems from the standpoint of commitment and coordination will become the dominant orientation in the industry within the next ten to fifteen years.

Articulating and shifting identities: A recurrence of leadership

Today, largely due to the global connectivity and vast access to information that technology has brought to us, executives have another crucial concern that goes beyond their operational concerns. Business leaders find themselves addressing a much broader range of stakeholders as they shape their companies' identities in the marketplace. Not only do they have to articulate their identities to customers, suppliers, investors, and employees, but they have to articulate their identity to banks, the media, politicians, etc. Today, more than ever before, practices for excellent recurrent coordination are not enough to ensure the future viability and success of an organization. Practices for the *continuous* reinvention of a company's future and for bringing meaningful change are necessary as well. When an executive acts on these concerns, we say that the executive is acting with the concerns of a "leader." The rest of the time, an executive acts on his or her management concerns.

There have been numerous examples in recent years of leaders reinventing their organizations, such as Charles Brown's monumental act of breaking up AT&T or Andy Grove's decision to get Intel, the "memory company," out of the memory business and focus on the processor business. Some of these actions have been highly successful and others less so. Despite the fact that we all can cite examples of this kind, most people cannot explain the *process of rearticulation*. How did these business leaders arrive at these decisions? Even those who have successfully rearticulated the identity of their companies and brought their companies into more prominent positions have difficulty articulating their accomplishments beyond the invocation of "luck" or "instinct" and are not confident that they would be able to do it again.

Shifts in identity, and change in general, are often regarded as great perturbations in the life of otherwise "stable organizations." The general common sense is that these are one-time events, and once they are completed, the company will "go back to normal" until some other change is imposed. In this common sense, both the need for change and the right direction for the future are mysterious. As such, it is easy to understand why the rearticulation of a company's identity is usually accompanied by apprehension and anxiety.

This uneasiness towards change need not be the case, and it cannot be the case if organizations must respond to change rapidly. A different approach to change requires us to observe the following. First, that the articulation and rearticulation of a company's identity is not a one-time thing, but rather it is a continuous activity of leadership and one that is undertaken in the normal course of business. Second, we can also observe a *recurrent structure* in the way the process of articulation and rearticulation is done in companies, recurrences which can be built upon to produce an ongoing, much less perturbing process of change.

We strongly suspect that leaders that are able to observe this recurrence and build a process of rearticulation into their organizations will build several competitive advantages simultaneously. One is the capacity to anticipate critical changes coming to the industry before they become competitive necessities. This will allow leaders to put their organizations in condition to shape change in their own favor, rather than being forced to react to it. Equally important, a process of constant rearticulation within the company will lessen anxiety and help people build a sense of serenity and stability as change becomes the normal order of things. The leader will be able to implement changes more quickly and with less loss of productivity. This in turn will allow the company to take advantage of the sometimes very brief windows of competitive opportunity as they arise.

These issues of leadership, identity, and corporate anxiety may seem distant from the usual concerns of IT professionals. But in this game, the stakes are high for the IT industry. We claimed in our introduction that *we are entering a third era, in which computers, and especially networks of computers, will be the medium through which companies and individuals will articulate and shift their identities in the world.* If our observation about the recurrence of these conversations is correct and the computer industry learns to be sensitive to this structure and builds tools to support it, the computer industry will be responding and making a great contribution to pressing concerns of business leaders today.

In the next section, we lay out as concretely as possible our initial interpretation of the recurrence that we have begun to observe in the process of articulation and rearticulation of an organization's identity and the structure of conversations leaders can build into their organizations so that they can regularly change from within rather than simply react to external pressures.

The future company and recurrent conversations for shifting identity

The first step in understanding how change takes place in a company is to look at how change happens in a company that regularly changes its identity from within. For our purposes, change is most easily understood in terms of six basic steps.

1. There is some "marginal"* or out-of-the-ordinary activity happening (a) in the mainstream activities of one's own company or (b) in other companies or relationships in the industry or related industries or (c) somewhere on the fringes of the company, the industry, or outside of the industry (such as the activities of engineers or hackers toying around, academics, hobbyists, and artists, for example).

2. Someone in the company draws a connection between the marginal activity and a looming crisis or recurrent problem.

3. Some person or company interested in innovation makes a commitment to explore the marginal activity to see whether it could be a promising source for resolving the crisis or recurrent problem.

4. If the exploration uncovers a stable connection between the marginal activity and the prevention or correction of the recurrent breakdown, then someone institutes a new program to turn this connection into a product or service that can be marketed or some new internal business process that can confer an advantage.

5. Someone markets the new offer of a product or service or institutes new roles, processes, and practices in the company.

6. Competitors arise with improvements in the product or service, or copy the advantages of the company's new internal operations. Complementary industries arise, and new industry performance benchmarks are established.

From this description, we can see that business leaders who are constantly in tune with innovations and changes that are taking place in the world also bring practices and skills into the company for discovering these changes and incorporating them into their organization to the extent that they consider it worthwhile to do so. In the future, we see that business leaders will seek to build organizations that do this in a systematic manner. They will also organize their companies so that they can very quickly charter various semiau-

---

*By *marginal* we mean something that just can't be explained or doesn't make sense inside of the current understanding of the business. It could appear in the form of a kind of inscrutable problem, persistent complaint, itching issues that won't go away, or even just strange and unexpected comments from people you have grown to trust.

tonomous organizations whose mission it is to find a way to develop something new by exploring a weirdness for competitive opportunities. These experimental organizations will not just be an offshoot of the company's standard R & D, because they will be feeding directly into the articulation of the company's identity and strategy at the highest levels. They will also generally require different cultures from the core company: something that, by definition, is "out of the ordinary."

Once, however, any one of these semiautonomous organizations successfully develops a new product or set of business practices, the core business can either:

- absorb the semiautonomous organization;
- give it greater autonomy by divesting it;
- reconfigure itself around the semiautonomous organization, adopting a new core business and substantially altering the company's identity in the marketplace.

One example of the last option is Compaq's decision to make low-priced computers its core business, a decision taken after such a computer was developed by a semiautonomous organization within Compaq.

A company that systematically practices this kind of discovery and exploration of weirdness in the business will, over time, generate a very different mood about innovation and change. Members of front-line units that are involved in such explorations are typically given authority to "break the rules" of the organization, and they have more frequent conversations with company leaders than their colleagues. Anxiety and cynicism begin to evaporate as people participate in the process of changing the identity of the company, rather than having change pushed down to them by the corporate organization. But especially at first, operating as a semiautonomous unit within a larger corporate culture is difficult. One is always fighting the inertia of the traditional culture of the company.

If this kind of exploratory activity is going to survive, institutions need to be built into the company to promote and support it in the face of the resistance of the rest of the organization. *We propose that companies that do this successfully will have a characteristic structure of speech acts, conversations, and processes.* At each step along the way, activities of interpreting and articulating what is happening in the company and industry are grounded by activities for listening to the concerns of various stakeholders, investigating and collecting information, conducting exploratory projects, and analyzing the results.

Our current working hypothesis of the recurrence that is present in conversations for articulating and shifting identities follows. We are in the process of

Conversations for Articulating and Shifting Identities

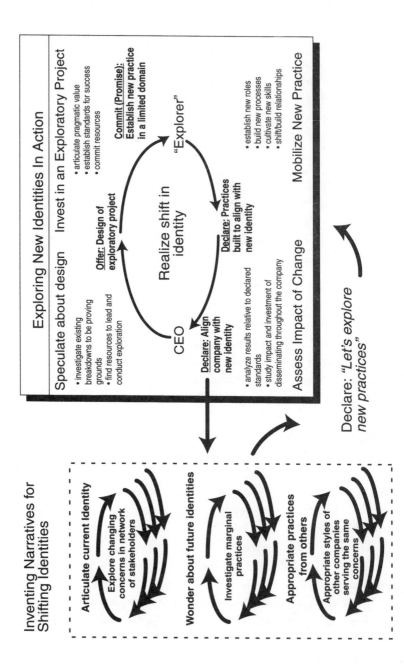

Figure 14.4. Conversations for articulating and shifting identities

elaborating these further and expect that we will modify these somewhat in the near future. However, they are a good beginning for opening up a dialogue about them. (We have mapped our initial speculation on the structure of this process. See Figure 14.4: "Conversations for articulating and shifting identities.")

Inventing narratives for shifting identities

The first recursive act that we have identified is that where the leader *describes* the business his or her company is in by describing the concerns the company addresses and how the company handles them. By focusing on concerns instead of simple needs, the leader deliberately avoids the trap of describing the company in terms of its main product. So for instance, if the leader's company produces cement, the concern his business answers is for solid, long-lasting structures. He meets this concern by the production of cement. But saying so much, even if it appears obvious, does not complete an act of thinking about identity. In order to ground a claim about the concerns that are being fulfilled, the leader must find the *exemplary activities of his or her company* that meet the concern that the leader takes to be the chief concern of his customers. This act alone, simple as it is, opens up a new way of being related to a company. The identity of a company is often understood in terms of its past, and leaders are as likely to take the past identity of the company for granted as anyone else. As soon as the leader starts grounding his descriptions, he may well find that the business activities that are exemplary of his description are not really the strongest in the company, that others have captured the imagination, which can cause the leader to reformulate his account of the business.

The second recursive act in the cycle of the thought and speaking of leadership is *wondering* about how the leader could redirect the operations of the company to better align it with the trends of the industry. Or the leader may have sensed the possibility for a greater ambition: to change the industry's understanding of the concerns it serves and so change the nature of the industry itself. These speculations about possible futures for the company and industry are grounded by finding and pursuing the kinds of weirdness described above.

Any business leader knows that as soon as he or she opens up relations with stakeholders where this sort of wondering takes place, wide-ranging suggestions will start pouring in. So the third activity in the leadership cycle is assessment. The leader must *assess* which of the marginal practices that could be developed could, in fact, respond and transform the concerns of his or her industry. Also, the leader must assess the amount of resources setting up an exploratory organization would absorb, how it would respect the interests of the various stakeholders, and so forth.

Exploring new identities in action

The next recursive act is then one in which a leader *declares* the establishment of an exploratory organization and its mission, and grounds that declaration in the *standards for its success or failure*. The conduct of such an exploration will proceed with the design of a project that meets the leader's standards and in which he or she is confident to invest. A new set of practices for the business is instituted in some restricted part of the company. While it is active and after it is completed, the leader will be making regular *assessments* of the project's progress in two domains: the immediate pragmatic business opportunities it is generating and the possibilities it presents for shifting the identity of the company in ways that confer an advantage.

Finally, the leader must *speculate* on the impact of absorbing the results of the exploratory project into the company, selling the results, or dealing with them in some other way. This speculation is grounded in the *dynamic analytic analyses* of business plans. That is, these analyses must take into account the way concerns of various stakeholders might change. This leads to a *declaration* concerning how the new organization will be dealt with, and this declaration is grounded in *precise plans for action*.

The leader ends this cycle by returning to the same kind of reflecting about the company's identity with which he began. But if he has pursued the elements of the cycle we have just outlined, he is no longer describing the future of the company in abstract terms. He is articulating a new narrative of the company, a new story that links the past and the future together to provide a sense of meaningful change. In doing so, the leader is not just listening to the concerns of stakeholders and working diligently to meet them. As often as not, in his conversations the leader will be *transforming* those concerns, changing the point of the game. And the narrative the leader tells is grounded in the way older exemplary practices in the core organization are giving way to *new organizations within the company and new organizations within the industry, new complementers, competitors, and so on*. A business such as the one we have described is not reactively changing its identity in response to events and circumstances. Rather, it will be in the business of continually changing its identity, even if only in small ways.

Information technology and the recurrent structures of leadership

Information technology can play a powerful role in producing a culture of companies that are constantly developing their identities. Very few companies have set up leadership organizations that give this process the structure we've articulated above, but since we know that business leaders are always involved in the process of articulation and rearticulation of their identities, we expect that business leaders in the future will seek to bring such structure to this process in their companies. So while we cannot predict the specific software and computer tools that can be developed to address this concern, we are confident that if the computer industry takes these recurrent structures seriously, it will make important contributions to corporations around the world.

One contribution is obvious from the previous sections of this paper. By supporting the conversation of developing our corporate identities and enabling corporations to do this in a more systematic way, the computer industry will bring competitive advantages to its customers. These companies will be in a position to anticipate change, implement innovations more rapidly, and lessen the anxiety associated with change as change becomes the normal order of things.

Another contribution may not be so obvious from the above text, but it is one that the recurrent structures of articulation and rearticulation of identity allow the computer industry to make. The computer industry can incorporate the recursive structure of leadership into thinking about systems much in the same way that it is beginning to incorporate the recurrent structures of coordination. And as such, if the commitment loops offer the natural subsystems for systems planning, the acts that constitute the leadership cycle mediate all connections of the commitment loops that run outside the company. Thus, only the leadership cycle offers us a systems approach to gathering that can be integrated with the dissemination that IT structures have had to date. For this reason, we believe that our cycle of leadership acts, which will no doubt undergo multiple revisions, will in coming years set contour to the potentially infinite and overwhelming amounts of information available today. As such, the computer industry will be in position to provide a sense of direction for people and organizations and enhance people's ability to build communities around shared interests and concerns. This is something that people are looking for. We have all heard visions about the creation of "virtual communities," but the Internet has yet to deliver them.

In talking about recurrences, we are aware that we are speaking fairly abstractly. And until we explore these distinctions further, including how commitment loops of an enterprise feed into the cycle of leadership acts, we will have to continue doing so. However, if we return to our story about DNA, we can say that structures of the sort we are describing themselves begin to open up whole new realms of activity that could not be guessed at ahead of time.

But once someone discovers a structure of stable recurrences, articulates how it works, and puts it into the context of concerns that people have, then we can be fairly sure that one important current of the future will lie in developing practices, objects, and systems based on that structure. Such a prediction is the best I can venture at this point.

LARRY DRUFFEL

Information Warfare

15

The phrase "information warfare" has recently reached the popular press. While the phrase may suggest hostile actions between two warring nations against one another's military information systems, hostile actions are limited neither to the military nor to nations at war. They may be undertaken by small groups of people or even individuals, and they may target civilian systems. The ideas of nation states and geographic boundaries are social artifacts that do not necessarily apply in the new world of networked computing. Neither are the responsibility and authority for protection clearly defined. As with physical systems, individuals must assume responsibility for their own protection but must also relinquish certain powers to properly authorized groups for greater protection. Professionals have a civic responsibility to warn the general population of the risks and to help them cope with those risks.

Networked computing provides enormous power—for good or evil

As we travel down the information highway toward the vision of a national information infrastructure (NII) or even the global information infrastructure (GII), we are experiencing new services and exciting opportunities. Even greater capabilities are expected. The range of services that are being announced is increasing at a dizzying pace. One need only read the *Wall Street Journal* to sense the rush to announce mergers aimed at new offerings.

The Internet is an example of this phenomenon. Systems have been attached to the Internet at such a pace that it is virtually impossible to keep track of what is connected. For valid technical, social, and business reasons, many systems—transportation, energy distribution, health care, banking, investment services, and military systems as well—have become part of the Internet, or have been otherwise made accessible, if only by dial-up.

With these opportunities come a variety of challenges, including an increasing need to protect ourselves and our systems from malicious actions. Our computers contain intellectual property that may have significant value. That value may be vested in the company for which we work or it may be personal. When connecting to a network, we must take steps to protect the intellectual property from unauthorized access.

The technology that underpins the Internet (which is also the basis for many new services) was developed with an open, trusting style. Early users developed a culture that was self-regulating. There was little need to protect systems or information. But now, with increased availability and significantly reduced cost of access, the user profile much more closely reflects the general population. Unfortunately, this includes those who would use the net for malicious purposes.

Nearly everyone has experienced the loss of information or time because of malicious codes such as a virus or worm. Viruses and worms are self-replicating programs whose execution causes undesired side effects. A virus is passive until invoked. A worm continues to replicate once it acquires control. Some viruses or worms lock up the system, and the user's attempts to regain control are frustrated. Others delete files. A common virus is the concept virus, which infects those who use Microsoft Word. I experienced this virus during preparation of this paper. An infected file appears to be there but cannot be opened. Once a specific system is infected, other files that are opened are similarly affected. If an infected file is sent to someone else, that person's system too can be infected. The consequence is that the user has effectively lost the file, even though it appears to be there. The file may represent days of work and contain information that is difficult to reproduce. (Fortunately, there is a program available that can find the virus and repair the damage.) As maddening as the concept virus is, many more serious experiences are in store for us.

In 1988 the Morris Worm,[1] named for the graduate student who developed it, nearly brought the Internet to its knees. In the aftermath of that event, the Defense Advanced Research Projects Agency established the CERT[SM] Coordination Center (CERT/CC) at the Software Engineering Institute. The CERT/CC assists organizations that experience disruptions because of intrusions, whether automated or directed by humans. Figure 15.1 depicts the increasing number of incidents reported to CERT/CC and illustrates the increasing trend to use the Internet for malicious purpose. The increase in the number of intrusions is closely correlated with the growth of the Internet. While the trend is clear, what is not as clear in the figure is that the severity and sophistication of the activity have also increased. Intruders now regularly use sophisticated tools, and knowledgeable intruders share their expertise with novices.

Important systems upon which many people depend are both accessible and vulnerable. The consequences of malicious activity on these systems range from annoying to catastrophic, including loss of life. A prankster can gain access to an individual's system and leave messages that have no effect other than

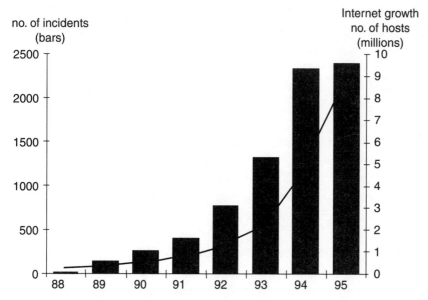

Figure 15.1. Incidence of disruptions to computer systems due to intrusions

to annoy the recipient. More seriously, an intruder gaining access to the control system for a power station might cause a power disruption, resulting in disruption of the air traffic control system, collapse of the security trading system, serious loss of business, and even a serious accident. New Scotland Yard[2] has reported a case in which someone got access to medical records and changed the pap smear results on women's records from negative to positive. Several women began treatment and suffered the attendant anxiety before the problem was discovered. Someone gaining access to a health record could change a person's profile to conceal a severe illness, which could lead to subsequent prescription of fatal medication by an unsuspecting physician. It is easy to hypothesize even greater calamities.

Who would inflict such experiences on people they do not even know? In the case described above, the perpetrator intended to play a prank and gave no thought to the consequences. But not all malicious activity can be attributed to pranksters. Some have suggested that there is no evidence of people engaging in malicious activities in a serious, coordinated way. On the contrary, there is ample evidence. Even if there were not, such a perspective is naive. Given that people regularly commit heinous crimes against other humans in the physical world where they directly observe the pain of their victims, why would we expect that they would not perpetrate crimes when they can do so more anonymously, and from a distance? The following paragraphs contain additional examples that have been reported by CERT/CC.

An intruder installed a packet sniffer that monitored packets going through a communications server at a site in another country where a conference was being held. As the conference attendees logged into their systems at home from the facilities provided at the conference, the intruder was able to capture authentication information. Some of the attendees were from the U.S. As a consequence, the intruder was able to gain access to a number of sites in the U.S., including military, government, and academic institutions.

A large scientific and engineering firm had a significant number of its systems compromised. As a result, they were forced to disconnect their entire network from the Internet for a week while they rebuilt their systems. The costs included the time to rebuild systems, the loss of productivity of fifteen hundred employees, and the disruption of information flow caused by the week-long disconnection.

A publishing company identified an intrusion that had been ongoing for about four weeks. The company disconnected from the Internet for about one month while they recovered from the incident. The company was unable to identify whether the intruders had obtained texts, valued at about $100,000, that resided on the compromised systems.

A major high-tech manufacturing organization had forty systems compromised by an intruder. Although the intruder appeared to be simply using their systems as a base from which to attack other sites, their analysis of the impact of the incident revealed that ninety-three percent of the organization's resources were spent on recovering the compromised systems at their site and seven percent of their time was spent on investigative activities associated with the incident. In total, the incident resulted in more than fifteen thousand hours of lost productivity for the organization.

Several incident reports indicate that Internet service providers (ISPs) had customer credit card numbers stolen from their sites by intruders. One ISP was notified that 6,500 of their customers' credit card numbers were found at another site. The ISP expressed minimal concern and did not think it necessary to notify their customers of this activity.

When attaching to a networked infrastructure, a user is entering a global space. In this space, there is no notion of geographic "place," no physical or political boundaries, no single culture, no consistent system of ethical standards, and no police force. There are unscrupulous people, such as those who would prey on the very young. There are people of radically different cultures, some of whom may have a real or perceived grievance against others—perhaps another culture, race, or religion. There are people who have a different set of ethical standards; what is unacceptable in one culture may be acceptable in another. National laws are inconsistent. In some countries, it is not considered a serious crime to gain unauthorized access to a computer system or even to pirate software.

Our systems are vulnerable to a variety of threats

Systems can be exploited in a variety of ways. In many cases, a human intruder is able to gain unauthorized access to a system using a number of mechanisms, including dial-in and e-mail. In other cases, rogue programs get control of a system. A 1991 National Academy of Sciences study report[3] describes the threat. A recent Air Force Science Advisory Board Study[4] described threats and countermeasures in the military context. The following are some examples of the kinds of threat and their potential impact.

Service may be denied

The services of the network and its servers can be interrupted. Denial of service is often the result of an automated attack. It can be accomplished by flooding a network with a stream of messages. While the system is still technically available, useful messages cannot get through. Denial of service can also be accomplished by a virus or worm that gains control of the operating system by exploiting any number of system vulnerabilities. The Morris Worm of 1988 had the effect of denying service to many Internet users. Denial of service is almost always detected even though it is difficult to stop. It can have serious consequences for a potentially large number of users, for example when the target is a telecommunications system or the control system for a factory or power plant.

A computing resource may be abused

An intruder may gain control of a system and use its computational resources. A frequent occurrence is the unauthorized use of a supercomputer to break password files. This is usually not detected and can continue undetected for a significant time. This abuse is usually directed by humans, but we should expect that intelligent agents will be used in the future to consume resources.

Data may be corrupted

Data elements may be changed so that the integrity of the information derived from the data is suspect. This can occur while data is in transit. It can also occur if an intruder is able to gain access to files and make changes. In one example, an intruder was able to gain undetected access to a collection of nearly two hundred computers at a major research university for a period of nearly three months. Data from several experiments were made suspect. In effect, three months of work was in jeopardy. Fortunately, the perpetrator agreed to disclose his actions to avoid prosecution. Such cases are usually the result of human-directed attack and are difficult to detect. The malicious modification of information that describes commercial offerings on the World Wide Web could have serious financial consequences.

Data may be lost

A virus or human intruder may destroy files or the pointers to those files. The consequence depends on the value of the data to the user and its urgency. A good illustration is familiar to anyone trying to check into a hotel where the "computer is down." This is not much different from corruption (only an extreme case) and can have much the same impact. One key difference is that destroyed data is often attributed to hardware or software failure rather than explicit human action, whereas malicious modification is not usually mistaken for an accident.

Data may be stolen

The case of stolen data is different from loss of data or corrupted data. When data is stolen, the owner continues to have access to it. In many cases, data has value to an individual so long as it is kept private. When it becomes available to others, the value is lost or compromised. It may be a proprietary design, a financial record, or a personal fact that would be embarrassing if made public. The result of its being discovered may be loss of competitive advantage, financial loss, or embarrassing loss of privacy.

Emerging technologies are increasing our vulnerability

The very technology upon which we depend for increased capability and services provides new avenues for exploitation. Many applications, such as PowerPoint, allow embedded commands that invoke some process. A file with embedded execution instructions may be sent to another user; when opened, the process executes on the user's machine. Similarly, when subscribing to online services, the user's software is regularly updated with new versions automatically. Some applications even open files on a user's machine that are updated and later queried. All of these applications are well intended, but the mechanisms that allow these techniques offer no protection against their use for malicious purposes. This general scenario is now being propagated to network services with the advent of Java, plug-ins, active X, and other network technologies.

In addition, systems are increasingly dependent on commercial software products. While this is a healthy trend, it can also increase vulnerability. A clever technique that has been used effectively by many vendors is to leave a trap door in their software to permit them to diagnose customer problems remotely. While the motivation for such troubleshooting aids may be in the customer's best interest in a perfect world, they make the customer unwitting prey. Other "undocumented features" or bugs in commercial software leave us at the mercy of the vendor or others who discover the feature.

Use of information in warfare is essential to military success

The use of information has long been a component of military strategy and tactics. Significant resources are invested in intelligence to gain complete information while confusing the enemy with disinformation. Students of WWII will recall that the Allies went to great lengths to conceal the Normandy invasion and to make Hitler believe that the invasion would take place elsewhere. Other important Allied successes were attributed to the ability to break coded messages and use the information to anticipate enemy actions.

During the Cold War, the military developed a variety of systems based on electronics technology, particularly to support air operations. Both sides evolved a sophisticated capability in signal processing to exploit the other's electronics. These techniques include intercepting enemy communications, deciphering encrypted messages, use of electronic signatures for identification and direction finding, and electronic jamming of an enemy's transmissions. Specially trained electronics warfare officers employ tactics for the use of electronics and countermeasures against the enemy's use of electronics. The success of the U.S. in the Gulf War has been attributed to the successful use of such tactics.

Although the Cold War is over, the world has certainly not become safe. Guerrilla warfare and terrorism are on the rise. The military must adapt to these new threats. At the same time, the technological options are expanding rapidly. Not surprisingly, the military has made heavy use of information systems and networking. As the communications and computing infrastructure has become ubiquitous, we find civilians and the military using not only the same technology but common systems. For instance, a satellite communications system might carry television signals, phone conversations, electronic funds transfer, military messages, and a computer link for a drug lord or terrorist organization.

In the past, military requirements demanded unique equipment and special training. It was reasonable to assume that short of warfare, civilian systems would not be affected by military activities. Today, as the military makes greater use of more accessible civilian technology, that assumption is no longer valid. The educational system is producing people who are capable of using the technology without additional training and at a very affordable cost. Anyone, for a variety of possible motivations, can wreak havoc on military or civilian systems and cause serious and unpredictable consequences. The military has recognized the threat and is preparing to protect its systems as it anticipates information warfare. Unfortunately, information warfare will not be limited to the military.

Anyone is a potential combatant, or victim, in information warfare

The rapid expansion of malicious activity on the Internet has led to concern over "information warfare." While information has traditionally been exploited in warfare, the increased dependence on information systems in many societies has led to the specter of warfare waged among users of networked computing. Anyone who uses a computer on a network is a potential combatant or victim of information warfare. Certainly, in the case of a broad engagement, there will be significant "collateral damage" to those who are not directly involved.

Information warfare exhibits many of the characteristics of traditional warfare, but there are also some important differences. For purposes of discussion about information warfare, the following paragraphs will describe several activities of traditional warfare and then relate those activities to information warfare in a military context. These same activities may also be present in the broader context of information warfare waged by terrorists or criminals. We can learn from the military experience in protecting civilian assets.

Indications and warning

In traditional warfare, two nation-states decide to engage in hostile action. These situations seldom occur precipitously. Some grievance, often historical, festers. One side will begin preparations and the other will counter. Each side will attempt to gather support from allies for its position, using intelligence and misinformation. Prior to any hostility, there are indications and warnings that an alert nation and its military intelligence will detect. These might be clear indicators such as the movement of troops to a forward area, or a combination of more subtle actions that must be pieced together.

In the information systems domain, there may also be indications and warning. If a potential enemy were contemplating a coordinated attack on the information resources of another country, they might conduct a series of intrusions to understand what vulnerabilities they could exploit. They might also leave trap doors such as an altered access table, to exploit later. These actions would not necessarily be aimed at military systems. They might be aimed at power, transportation, and communications, and undertaken with the intent of paralyzing the enemy. Consequently, the indications and warnings become much more difficult to detect. Or they may seem unrelated and even nonthreatening because they cause no real damage.

There is a need to look globally for correlation among observations, i.e., to piece together the big picture. Detection of a single intrusion might be accomplished manually. But it would be much more effective to have a system of monitors that can detect a violation of access policy and provide notification to an organization that can correlate seemingly independent violations. While the notion of monitors raises the specter of "big brother," it is possible to monitor network primitives; this monitoring does not invade privacy and yet detects certain violations of access policy. The ARGUS software available from CERT/CC is an example of this approach.

Increased state of readiness

Once a nation detects signs that an attack may be imminent, the nation assumes a higher level of readiness. Most countries maintain a military force, and the government may give the military increased authority in times of crisis. Security is heightened.

If the threat is against information systems, it is possible to implement increased security only if the protection mechanisms have been planned and people trained in their use. Also, there is no "force" upon which to invest the increased security responsibility. If the technology has not been provided and people have not been trained in its use, a state of increased readiness may simply become a state of increased hysteria. The use of information warfare tools on the infrastructure, such as filters and monitoring, may provide increased protection during heightened tensions, but at a high (perhaps unacceptable) civilian and business cost in terms of privacy and performance.

Hostility

At some point, threatening action turns to hostile action: warfare. One country attacks and the other responds. There may be a series of independent battles or one protracted encounter.

In the context of attack on information systems, the attack must be detected. If the attack comes as a series of human-directed attacks, each intrusion must be detected and countered. The human-directed attacks are likely to be more focused, or "surgical." Automated attacks are likely to affect more systems and be less controlled. Collateral damage (damage to systems that are not direct targets) is likely to be severe. Given the extent to which systems are interconnected, collateral damage is likely to extend beyond the target country. For instance, a virus intended to disable a military system might propagate to medical or financial systems of a neutral country.

Whether the attack is directed by humans or automated, it may not be possible to identify the attacker; therefore it will be difficult to counterattack. Much of the activity will necessarily be defensive, aimed at blocking or containing the intruder's actions and protecting systems against damage. While individuals can take actions to protect the system over which they have control, the average user will be as powerless as a noncombatant in a shooting war. Those under attack will need trained and prepared professionals to protect them. Automated tools can provide some leverage to the defenders, but leverage favors the attacker.

Damage assessment

In traditional warfare, during the attack and after, damage assessment is a key activity. It is essential to know what resources remain to prepare for the next engagement, or simply to rebuild and continue with normal activity.

Again, this is more difficult with information systems. It is not enough to simply determine what is working, although that is important. It is necessary to determine what information has been corrupted, what data may have been compromised, what Trojan horses or trap doors may have been left to be exploited later. Again, automated assistance will be key. Intruders simply do not leave tracks that can be analyzed later. Any hope of assessing damage will depend on observing and logging actions. Damage may even be a future event such as logic bombs that are keyed to detonate during the next exchange.

This discussion is an attempt to relate information warfare activities to traditional warfare. The scenario assumes one nation waging war against another nation. In traditional warfare, we think in terms of force against force. Nations invest in a military. They train soldiers and develop weapons as force multipliers that take advantage of technology to counter larger forces. They worry about the logistics trail. They have rules of engagement that limit the use of certain weapons of mass destruction, such as chemical weapons. They try to limit collateral damage to civilian systems. Those engaged do so at significant personal risk. Combatants die.

Information warfare does not exhibit these same characteristics. Information warfare may be initiated by a relatively small number of highly skilled people. The technology itself provides an enormous force multiplier. The attacker does not need the resources of a nation-state. They may operate in a country (or group of countries) whose laws do not prohibit their actions. They may not even be from a single nation. They may be part of a cult, be employed by a drug lord, or be opposed to some race or religion. They may target specific individuals or groups. They may simply release malicious code that operates at random without regard to collateral damage. There are no rules of engagement. They do not have to worry about the logistics trail. They incur little personal risk of retribution. They might not even be identified.

These factors tend to favor groups and countries that are not as reliant on a computing infrastructure. A small group not dependent on a correctly functioning infrastructure may attack with impunity. A country with a sophisticated and interconnected computing infrastructure may not be able to use the same attack technologies without threat of "friendly fire."

Hostile actions are not limited to warfare

A small group of people might actually conduct all-out information warfare against a nation, but there are other more limited kinds of hostile actions. While they do not qualify as information warfare in the military sense, they exhibit many of the activities of warfare and will require the same kinds of protection mechanisms. These lower-intensity types of hostility can be categorized in the same terms we generally use to describe threats in the physical world: vandalism, invasion of privacy, fraud and theft, and espionage.

Although there are some similarities, there is one very distinct difference. Military systems are designed to keep the enemy out—only those who are known to be friends are trusted. Even then, precautions are used to afford some protection against insider actions that would compromise the system. In the case of most civilian systems, the situation is reversed. The circumstances require a certain level of trust. Banks invite their customers in—they want the business. Health care providers want a broad variety of professionals, administrators, insurers, and others to have access, all of whom must be trusted by the system. Transportation systems providers want their customers to have access to online ticketing and scheduling systems. In effect, the distinction between insider and outsider is blurry.

Vandalism

This is currently the source of most malicious activity today. It is normally carried out by people who have plenty of extra time on their hands, may be poorly adjusted to society, or may harbor some grievance. They might simply be young people who mean no real harm and who carry on their activities in random fashion as an intellectual challenge. One example of vandalism is e-mail spoofing, in which perpetrators make e-mail appear to originate from someone in authority asking for information, e.g., from the system administrator asking for a password. While they may see their actions as a "prank," they can cause serious, even if unintended, damage—just as a "prankster" throwing a rock off an overpass may seriously injure a driver passing underneath. This type of vandalism is carried out against targets of opportunity.[5] They are not normally concentrated or even persistent.

Another source of vandalism is the person who has a reason for causing harm. The individual might be a disgruntled employee operating alone or a political activist operating in concert with others. In this case, the damage is likely to be targeted. The damage may be serious or it may be symbolic. Examples include the use of a logic bomb, e-mail bombing, or e-mail "spamming." A logic bomb is a program that is triggered by some future event, often a date. E-mail bombing involves repeatedly sending an identical message to the same address. E-mail spamming is a variant in which a message is sent to thousands of users—the effect is exacerbated when the recipients attempt to respond.

Invasion of privacy

As in the physical world, individuals seek access to information about one another for a variety of reasons. The reason may be a well-intended but misguided desire to collect marketing data. The desire for information may be motivated by a group with a political or social agenda, targeting a particular racial, ethnic, or religious group. A search for information may also be aimed to expose or embarrass a specific individual. Or a legitimate law enforcement activity meant to expose wrongdoing may invade the privacy of individuals.

Examples of invasion of privacy include penetrating personal files on an individual's machine; accessing health, insurance, or financial records in corporate databases; and collecting information about personal activities, such as credit card use or credit history, buying habits, or even Web sites accessed. In one case, an undergraduate student monitored access by faculty and students to pornographic web sites without their knowledge. Another example is the use of a sniffer that reads e-mail as it passes by.

Fraud or theft

Fraud and theft are activities aimed at financial gain. The perpetrators attempt to gain personally from the endeavor. Examples of fraud include the spoofing of the telephone system to avoid toll charges, use of remove computers (particularly supercomputers) without authorization, use of another's credit card number to make purchases on the net, and use of fictitious and stolen credit card numbers to obtain accounts from ISPs.

While fraud and theft often result from individuals who exploit targets of opportunity, increasingly, professionals and teams of people cooperate to steal and defraud. They even have a publication called "2600" and a newsgroup called "alt.2600" dedicated to sharing information for this purpose.

Cases of fraud and theft are often not reported. When a bank or large company that depends on public trust is defrauded, there is a tendency not to publicize the loss, lest the publicity cause people to lose trust in the institution. At least one bank, Citibank, has taken a refreshingly different view. In a recent instance of theft, they have made public their activities to find and prosecute the perpetrator even across national boundaries. The message they want to send is that if you mess with Citibank, they will go after you.

Espionage

Individuals engage in activities aimed at learning strategically important information about an enemy or competitor. Military organizations of most technologically advanced countries are extensive users of networked computing. As the military brought more of its systems online, their networked information became vulnerable to foreign sources. In addition to concerted efforts to gain access to military information, the military has been a ready target of opportunity. Some individuals who have "stumbled across" military information in their other activities have tried to sell the information to others. Perhaps the best-documented and celebrated case involved the tracking and identification of a Russian spy.[6]

Espionage is not limited to military concerns. Companies possess information that is essential to their competitive advantage, e.g., the design of a new automobile or the manufacturing process, marketing plan, or production capacity for a specific product. All are examples of information that would be both valuable to a competitor and generally available on the corporation's computers, many of which are accessible via the Internet. When the information is stolen, the theft is seldom detected.

Even this incomplete case analysis suggests that much more attention needs to be given to the protection and valuation of information and resources. In each of the cases, the activities described as conditions of warfare (indications and warning, increased readiness, defense against hostile action, damage assessment and containment) will be present to some degree.

The need for protection is based on the (perceived) threat

The notion of protection assumes a threat. Individuals protect themselves against identified threats, whether real or perceived. We lock a door to prevent an intruder from entering. The strength of the lock depends on the perceived threat. An interior door in a home or office will not stop a serious intruder for more than a few seconds. Its purpose is to protect our privacy. An exterior door with a deadbolt protects us against average intruders. If we perceive the threat to be greater, we increase the strength of the protecting mechanism and add alarms.

When the threat becomes so great that an individual or family cannot provide adequate protection, groups band together for added protection. Some people live in protected neighborhoods with security guards. Cities have police forces. Nations have militaries to protect their people, geographic boundaries, trading routes, and economic interests. Nations band together to form alliances for greater protection. In each case, the protection mechanism is designed to counter a threat. Also, in each case, individuals assume certain responsibilities for their own protection. The individual also assumes responsibility for participating in the protection of others. In many cases, a group of individuals agrees to entrust others with controlled authority over them, in a sense relinquishing certain rights to gain a greater level of protection.

At least one exception to the geographical basis for protection is the multinational corporation whose interests transcend geographic and national boundaries. While relying on the protection mechanisms of the countries within which it resides, the corporation may build additional protection mechanisms, but these still follow a hierarchical model.

The responsibility for protection is first an individual responsibility

Regardless of the threat scenario, the amount of protection depends more on the individuals who interact with computers over a network than any other single factor. No amount of technology will protect a user who does not take the necessary precautions to use the technology properly.

In general, protection is based on access policies, both manual and automatic. Intruders exploit some weakness in the system to violate one or more of those policies. If users make a poor choice of password, are careless about running virus checkers, do not use encryption, they make themselves more vulnerable, just as certainly as if they walked down an unlighted street late at night or left the house unlocked.

As individuals, we must take responsibility for our own protection. We must do so for the very practical reason that no one is going to do it for us. While network service providers can take some responsibility for address checking and other transport-related security concerns, they will not do so unless individuals demand it. In addition, if we collaborate with others as part of a subnet, such as for the company where we work, we must protect ourselves as responsible members of that organization. Normally, if someone is able to penetrate one element of a subnet, they are able to gain access to the entire subnet. In such cases, our failure to use appropriate precautions is no different from leaving the door to an apartment complex unlocked.

Individuals can't do it by themselves

While the individual has the ultimate responsibility, the individual needs help. The company or organization that provides access to a subnet has a responsibility to build protection mechanisms into the subnet—and to enforce those mechanisms. They need to give the individuals the tools to protect the system and take action to make sure that no one violates those mechanisms, thus exposing others.

When we participate as part of a subnet, we must be prepared to relinquish certain rights for our mutual protection. In return for the expectation that our system will be protected, we must understand that the provider (through the system administrator) must perform certain actions to fulfill that responsibility. For instance, we might agree to allow the system administrator gain access to our system each evening to back up all files that have been created or changed. We might also agree that the administrator monitor the use of the system for violation of some access policy and if any is detected increase the level of monitoring to identify unauthorized users. In such cases, we willingly give up a certain amount of privacy to achieve a level of protection. The provider, perhaps the company we work for, is trusted not to misuse the information. Even so, these functions should be well defined and understood by all.

As we become accustomed to investing such rights of access to others, we must be careful to understand that we are opening ourselves up to new vulnerabilities. For instance, when individuals decide to use one of the new services being provided to banks to access account information and perform certain financial transactions, they trust the bank. When they load the software provided by the bank, several files are created and several programs are loaded that will run when they connect to the bank. They must trust that the bank software will only execute the functions they expect and will not write any files that keep unexpected information. In most cases, the trust is well placed.

Similarly, we are becoming comfortable signing up for other services, such as those that provide network services. When we load the software provided, we again create files and load programs that will be invoked later. When logging into some network providers, the provider will automatically query the version of software being used and download updates. The network provider may also download graphics packages and write to files on the user's private disk. The user is giving unprotected access to the service provider—which requires a significant amount of trust! By comparison to the amount of regulation imposed on a bank, the amount of regulation on these providers is minimal.

Institutional actions can be taken to help people help themselves

We can help people to help themselves in a number of ways and help those who are going to help others. The most obvious way is to make protection mechanisms for applications and networks more accessible and to provide training for the individual user. Individuals need to understand the nature of vulnerabilities and need a self-defense course. Likewise, more attention needs to be given to the professional development of systems administrators. This group of people must deal with a complex, confusing, and rapidly changing environment. The success with which they implement a protection program and keep the systems releases up to date determines the vulnerability of the systems they administer. A curriculum to support the entry level of this profession and continued professional development should be a high priority.

Vendors and standards organizations need to work toward building products and standards that are less vulnerable. We also need the capability to evaluate the vulnerability of products to malicious intrusion attempts and invasions of privacy. There is a need for a public encryption standard that is widely accepted and incorporated into systems in modular fashion.

Help! Police!

When faced with a hostile action in the physical world, an individual will do one of two things (or both). They will take action to protect themselves or they will seek help from someone they trust. In many parts of the world, we have come to trust the local police, even if we are in a foreign land. Similarly, if we find ourselves the victim of hostile action in our computer system, we will take immediate action if we can, but here is no equivalent of the local police.

The Forum of Incident Response and Security Teams (FIRST) system has grown to the point where there are more than fifty organizations that cooperate in assisting in the case of hostile action. Necessarily, the assistance is provided to systems administrators, not to individuals. The service is more like a volunteer fire department than a police force: it has no authority. It can provide only technical assistance and advice, and it cannot exert force against the intruder. (A wealth of information about FIRST and related protection is available by browsing http://www.first.org.)

Not only is there no police force to protect citizen users of the net, there is no military to protect its citizens. Most countries have an army to protect them against hostile action from across their borders. Many also have a navy that would protect them if attacked by sea, and most have an air force that would protect them against an attack by air. Today, no country has a force that would protect its citizens if their automated systems are systematically attacked.

This lack of protection is not simply an interesting hypothetical question. It requires resolution of a number of difficult and complicated problems.

First, a police force or military organization must have authority to act. In doing so, it must have privileges that give it access to systems. It must have the authority to monitor. It must have the authority to trap an apparent attacker or to divert or lure the apparent attacker to another system. (The word "apparent" is appropriate, because, as in the physical world, an innocent and legitimate series of actions by an individual may appear hostile to an observer.)

Over whom would the police force or military have authority? The ready answer that it would have authority within the jurisdiction of its national boundaries is too limited. Networks use a variety of available communications paths, including satellite communications, many of which cross national boundaries. These communications services are provided by multinational companies. Likewise, the community of users affected by a hostile action may not necessarily all be in one country. They may be members of a multinational company residing in several countries or members of a task force composed of individuals from several countries.

Likewise, the perpetrators may be operating from outside the geographic boundaries of the users who are affected, or they may be operating within the geographic boundaries of all the countries where the affected users reside. How would a police force or military have authority to act?

If we were to suggest an NII or GII police force, then from what source might they derive their authority? What governing body could endow them with authority? Whose laws would they follow?

Some of these issues are beginning to find their way into the agendas of legislative bodies as the world considers the consequences of the GII. Unfortunately, they will probably not receive serious attention until after one or more crises must be handled in the absence of clear consideration of the alternatives.

There is clearly a role for government, even if the implementation is not clear. It certainly includes funding for research, such as that conducted by the Defense Advanced Research Projects Agency. The government role also includes the creation of appropriate laws, provision for their enforcement, protection for its citizens and infrastructure on which those citizens depend, and negotiation for reciprocal agreements and alliances with other governments. However this government role evolves, individuals will face serious questions about how much power they are willing to relinquish for protection, and how much trust to place in their protectors.

Professionals have a special responsibility

Increasingly, typical users do not have the technical background to understand the power they are investing in others by connecting a computer to a network. Neither do they understand the technology available for protection. Professionals have a serious responsibility to assist these users.

They have a responsibility to make the technology more accessible—easier for the average person to use; and a responsibility to inform the public about the various rights they are relinquishing when they give a provider access to their system. Finally, professionals have a responsibility not to abuse their knowledge by taking advantage of unsuspecting users.

This responsibility extends to the designers and vendors of products and network services upon which the public is dependent for information safety. Just as we expect industries, such as the automotive, construction, electrical, and nuclear industries, to follow stringent standards and codes, we must hold the information industry to similar standards. This is another area in which government has a legitimate role, albeit an unwelcome one: to protect the safety of its citizens.

Conclusion: The world is a dangerous place—the world of networked computing is no less dangerous

Most of us do not think of the world of networked computing as dangerous. It is just as dangerous as the physical world—perhaps more so simply because we do not perceive the dangers. As users and as professionals, we have a responsibility to protect ourselves and our fellow users. The government has a legitimate role that is becoming increasingly complex. We have to protect our individual rights, but we must be prepared to give certain rights to others whom we can trust for our mutual protection. This is a serious problem but is not currently being addressed seriously. We must change our attitude of complacency.

Acknowledgment

Several people reviewed an early version of this paper and made useful suggestions toward its improvement. These include Al McLaughlin, Peter Blankenship, and Cliff Weinstein at MIT Lincoln Labs; Kathy Fithen, Eileen Forrester, Tom Longstaff, and Rich Pethia at CMU Software Engineering Institute; Greg Druffel at Computer Sciences Corporation; and Cathy Druffel at Rational Software.

References

1. ACM. *Communications of the ACM* 32 no. 6 (June 1989): entire issue devoted to the subject of the Morris Worm.

2. Austin, J. Law Enforcement Issues Panel at FIRST 5th Computer Security Incident Handling Workshop, 1994.

3. "Computers at Risk." National Research Council (U.S.). Computer Science and Technology Board. System Security Study Committee, National Academy Press, 1991.

4. Druffel, L. "Defensive Information Warfare in the 21st Century." Air Force Scientific Advisory Board New World Vistas, Information Systems Applications Volume, Chapter 2, 1995.

5. Fiery, D. *Secrets of a Super Hacker.* Port Townsend, WA: Loompanics Unlimited, 1994.

6. Stoll, C. *The Cuckoo's Egg.* New York: Doubleday, 1989.

ABBE
MOWSHOWITZ

Virtual Feudalism

16

Taken as a whole, the practices of many companies today reflect a sea change in the relationship between business and government. Companies are increasingly relying upon outsourcing, strategic alliances, acquisitions and mergers, relocation of plant and equipment, and aggressive money management to compete in the global marketplace. Although these practices and not entirely new, they have only recently become "normal" management instruments.

The absorption of these and related instruments into standard operating procedure—made possible by computer-communications technology—is creating a fundamental realignment of economics and politics. The nation-state will decline in importance, sovereign power will come to be exercised by private organizations, the welfare and security of the individual will depend on contracts with these organizations, and personal relationships will become ever more evanescent.

This realignment appears to be the mirror image of an earlier historical transformation. Classical feudalism, the political economy of the

Middle Ages, gave way to modern society, which is now returning the favor by ushering in virtual feudalism. The old and new forms have much in common but are not identical. Virtual feudalism is based on the ownership of abstract forms of wealth that may be located anywhere and moved at will, whereas classical feudalism was based on the ownership of (immovable) land. Common to both variants is the exercise of public power by private parties. The emerging future, like the medieval past, will be a prolonged period of fragmented political authority in which "the basic powers of government (justice and defense) are controlled by private contracts." (Strayer, 1985)

Virtual feudalism is an inevitable consequence of changes in the organization of economic activities stimulated by the deployment of computer communications technology. Applications of information technology in factory and office make production less dependent on human workers. Moreover, location is transformed into just another resource, like raw materials and labor, to be weighed in the balance of cost vs. effectiveness.

Industrial society will be transformed in the next half century because economic and political actors will continue to seize upon the opportunities afforded by computers for competitive advantage. Managers and entrepreneurs are dazzled by the ability of computers to lower costs, improve product quality, generate innovative products, and ultimately increase market share and profits.

How are political and economic forces bringing us into a world of virtual feudalism, and what will it be like?

Virtual organization

The key to understanding this emerging world is a new paradigm, *virtual organization,* which we use here as a means for interpreting the role of information technology in contemporary society. Virtual organization is a way of thinking about organizing that enables managers to take full advantage of the opportunities afforded by advanced technology.

The popularity of *virtual reality* has led to the coupling of "virtual" with any number of nouns to characterize the changes brought about by networking in various familiar settings. Virtual reality allows one to interact with a simulated world via computer. A "virtual office" is a working environment that extends beyond the space defined by a room or building. Office functions can be distributed over many places, possibly far from each other, and the functions need not all be performed between 9:00 and 5:00. A "virtual classroom" is similar. Organized learning need not be confined to a fixed location. Students can interact with the teacher and with each other by means of electronic mail or a computer conferencing system without being in the same place at the same time.

Virtual organization is not a simulated world, nor is it necessarily a computer-mediated environment, although it shares some of the characteristics of both. Rather, it is a *way of organizing goal-oriented activities* that supports an innovative principle called *metamanagement*.

This principle has much in common with the idea of virtual memory in computer systems. In virtual memory a distinction is made between physical and logical storage space. The relation between the two is recorded in a table that gives the current physical locations of items assigned logical space.

Programmers using such a system need not concern themselves with the actual physical space assigned to their programs. Indeed, virtual memory was developed in connection with time-sharing so that the physical location of a program—instructions, data, intermediate results, etc.—may be *switched* from moment to moment under control of the operating system. The table of correspondences between physical and logical space keeps track of the changes.

The essence of metamanagement lies in this switching. Consider, for example, a company that makes a product consisting of parts a, b, c, and d. Suppose each of these four parts must be obtained from an outside supplier. The parts, specified independently of any particular maker, are production requirements that may be satisfied by any of several possible suppliers. At any given time, the choice of suppliers for parts a, b, c, and d defines a correspondence between (abstract) requirements and (concrete) satisfiers.

The idea of assigning satisfiers to requirements is similar to that of matching needs with resources, a well-known operations research problem. By making the task of the manager analogous to that of the operating system of a virtual-memory computer, virtual organization gives switching a central role in management. To accomplish this, virtual organization draws a logical distinction between the management of requirements and the management of satisfiers. Switching then becomes standard operating procedure, rather than an ad hoc solution to a special problem.

This approach to managing goal-oriented activity is consistent with centralized and decentralized, organic and inorganic forms of organization. The logical distinction between requirements and satisfiers, drawn by metamanagement, promotes self-reflection or continual reexamination of goals. Judicious use of switching assures effectiveness and efficiency.

Making virtual organization practicable

Virtual organization has been made practicable by three major innovations: information commodities, standards for social interaction, and abstract forms of wealth.

Computer-based *information commodities*—products and services using computers to furnish information—have transformed the information marketplace into a major economic arena. The role of such markets is analogous to that played by labor markets in the industrial revolution.

To reap the advantages of switching, a manager in a virtual organization must be able to shift effortlessly from one means to another for the satisfaction of organizational goals. The most efficient and effective switching process is one accomplished automatically, without human intervention. As information, knowledge, and skill are removed from human beings and turned into commercial products and services such as software and databases, this kind of seamless switching is brought closer to reality.

By embedding knowledge or skill in software or databases (e.g., training a robot to spot-weld automatically), such knowledge or skill becomes accessible to and can be used by a variety of different processes, either person-based or machine-based. This increases the flexibility of organization.

Computer-based information commodities include hardware, software, and databases in varying combinations. Concrete examples are personal computers, electronic spreadsheets, word processing packages, specialized programs, Internet browsers, CD/ROM databases, and online services.

By replacing human functions, information commodities create new opportunities for organizing work. This holds for managers and programmers as well as assembly-line workers. A revealing example is that of programs to control the operation of machine tools. The deployment of computer-controlled machine tools introduces a critical change in the making of discrete parts. Initially, the only noticeable change is the redefinition of the machinist's job description. The skill of the machinist is embedded in a computer program designed to control the operation of the machine tool. In this way the machinist's job (which may eventually be eliminated) is deskilled into one of monitoring the computer-controlled tool.

More far-reaching change is possible. The replacement of a skilled worker by a computer program generates new production and business opportunities. The program itself can be turned into an information commodity, a product that can be marketed to other manufacturers. Moreover, if the program can be marketed, it can also be purchased, i.e., the expertise needed to machine a part can be obtained in the same way that raw materials and capital equipment are acquired—either by purchasing them from outside vendors or building them in-house.

Information commodities thus open up new possibilities for outsourcing. Currently, eighty-six percent of major corporations make use of outsourcing for some of their service requirements. A wide variety of services are obtained in this way. DuPont Co. contracts with Forum Corp. for corporate training and development. Pepsico provides personal financial planning to its employees through UPMG Peat Marwick. AT&T and Continental Airlines both outsource to TeleTech Holdings Inc, the former for taking customer-service calls, the latter for booking seat reservations.

Outsourcing is not without its problems. Conflicts with unions have arisen over possible job losses. The payoffs expected from outsourcing have been disappointing in many cases, and delays in obtaining services from outside firms have been encountered. On balance, however, outsourcing has been a powerful management tool, and its use will continue to expand with the development of information commodities.

The basic ingredients needed to support information markets are already in place, and refinements are on the horizon. Software such as IBM's Informarket will provide a convenient and effective way to charge for information on the Internet. The "network computer" (an inexpensive, stripped-down PC designed for accessing the Internet) or the "information appliance" (a device for making a Web browser out of a TV set) will put the offerings of information markets within reach of nearly everyone.

While information commodities enlarge the possibilities for differentiating activities conducted within an organization, *standardization* provides the requisite interfaces between activities. Switching in virtual organization requires standardized organizational structure and behavior to achieve *interchangeability* and *compatibility*. Interchangeability facilitates the replacement of one organizational unit (or individual) by another with essentially the same functionality; compatibility enables two different units, with a minimum of effort, to interact with each other in the performance of a common task.

Standardization is in the long-term interest of all the actors in the marketplace. Competition between suppliers may retard the adoption of standards, but it does not alter the secular trend.

Effective telework requires standardization. Many companies, like AT&T, are turning to telework to reduce office and related support costs. Teleworkers rely on computer-mediated communication to exchange information with colleagues and clients. Technical networking standards are necessary but not sufficient to make such exchange cost-effective.

Tasks must be defined in a uniform way, instruments (like word processing and spreadsheet programs) must be standardized, and language and behavior must also adhere to certain conventions. If tasks differ from one unit to another, different software packages are used, and a lot of explanation and background information has to be provided for each new conversation, the cost savings expected from telework would evaporate.

The use of electronic mail for exchange of messages and of electronic data interchange (EDI) for computer-to-computer exchange of structured business forms created de facto organizational standards. EDI, originally supported on private networks, has proved highly effective in lowering the cost of paperwork in business and is now blossoming as e- (electronic) commerce on the Internet.

E-commerce stimulates the adoption of conventions governing interaction between organizations. The practices and procedures designed to accommodate computer-mediated communication lead quite naturally to organizational practices and procedures that define de facto standards. For example, facsimile and e-mail used in business correspondence offer new means for interaction between individuals. Over time, social protocols for the "proper" use of these instruments will be elaborated.

The desirability of behavioral and organizational standards is especially noticeable in the conduct of global firms. Whirlpool Corp., an American-based multinational, makes appliances in twelve countries, sells them in 140, and derives thirty-eight percent of its revenues from sources outside the United States. In its new joint-venture plant in Shanghai, Whirlpool has been setting up washing machine production. American, Italian, and Chinese engineers have been working together on this project, requiring three translators to facilitate communication.

Differences in behavior and organizational practices compound the difficulties of language barriers. All of these impediments to globalization of business can be eased by establishing standards and using information commodities to substitute for human performance.

The switching principle also requires the capacity to shift wealth or assets freely from one form to another and from one place to another. These shifts are occasioned by the ever changing economic scene—fluctuations in supply and demand for products and services in different markets, variable exchange rates and borrowing costs, etc.

The need to manage and exploit such fluctuations has fathered the invention of a host of new forms of *abstract wealth* that complement and extend existing financial instruments. Concrete wealth includes tangible assets such as land, buildings, and equipment. Abstract forms such as stocks, bonds, options, futures contracts, etc. have been used extensively since the seventeenth century, when Amsterdam was the financial capital of Europe.

Computers have made it possible to extend the range of financial instruments by facilitating the development of *derivatives,* to increase the volume of trade in such instruments, and to use them to service a variety of users for widely varying purposes. Despite the occasional failure in control (e.g., the demise of Barings Bank and the bankruptcy of Orange County, California), these new forms of abstract wealth are designed to assist investors and corporate treasurers in managing assets and minimizing risk.

Abstract wealth supports the transfer of resource ownership on a global basis and is thus indispensable to the practice of switching.

Living standards

The increase in productivity accompanying deployment of technology has resulted in a net decline in the labor needed to produce a unit of output for many products and services. But over the past century labor-management agreements have compensated by reducing the average time required to earn a living through work. Compensation has meant shorter work weeks, longer vacations, earlier retirement, ample sick leave, maternity and paternity leaves, etc. *without pay reductions.* Benefits such as health insurance and pensions have been rising but are not counted in the "average wage."

Social policies have been adopted that in effect change the definition of working conditions in order to allocate the available work and maintain buying power. So the creation of new economic activities in the course of industrialization—and more recently in the spread of automation and computer applications—has not by itself compensated for the reduction in the need for human labor triggered by increased productivity.

Like earlier innovations, virtual organization will improve productivity and efficiency in the world's industrial economies. However, it is doubtful that new economic activities coupled with the kind of social adjustments made in the past will be able to compensate effectively for such improvements in productivity. Certainly, new activities will continue to be created; but their ability to add to the employment balance is limited, because they too are susceptible to the use of the tools of virtual organization to reduce their own labor requirements.

How short can the work week become? Below a certain threshold number of hours, the transaction costs of shifting between workers will introduce significant transaction and management costs. At the same time, an employment contract calling for, say, one hour or less of work per week is no longer a job in any meaningful sense—it is welfare in disguise.

Automation in the manufacturing sector in the post–World War II period did not lead to massive unemployment, and living standards improved in the 1950s and 1960s because automation was accompanied by an enormous expansion of earning opportunities in the service sector. Now that computer communications can be used to reduce staffing requirements in the service sector, yet another avenue for earning money is at least partly blocked. No sector of the economy is immune to productivity-enhancing technology. This is a structural problem that will not be cured by stimulative monetary and fiscal policies, nor by job training programs.

Opportunities to earn are not likely to keep pace with the need for making a living. New jobs will be created, but only the favored few will enjoy a living standard comparable to that of their parents and grandparents, and these lucky ones will probably have to work harder to boot.

Assuming steady growth in population as well as the labor force, maintenance of the status quo in living standards will require companies to share with employees an increasing portion of the savings achieved through productivity gains. That is to say, employers will have to agree to further reductions in the work week to accommodate jobseekers. Moreover, to insure steady buying power, employers will have to pay proportionately higher hourly rates.

As long as the intense pressures of the global marketplace persist, such concessions are not likely to be made. Thus, an erosion in living standards is inevitable, contributing to a weakening of public confidence in government.

In the short run, the effects of virtual organization on living standards will vary greatly across regions, as companies learn to exploit differences in labor and other local costs more effectively. Unemployed or poorly paid workers may not be able to afford what they produce, but globalization has made it possible to sell anywhere on the planet. Companies will be able to thrive for some time by producing in low income areas and selling in high income areas. Persistence of such business practices would tend to make the lowest living standards the global norm. Barring effective countervailing power, the economic gains of virtual organization are not likely to be shared by the mass of humanity for some time.

Personal relations and family values

Personal relationships often influence the outcomes of organizational decision-making in ways that have nothing to do with organizational objectives. For example, manager John may buy from supplier Bob, not because Bob gives the best value for the money, but because John and Bob know and trust each other. Virtual organization would eliminate such extraneous considerations from decision-making.

To get maximum advantage from switching, it is essential to expunge subjective, personal loyalties from management procedures. The same applies to subjective regional loyalties. Patriotism, nationalism, and other forms of subjective place-loyalty must also give way if the benefits of switching are to be realized fully. If the objectives of an organization can be met better in Florida than in New York, metamanagement would not allow a personal attachment to New York to block the decision to shift operations to Florida.

Over the long term, the weakening of subjective, personal, and regional loyalties in the conduct of business can be expected to influence human relationships in other spheres. This observation is justified on historical grounds, by analogy with the generalized influence of economic individualism. The market economy led eventually to the collapse of feudal relationships, first in the economic sphere and later in religion and politics.

Once it became possible to sell surplus produce, individuals acquired the option of creating wealth and of changing their circumstances. The rigid bonds of the feudal system began to unravel. Economic individualism—the ideal of being free to ply one's trade in open markets—laid a foundation for the religious individualism of the Reformation (Nisbet, 1953). Moreover, it supported the concept of democracy by providing a measure of the value of the individual, based on performance in the marketplace.

At this moment in history, relatively few organizations are able to exploit metamanagement effectively. But just as modern commercial practices were forged in the primitive markets of the early Middle Ages, so will metamanagement be elaborated and refined in today's global markets.

Like all new ideas, the paradigm of virtual organization will be grasped initially by just a few virtuosi. As indicated earlier, this vanguard group currently consists of international business managers, but no group will have a monopoly on metamanagement practices for long. With the growth of global trade and industry, even more people will become participants in virtual organizations, and familiarity with these practices will spread.

The transformation of medieval society occurred over a long period of time, and the benefits of economic individualism were realized very slowly. Nevertheless, economic individualism had a profound effect on the development of democratic institutions. It is a great irony that quantitative measures of human qualities (such as skill and knowledge) are often disparaged and that dehumanization is equated with "turning people into numbers."

Abstract measures of human worth are essential to conferring humanity on all human beings, and the experience of the marketplace has contributed to widening the circle of humanity. Central to the marketplace experience was the ability to trade or produce, and that experience suggested a standard of measuring human worth that transcended the rigid social hierarchy of the medieval world.

Virtual organization, by promoting objective rather than subjective loyalty, can be expected to extend the social transformations triggered by the market economy. Greater reliance on explicit and objective criteria in human relationships will help to reduce the importance of extraneous social differences linked to race, religion, and ethnic origin. In this sense, virtual organization is a crucible for universal equality, that most elusive goal of democratic ideology.

Basic institutional changes are also in the offing. The transformation of the family that has been occurring since the early days of industrialization will continue. The factory system of production led to the decline of the extended family; now the nuclear family is under siege. A social institution can outlive its function for a time, but unless it adapts to altered conditions, it is doomed to extinction.

The institution of the family has adapted to a drastically altered economic function by downsizing, i.e., contracting from an extended to a core (or nuclear) unit. In the preindustrial era, almost all goods and services were produced by the extended family. Industrialization changed the locus of production from the home to the factory, and in so doing separated economic from other activities conducted within the home. This separation meant that individuals, rather than family groups, were called upon to fill production roles. Factory owners hired individuals, not family units.

Now dependence on the human being as a carrier of skill and knowledge is diminishing, so there is less need for the family unit to reproduce the skills and knowledge required by the economy. Although not the only justification, economic necessity is a critical one for all human institutions. Just as the extended family adapted to industrialization by downsizing, the nuclear family is adapting to the postindustrial world by splitting into its elementary constituents.

In effect, the human being is becoming ever more liberated from—or thrown out of—the process of production and is thus losing ground in the

Figure 16.1.

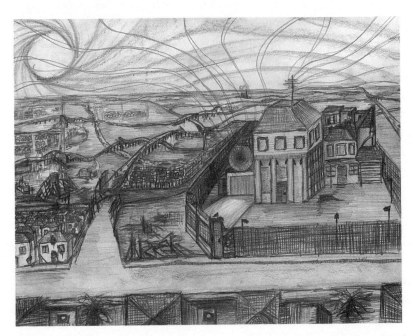

Figure 16.2. "The Eternal Recurrence," original pencil drawings by Jed Mowshowitz.
Above "Past." Below "Future."

labor market. Since the family's primary economic output is being devalued, the enterprise itself is being devalued. Concretely, this means that couples find it increasingly difficult to stay together. Romantic attachments and bonds of affection are evidently not enough in themselves to sustain the nuclear family.

High divorce rates and the rapid growth of single-parent households are strong indicators of the transformation of the family. New, stable forms may emerge, but they are not yet in view. Inner-city communities in the United States have a high proportion of single-parent households, many of which are headed by adolescent females. In middle-class communities, serial marriage is quite common. Perhaps something like the child-rearing institutions featured in negative utopias such as Huxley's *Brave New World* will replace the family altogether. The only certainty is that stability requires form to follow function.

An emerging political economy

Fundamental political changes are also likely to accompany the spread of virtual organization. The weakening of subjective, regional loyalties enables organizations to operate on a global basis. This spells the end of the nation-state. Indeed, the handwriting has been on the wall for some time now.

For many multinational or transnational enterprises, the notion of regional or national loyalty is already an anachronism. Boeing and other American firms carefully cultivate the Chinese leadership in hopes of lucrative contracts despite political or trade frictions between the United States and China. Similarly, German firms such as Siemens and Volkswagen actively pursue their business interests in China, seemingly oblivious to the German parliament's rebuke of China's Tibet policy.

What matters is the bottom line. If a company based in the United States discovers that it can produce some item more efficiently in Mexico or South Korea and the transaction and management costs associated with a shift in production are not excessive, that company is likely to curtail production in the United States and establish or enlarge operations in Mexico or South Korea. There are intermediaries, such as brokers and bankers, whose living derives from transaction costs, but they cannot keep such costs artificially high, as shown quite clearly by the trend toward disintermediation in banking and the elimination of many intermediaries in commerce due in part to the adoption of EDI.

Inevitably, the nation-state will decline as a political entity. Globalization of business, stimulated in large measure by virtual organization, has compromised its power and authority and has drastically reduced its ability to meet the challenges of unemployment, declining living standards, inequitable distribution of wealth and income, regional disparities, and social disintegration. In particular, as argued above, declining living standards are a long-term, structural problem that will worsen as businesses adopt the methods of meta-management. Paradoxically, nation-states are likely to continue pursuing policies that reward global enterprises for reducing average family buying power within their borders. Tax incentives and subsidies will continue to be offered to companies to conduct R & D domestically, with no constraint on where volume production is ultimately established. With such policies, the benefits of public largesse may be (and often are) exported.

Social disintegration is evidenced by increases in homelessness and crime, failures in education, and the breakdown of the family. All of these are symptoms of the increasing inability of the nation-state to manage effectively in a fundamentally altered economic environment. In time the legitimacy of the nation-state will be undermined by its inability to cope with mounting distress of large segments of its population.

Persistently low participation rates in elections may be a leading indicator of the nation-state's decline. Apathy and mistrust of politics are rampant in the Western democracies. Whether or not this rejection of the political process signals the end of the nation-state, it is clear that politics and economics are diverging.

The nation state arose in a period in which territory, reinforced by language and culture, made a great deal of sense as a basis for a political entity. That is no longer true because of the globalization of the economy. Economic relations can no longer be contained within the framework of the nation-state.

This divergence of economics and politics is strongly reminiscent of developments in an earlier period of history. The political structure of the late Roman Empire also proved to be an inappropriate framework for the economic conditions of that period. Imperial government, unable to collect enough revenue to provide essential services, gave way to the feudal system, in which public authority was exercised by private parties (e.g., landowners).

Contemporary governments are reeling from the same kind of structural revenue shortages and are gradually ceding effective authority to private organizations (e.g., transnational companies). The result, assuming the trend continues, will be *virtual feudalism,* a system possessing all the earmarks of classical feudalism except that it is based on globally distributed resources rather than land.

Nation-states are short of money because they are no longer able to exercise effective control over the economic activities within their borders. With the globalization of the marketplace, opportunities for moving (abstract) wealth from place to place have increased enormously. These opportunities allow transnational companies to minimize their tax obligations—through transfer pricing and other mechanisms. Since large corporations account for a large share of gross domestic product, chronic tax-revenue shortages are inevitable. Obviously, such shortages limit the ability of the nation-state to pay for public services.

Revenue shortages are evidenced by the fiscal insolvency of key welfare programs such as health insurance and social security. The U.S. Social Security Trust Fund, for example, is expected to be in deficit by the year 2020. Moreover, welfare benefits are being reduced, or else responsibilities are being shifted to individuals and private organizations or from central to local government (without corresponding transfer of resources).

Even the welfare states of Europe are being dismantled piece by piece. Germany and Holland are making substantial cuts in social security, health insurance, unemployment compensation, aid to students, and other benefits. Moreover, employers are being given greater leeway in firing employees.

Power in virtual feudalism will be wielded by those adept at switching. Giant multinational companies have been the first organizations to use this principle effectively. However, enterprises of varying size—regional as well as international—may very well play a prominent role in the future. These entities will gradually become political as well as economic units.

From our vantage point, the multinational company, for example, is a private entity that is chartered by public authority. Slowly, the definition of private and public will shift, so that what is now deemed to be political power will eventually come to be exercised by entities that are currently defined as private. This transformation is inevitable because the nation-state will not be able to provide an adequate system of justice and defense. The resources needed to maintain public order and to prosecute breaches of the law by large corporations will simply be unavailable. National governments will not disappear, but their functions will be drastically curtailed.

As in medieval feudalism, the basic functions of government will come to be exercised by private parties. This is not just a change in the names of the providers of public services. With the shift in function will come a shift in power and legitimacy. Private parties will exercise authority in their own name, not in the name of a law that transcends their own power. This is the essence of feudalism.

The devolution of public functions to private organizations is evident in education and training, dissemination of government information, prison management, payment mechanisms, and in other services.

Many large companies are providing their own training and education programs because they are not satisfied with the results of public or nonprofit institutions. Moreover, a number of private companies (e.g., Education Alternatives Inc. and Sylvan Learning Systems Inc.) are in the business of managing public schools. This business appears to be on the verge of expanding rapidly, just as the managed health care industry was some twenty years ago.

Since the early 1980s, the U.S. federal government, in an effort to cut costs, has moved to contract with private companies for the distribution of documents, reports, and statistical (e.g., employment and census) data to the public.

Private companies have been engaged to manage public institutions such as prisons—again, in the hope of saving money. This is perhaps the most telling example, since prisons are generally thought to be preeminently public institutions.

In the payments arena, government still has exclusive control over the minting of coins and paper currency, but these forms of money are overshadowed by credit and debit cards offered by financial service firms. New media of exchange (called electronic- or e-money) are being introduced by Citibank (Electronic Money System), Digicash, Natwest (Mondex International System), and Visa (Visa Cash System).

These new media take the form of smart cards with embedded microchips that can be loaded with electronic money via automated teller machines or through PCs connected to the telephone network. An estimated twenty percent of all household purchases in the United States (amounting to about $3 trillion) may be made electronically by 2006. E-money seems poised to catch on in Japan as well.

The above examples signify a significant transfer of public functions to the private sector.

Virtual feudalism shares the political features of classical feudalism, but its economic basis is abstract wealth, and the social system erected upon it may be very fluid. The central institution of virtual feudalism will be the virtual fief, rather than the manor or landed estate of European feudalism. Assets will be distributed on a global basis as "virtual resources," i.e., the particular form of abstract wealth may change from moment to moment depending on the institution's financial needs and market conditions. Excess cash, for example, may be kept today in a Deutschmark-denominated money market fund but switched to Japanese Yen tomorrow because the Deutschmark is expected to decline against the Yen.

Virtual organizations such as multinational companies could in principle take political responsibility for ensuring freedom, justice, security, and opportunities for the pursuit of happiness. But how is this acceptance of responsibility to be brought about, first for the lucky retainers of the virtual fiefs and then for everyone else? Power will accrue to the virtual fiefs simply because of their preeminent role in the global economy. Acceptance and exercise of responsibility are entirely different matters. What will induce the new centers of power to act responsibly?

Not too many firms are likely to follow the example of Malden Mills Industries, whose head, Aaron Feurerstein, has promised to reemploy 3,200 employees who were idled by a fire at the firm's Massachusetts plant in early 1996. Even fewer would go the extra mile and pay most of the idled workers for ninety days while a replacement plant is built.

So long as enterprises can gain advantage from applying the principles of metamanagement, there is little to stop them from playing a zero-sum game with competitors, employees, and the general public. A company can close down a plant and thereby idle twenty thousand workers without worrying about the effects of such a move on the local community if there are other places to produce its products and other markets in which to sell them. The ability to operate in this way (i.e., to produce in politically stable, low-wage markets and sell in relatively affluent ones) will continue until disorder and poverty become nearly universal.

In the absence of assistance programs, declining living standards will breed widespread social unrest and thus create uncontrollable security problems. Global business is highly vulnerable to disruptions in transport and communications, which cannot be protected adequately by police and military power alone—history shows that power without legitimacy is inherently unstable.

At some point, the virtual fiefs, for reasons of survival, will have to take responsibility for the consequences of their actions. For the moment, the scale of global switching is relatively modest, and governments are still able to bear the burdens of dislocation. But these burdens will become increasingly unbearable. When will the virtual organizations realize that they must act in the public interest? And what will bring them to that realization?

Absent radical intervention, it could take a long time before the global economy becomes so volatile that firms can no longer make any profits because of crime, social disorder, and unstable markets. This kind of disintegration has already occurred in many inner-city areas in the United States.

Nevertheless, there is business as usual in the more affluent neighborhoods. Why? A cynical interpretation is that the inner cities have been written off because the buying power they represent is relatively insignificant. Business and political interests may reason that because a particular community does not have sufficient buying power to warrant substantial investment in infrastructure and security measures, it can safely be left to implode.

The only effective guarantee of responsible action is countervailing power, but who knows from what corner it will arise, or what it will demand?

It is possible for individuals and communities to reap the benefits of the productivity and efficiency gains to be expected from virtual organization. In the long run, a stable social order will emerge—but a great deal of dislocation, chaos, and misery may be experienced on the way. The amount of disorder and misery will depend on the actions that are taken to establish political forms consistent with the evolving economic reality.

History gives some idea of what to expect. The robber barons of the industrial revolution were not eager to share the fruits of improved production with employees and the public. Mobilization of countervailing power in the form of labor unions helped to achieve more equitable arrangements. Similar movements—of consumers, perhaps—will be needed to impress the overlords of the coming virtual fiefs. The mere threat to boycott a company's products is sometimes enough to change corporate policy. Under threat of boycotts by American consumers, Pepsico withdrew from Burma in April 1996, and Heineken followed suit a few months later.

Old power does not readily yield to new power, and the nation-state—when it finally realizes the challenge posed by virtual enterprise—will try to fight back. This could lead to a protracted struggle, reminiscent of the contest between the feudal barons and the monarchies in the early modern era.

There is relatively little tension at the moment. Nations and supranational bodies such as the European Union encourage business development without paying much attention to the results. For example, companies receiving tax subsidies are not punished for relocating plants outside the country.

However, governments do sometimes restrict international business transactions that are deemed to be contrary to national interests. Export controls have been imposed on the sale of advanced military equipment, and foreign acquisitions of domestic firms (e.g., sole producers of militarily or strategically critical products) have been blocked. Unilateral actions, such as the levying of tariffs on selected imports, have long been used by nation-states to protect domestic business interests. The threat of retaliation and escalation into a trade war inhibits the use of this mechanism, however.

Antimonopolistic policies are another means for controlling international business activity. For example, the U.S., the U.K., and the European Commission must all approve the recently announced alliance between American Airlines and British Air.

These kinds of controls could be used in the future to rein in the global economy, but the prevailing sentiment is to encourage, rather than inhibit, globalization. The ability of multinational firms to relocate productive and financial resources anywhere in the world makes a hostage of the nation-state. Governments fear—justifiably or not—that companies will relocate facilities to other countries, resulting in possible losses of tax revenue and domestic jobs. This holds as much for the great powers as for the small ones.

The main weapon of the nation-state is its power to levy taxes. Since it is becoming more difficult to generate revenue by taxing producers, governments may try to increase taxes on consumers. But what is to prevent people from moving to avoid onerous taxation? Attempts to prevent people from moving will fare no better than comparable actions by imperial Rome.

As virtual feudalism unfolds, the economic prospects of individuals can be expected to vary substantially from one region to another. Job prospects and living costs, for example, may for a time be far more attractive in one country than in another. Such regional variations are likely to increase migration pressures, amplify tensions between countries, and promote social instability.

Problems arising from migration pressures have already proved difficult if not intractable—witness illegal immigration to the United States from Central America and the Caribbean, to Germany from Eastern Europe, to Europe and the Americas from Asia, and the gathering wave to France from the Southern Mediterranean region. Individuals too can learn to exploit virtual organization.

Systems in transition are often unstable. If wise counsel prevails, the negative effects of instability can be avoided, and the benefits of a new order can be secured with a minimum of disorder.

Conclusion

Virtual organization makes it possible to organize human activity in new ways. It is the child of three major innovations: information commodities, standards for social interaction, and abstract forms of wealth. The new paradigm carries profound social changes in its wake. Divergence of economic from political reality in the industrialized world is leading to the decline of nation-states. In the long term, the social changes will crystallize in virtual feudalism, a system of political authority centered in private, virtual organizations and based on the management of abstract forms of wealth.

The transition to this new order may be marked by diminished living standards, social disorder, and conflict between the old and new regimes. But at the same time, these social changes may extend and refine the accomplishments of economic individualism and carry the values of democracy to all human beings.

Further Reading

Barnet, R.J., and Cavanagh, J. *Global Dreams*. New York: Simon & Schuster, 1994.

Brown, P.G., and Shue, H., eds. *Boundaries: National Autonomy and Its Limits*. Totowa, NJ: Rowan and Littlefield, 1981.

Braudel, F. *The Wheels of Commerce: Civilization and Capitalism 15th–18th Century* (Volume 2). New York: Harper & Row, 1982.

Nisbet, R. *The Quest for Community*. Oxford: Oxford University Press, 1953.

Porter, M.E., ed. *Competition in Global Industries*. Boston: Harvard Business School Press, 1986.

Davidow, W.H., and Malone, M.S. *The Virtual Corporation*. New York: HarperCollins Publishers, 1982.

Giuliano, V.E. "The mechanization of office work." *Scientific American* **247**(1982): 149–164.

Hammer, M., and Champy, J. *Reengineering the Corporation*, New York: HarperCollins Publishers, 1993.

Leontief, W.W. "The distribution of work and income." *Scientific American* **247** (1982):188–204.

Mowshowitz, A. "Virtual feudalism: a vision of political organization in the information age." *Informatization and the Public Sector* **2**(1992):213–231.

Mowshowitz, A. "Virtual organization: a vision of management in the information age." *The Information Society* **10**(1994):267–288.

New York Times. The Downsizing of America. New York: Random House, 1996.

Reich, R.B. (1992). *The Work of Nations*, Random House, New York.

Rheingold, H. *The Virtual Community*, Reading, MA: Addison-Wesley Publishing, 1993.

Strayer, J.R. "Feudalism," in *Dictionary of the Middle Ages*, J.R. Strayer, ed., New York: Charles Scribner's Sons, 1985.

Thurow, L.C. *The Future of Capitalism*. New York: William Morrow & Co., 1996.

Turoff, M. "Information, value, and the internal marketplace." *Technological Forecasting and Social Change* **27**(1985):357–373.

DONALD D. CHAMBERLIN

Sharing Our Planet

17

The laws of thermodynamics tell us that in a closed system, order tends to be replaced by disorder and randomness. But approximately three billion years ago a chemical structure appeared on the earth with a tendency to organize itself into increasingly complex forms. This structure, made mostly out of carbon and hydrogen, is called DNA. Of course, the tendency of DNA toward increasing order is not a thermodynamic anomaly, because the earth is not a closed system, receiving as it does a steady rain of energy from the sun. Nevertheless, the behavior of DNA is unusual enough that we give a name—"life"—to its complex forms, and devote a science—biology—to their study.

If we were to take snapshots of the earth's surface at various points during the last three billion years, they would tell a story of the evolution of increasingly complex DNA structures. An early snapshot might show single-celled microbes inhabiting the oceans. A later one might show the emergence of multicellular organisms, and a still later one might reveal land surfaces populated by giant reptiles. Over time, a large variety of species evolved, covering the planet with DNA and its byproducts. These species came to exhibit complex social behavior and to compete with each other fiercely for resources. The science of evolutionary biology studies how species change and attempts to discover the rules that govern how much and what kinds of DNA will be found on the earth at any given time.

Fifty years ago, a new medium appeared on the earth that, like DNA, is able to carry large amounts of information: the medium of digital storage in electronic and magnetic devices. We might think of all the digital devices in the world as forming an ecosystem. Occupying this ecosystem are digital individuals: the programs that give our devices their function and personality. Like living things, digital programs have shown a tendency to evolve more complex forms over time. We can imagine a taxonomy of programs similar to the one used to classify biological life. It would include humble fixed-function programs found in watches and calculators, as well as larger and more flexible programs such as operating systems, database systems, and word processors. Some of the "species" within this taxonomy have well-known names, such as Windows or Notes, while others are more anonymous, such as the programs that route our telephone calls. These digital species commonly consist of millions of individuals, and the most successful species number in the hundreds of millions. Like biological species, digital species evolve over time, form symbiotic relationships, and compete for survival in various ecological niches.

In fifty years, the digital habitat has expanded from a few bits of storage in a small number of isolated sites to a richly interconnected global network. Some idea of the rate of growth of this habitat can be seen in Figure 17.1, which shows the storage capacity of the hard disk drives manufactured (or expected to be manufactured) worldwide during the years 1990–1999. During the last decade of this century, manufacturers will ship about 2×19^{19} bits of digital storage on hard disks. But this is only part of the digital habitat, which also includes semiconductor chips inside all sorts of computers, appliances, and vehicles, as well as enormous amounts of data stored on archival devices such as tapes and compact discs.

Like biological evolution, digital evolution might be illustrated by a series of snapshots. An early snapshot would show relatively simple programs inhabiting isolated mainframes and propagating by cumbersome methods such as magnetic tape. A later snapshot might include species that can thrive on a variety of platforms and that propagate by various planned and unplanned methods, including teenagers exchanging bootleg copies on floppy discs. A still later snapshot might reveal species that exist somewhere in cyberspace,

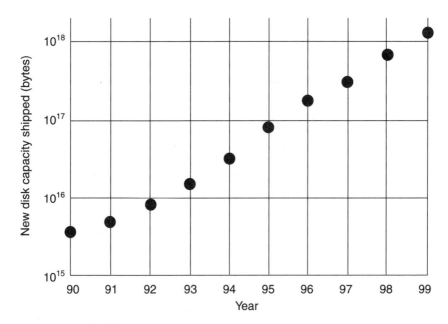

Figure 17.1. Worldwide shipments of hard disk drives. Source: *Disk/Trend Report,* 1990–96

downloading copies of themselves on demand to individual machines around the world.

It is important not to read too much into the analogy between digital and biological evolution. Clearly, software does not satisfy the traditional criteria for life, and I do not mean to imply that programs possess consciousness. Nevertheless, it seems clear that something important is happening here, and very quickly. Simple structures are being replaced by more complex and highly organized structures, in seeming (but not, of course, actual) contradiction to the laws of thermodynamics. This is only the second time that such a phenomenon has been observed on our planet. And this time, the snapshots that show the progression of the phenomenon are spaced not by millions of years, but by perhaps twenty years. The advent of digital software raises a question that the human species has not confronted before: if we are to share our planet with a new form of rapidly evolving entities, nearly as complex as ourselves, what long-term effect can we expect these entities to have on our environment and our society?

It is worth noting here that although I use the term "digital" to describe the entities that have come into existence in the last fifty years, this is not really the characteristic that distinguishes them from biological life. The genetic blueprint contained within each human cell consists of about 3×10^9 base pairs, each representing a "letter" in a four-letter chemical alphabet. Since each letter in a four-letter alphabet carries two bits of information, the total amount of information in the human genome is about 6×10^9 bits, less than one gigabyte. Interestingly, biologists believe that less than ten percent of this information is "switched on" in the sense that it plays an active role in the physiology of the human body. Thus the human genome might be considered to contain less than one hundred megabytes of usable information. This is the size of a large but not impossibly large computer program, though presumably the genome is written in a more efficient language. The genetic blueprint of a medium-sized bacterium, such as *E. coli,* is written in the same four-letter code and contains less than one megabyte of data, a rather small computer program by today's standards. Scientists in the human genome project are attempting to decode the digital language of DNA, in what is perhaps the world's largest reverse-engineering effort. Thus, computer programs are distinguished from living things not mainly because they are digital, but because they encode their personalities in electronic and magnetic rather than chemical media.

In his book *Bionomics: Economy as Ecosystem,*[3] Michael Rothschild draws an analogy between biological organisms and economic organisms such as businesses. Rothschild observes that the essence of both kinds of organism lies in the information that they contain. Biological organisms interact with their environment to generate an energy surplus, which they use to create more copies of their genetic information. Similarly, businesses interact with their environment to generate profits, which they use to fuel their growth. For example, the profits generated by a chain of stores might be reinvested to replicate the "genes" of the chain in new locations. Like biological organisms, economic organisms compete with each other for survival in various ecological niches. Both kinds of organism are subject to the law of natural selection, which causes them to evolve over time, becoming more efficient in generating surpluses and in replicating the information that lies at their heart.

We can extend Rothschild's analogy to apply to software "organisms" as well as to businesses. It is clear that the essence of a computer program lies in its information content, and that in order for a software species to prosper, this information must be replicated and widely distributed. As in the case of a business, the replication process for software is mediated by humans and based on providing value to humans. This is not, of course, the only known example of one species relying on another for its reproduction—another example can be found in flowers that propagate their genetic information by providing value (in the form of nectar) to bees.

Although digital machines can operate for limited periods of time without human intervention, I think it is likely that the digital ecosystem will remain under human control, having more in common with a farm than with a jungle. Some digital programs, called viruses, have evolved a means to replicate themselves without human control or intervention; but since humans find this trait to be unpleasant or threatening, it has not proved to be positively linked to survival. Thus, species of software can expect to occupy the digital ecosystem in direct measure as they create or conserve resources that humans find valuable, such as time, money, health, information, or amusement. In other words, serving human needs is the principal evolutionary imperative for digital forms.

I would like to examine three ways in which digital species will earn their habitat over the next fifty years: by allocating resources more efficiently, by moving information to the places and times where it is needed, and by having a globalizing influence on human culture.

Allocating resources

During the decade from 1975 to 1985, the average fuel efficiency of new cars sold in America increased by more than two-thirds, from about sixteen to about twenty-seven miles per gallon, with little decrease in comfort and with an actual improvement in the driving characteristics of the typical automobile. Part of this improvement resulted from reduction in vehicle weight and use of new materials. But a significant part of the improvement was made possible by a new individual riding inside every new car: a digital fuel injection program that meters out the precise amount of fuel needed for each piston stroke, taking into account various factors such as air temperature and pressure and the speed of the engine. Digital fuel injection is more efficient than an old-fashioned carburetor because it brings more information and intelligence to bear on the problem of allocating a resource: gasoline. Any allocation of a limited resource depends on information and on the ability to process that information quickly, and these are exactly the commodities that are provided in abundance by digital machines.

Japanese industry has become famous for its "just in time" principle, in which the materials necessary for each step in a manufacturing process arrive just as they are needed, eliminating wait time and minimizing inventory. Imagine the time and resources that could be saved if more human activities were conducted on a "just in time" basis, with the help of digital machines. I will illustrate these savings with a few examples.

A decade ago, students registered for university classes by standing in lines on registration day. In order to get a seat in a popular class, a student might need to stand in line for many hours or even overnight. Today, the allocation of class seats by standing in line has been replaced by phone-in registration systems that enable a student to register for classes by calling the university computer at an appointed time. Similarly, airline tickets, hotel reservations, campsites, and many other resources are now routinely allocated by computer.

Wherever people are found waiting for something, that activity is a candidate to be made more efficient by the application of digital technology. To illustrate this point, consider a theme park at which people wait in lines to ride on various attractions. Each person waiting in line for a ride is using his body as a token to encode two small pieces of information: the fact that he wants to take the ride, and his ordinal position in the list of people who want to take the ride. Clearly, a human body is not necessary to encode these pieces of information. By swiping a magnetic card, a person could make appointments to take as many rides as he likes at designated times. Details such as how many reservations a person may hold, or how far in advance rides may be reserved, or whether reservations may be sold or bartered, are matters of policy to be controlled by the theme park.

As a somewhat more fanciful example, consider a busy intersection with a line of cars waiting at a red traffic light. Each driver is using his car as a token to represent his position in the queue of people who want to use a resource: the physical space in the intersection. This resource is already being allocated by a digital device, which changes the traffic light every minute or so. Now, computers are very good at allocating resources in small slices, and all modern operating systems schedule usage of memory and processor time in units of milliseconds or less. In principle, the space in an intersection could be allocated by a dialogue between a computer in the intersection and computers in the approaching cars, providing each car with exactly the amount of space and time it needs. By dynamically allocating the intersection and automatically controlling the movements of the cars, it might be possible to interleave two streams of traffic without anyone slowing down—in fact, the faster the cars are moving, the less time each one needs to occupy the intersection.

I do not really expect to see cars whizzing past each other under computer control with inches to spare, but I do expect that digital systems will continue to improve the convenience and efficiency of many kinds of resource allocation in human society.

Moving information

Human society is largely based on the premise that information is scarce and expensive. Many human institutions, ranging from a small company to a large city, are primarily collections of information that have been concentrated in a particular place. Since information has traditionally been expensive to store and transport, humans have been forced to spend enormous amounts of energy on moving their bodies to places and times where information is available. For us, one of the most important implications of the new digital inhabitants of our planet is that information is becoming free and ubiquitous. Every human activity that is based on moving people to information is about to be replaced by an activity that moves information to people. The devices that we use today to move information through time and space, such as VCRs, cellular phones, voice mail, fax machines, and the Internet, represent the leading edge of a revolution that will transform human society beyond recognition.

I will illustrate the new independence of information from geography with a few examples.

The building where I work houses about five hundred people who spend much of every day pounding on their keyboards. Most of their keystrokes are processed on desktop computers in the offices where they originate, but a significant fraction of the keystrokes travel out of the offices on wires for processing elsewhere. Until recently, all these wires led to a large computer in the basement that provided certain shared services and access to the global network. One day the large computer disappeared and was replaced by a computer in another state about two thousand miles away. The computer room in the basement is now an echoing cavern, but the five hundred people don't know the difference. As far as they are concerned, their keyboards are interfaces to a computing resource whose geographical position is irrelevant.

Similarly, my son, who maintains a home page on the World Wide Web, wants to count the number of times his page has been visited. He accomplishes this by sending messages to a "count server" at a university in another state. To his generation, sending an electronic message across the continent to perform such a trivial operation as incrementing a counter seems like a perfectly reasonable thing to do.

Every day a newspaper is delivered to my home, containing many pages of classified advertisements for job openings, cars and houses for sale, and many other things. Except for lining birdcages, I have no use for all these printed pages on days when I am not looking for a new job, car, or house. On the rare days when I am looking for one of these commodities, I would prefer to conduct a focused search by specifying the parameters of the thing I am looking for and by varying these parameters to get a sense of what is available, not just in my home town but in other places as well. If the thing I am looking for is not currently available, I would like my computer to alert me when that thing, or a near match, comes on the market. This kind of search capability is now beginning to appear on digital media such as the World Wide Web. It represents the beginning of a revolution that will replace the current flood of useless information coming into our homes with a much more concentrated flow of information that is relevant to our needs and interests.

Digital devices that we carry around with us make many of our activities independent of location. Accurate timekeeping and calculating were expensive a generation ago, but are now nearly free and taken for granted everywhere. Cellular telephones and wireless modems allow us to communicate with our human and digital friends independently of where we are. We carry cards with magnetic stripes that enable us to identify ourselves and obtain money from cash machines all over the world. And if we really want to know where we are, we can buy a hand-held digital device that displays its current position to within one hundred meters, anywhere in the world, based on information broadcast by global positioning satellites.

Virtual conferences are beginning to take place, in which geographically dispersed groups of people meet in cyberspace to discuss a topic of common interest. As the bandwidth and processing power of our digital networks increase, these virtual conferences will soon include real-time audio and video, with simultaneous translation to the native languages of the participants. Eventually, much of the time and energy we currently spend on business travel can be saved, by moving information through wires rather than moving people through the air.

Virtual companies are beginning to form, in which the participants organize themselves, recruit employees, find customers, and perform services entirely in cyberspace. The first such companies are small groups of consultants and software developers. Ultimately, accounting firms, insurance companies, travel agencies, securities brokers, and other organizations that deal primarily with information will find that they no longer need to have a physical location.

Projecting these trends into the future, we can foresee a day when it will no longer be necessary to cut down forests and turn them into paper or to build buildings to hold the paper. People will live in cities and work in office buildings only if they choose to do so. The time, energy, and other resources that are currently spent on moving people to places where they don't really want to go will be vastly reduced, and our lives and our environment will be correspondingly improved.

Globalizing culture

Human culture is influenced by many factors, including history, genetics, physical environment, and information environment. One of these factors, the information environment, is being profoundly changed by digital technology. The historical barriers that have separated human cultures by limiting the propagation of information from one to another are falling away. It will, of course, continue to be colder in Finland than in Panama, but the information that is accessible to citizens of these two countries is becoming increasingly homogeneous. On the global network, communities are forming of people who are interested in topics such as stamp collecting, nuclear power, and women's rights, and these communities are largely independent of national boundaries.

Gutenberg's press was a seminal invention because it made it possible for the publisher of a book to communicate information to large numbers of readers, a "one-to-many" form of communication. Today, digital networks make it possible for everyone to be a publisher. The advent of "many-to-many" communication on digital networks is no less a watershed event in human history than was the development of the printing press.

In the digital world, everyone has access to a global market, both as seller and as buyer. Everyone can make requests for information or for goods and services, and have these requests disseminated to a large population. Everyone has access to the "world library" of interconnected computers and can contribute material to the library for others to see. Digital technology tends to make it difficult for a population to be isolated in its own private "reality." Opinions and priorities may differ, and the world library will certainly contain a lot of material that is incorrect, misleading, or offensive. Governments and other institutions will try to control the content of the world library and to limit people's access to it. But in a span of decades, the overall trend will be toward a free global market in which barriers to information flow are lowered and people can seek out the ideas that they find most useful.

The digital marketplace will tend to have a leveling influence on global standards of living by creating a worldwide meritocracy. Over time, for example, the income levels of a computer programmer in India and a similarly qualified computer programmer in California will tend to converge, since digital information can flow very quickly and cheaply from one to the other. Ubiquitous digital information will also make education more broadly available, enabling individuals around the world to participate in the global economy according to their skills and ambitions. These changes will be impeded by established political and economic institutions and may occur slowly as measured by a human lifetime; but measured against a perspective of planetary history, they will occur very quickly.

Enlightened self-interest, the "invisible hand" in Adam Smith's theory of capitalism, is a powerful force. Access to information enables people to vote with their feet and their money for social institutions that meet their needs and interests. Ubiquitous information tends to make markets more efficient and political processes more responsive, and to reinforce distributed rather than centralized solutions to problems. For this reason, digital networks may have played a larger role in the collapse of Communism than any weapon of destruction.

The long-term effect on human culture of the digital networks that now encircle our planet is unpredictable. At worst, some of the diversity that enriches our species may be lost. At best, conflicts between groups may become less likely and more tractable. At minimum, the world will become a more closely knit community.

It has been clear for some time that humans have been consuming the resources of our planet at a rate that cannot long be sustained. Because the earth is finite, we know that the human population and its appetites cannot continue to grow indefinitely. The ecological crisis that is approaching will be resolved either by a disaster or by a fundamental change in human society. Perhaps the most hopeful development of the last fifty years has been the arrival on our planet of digital machines that are prodigious generators, organizers, and propagators of information. Information makes everything more efficient, and digital devices spread information everywhere.

By improving our allocation of resources, by moving information to where it is needed, and by helping us to pursue our enlightened self-interest, digital machines will earn their position as our partners on the planet. In the end, a symbiotic culture composed of human and digital individuals may be a more effective steward of the earth's resources than humans would be by themselves. The best outcome that we can hope for and work toward is that the arrival of digital machines will be the catalyst for the changes that are necessary to ensure our own survival on the earth.

References

1. Dawkins, R. *The Blind Watchmaker.* New York: W.W. Norton and Company, 1986.
2. Porter, J. N. and Katzive, R. H., eds., *Disk/Trend Report,* Disk/Trend Inc., Mountain View, California (annual reports: 1990–1996).
3. Rothschild, M. *Bionomics: Economy as Ecosystem.* New York: Henry Holt and Company, 1990.
4. Shapiro, R. *The Human Blueprint: the Race to Unlock the Secrets of our Genetic Script.* New York: St. Martin's Press, 1991.

WILLIAM J. MITCHELL
& OLIVER STRIMPEL

There and Not There

18

The economy of presence

We rarely choose to think of it this way, but presence consumes resources and costs money. Typically it costs us more (in hotel charges or office rents, for example) to be present in places where many people would like to be than it does to be present in places where few people want to be. And it costs us time and effort to get to places to meet people, conduct transactions, and see performances. Being in the right place, at the right time, can be expensive.

In the past, being "present" meant that your body was there, in a specific location, and that you could interact face to face with others who were also there. Now, electronic telepresence and asynchronous presence are additional possibilities; in general, these are less intense than full face-to-face presence, but they can be achieved with greater convenience and at lower expenditure of time and resources. So in our daily lives, we continually have to choose among different grades of presence with different properties and different associated costs. In other words, there is an emerging economy of presence; within it we make choices among available alternatives and allocate resources to meet demands that are made on us and to achieve what we want.

Theaters

Consider theatrical performances, for example. You can view them live, on stage, or you can watch transmissions to remote locations. And you can be part of the audience as a performance actually unfolds, or you can listen to a recording. The basic possibilities are summarized, with some examples, in the following cross-classification table, where traditional, "high presence" forms of theater appear at the upper left, and more recent, electronically mediated, "low presence" forms are at the lower right:

	Synchronous	Asynchronous
Presence	Live stage performances	Movie theater performances
		Video game parlors
		Location-based entertainment installations
Telepresence	Live broadcasts	WWW sites
	Videoconference events	Video on demand
	MUDs, MOOs	
	Network games (Doom, etc.)	

In past eras (and still, in some traditional societies), live performance was the only possibility: performers and audience had to assemble in exactly the same place, at precisely the same time. Theaters—in easily accessible locations, with stages and audience seating in carefully calculated spatial relationship—were built to accommodate this synchronous copresence. Performance times were fitted in to the temporal rhythms of the seasons and of daily life. Performance schedules were typically preestablished, widely known, and difficult to alter—yielding the tradition that "the show must go on." And going out to the theater was an important social occasion; you dressed up for it. Where the tradition of live theater thrives, most of this is still true today.

Broadcast technologies opened up the possibility of live radio and television performances to widely dispersed—and even mobile—audiences. The broadcast studio is still a "stage" of sorts, but the audience is no longer in a fixed relationship to it. Furthermore, scattered audience members have little or no awareness of each other, and performers and producers have no direct way to gauge audience reactions. (The Nielsen system, and other such surrogates, are a response to this.) But performances *are* still synchronous events, so printed radio and television guides continue to play an essential coordination role.

Teleconference and videoconference events are synchronous too, as anyone who has ever tried to coordinate them is acutely aware. But, in an event like a videoconference lecture, an electronic connection now substitutes for the proscenium as the two-way link between performance space and audience space. The result is a "virtual theater," made from separated architectural fragments. There are other architectural possibilities as well. For example, the TeleDining suites created by TelePort Corporation and IBM create a more symmetrical relationship and so blur the distinction between performers and audience; there is a video projection screen down the middle of a restaurant table, and you are electronically connected via a computer network to the distant other "half" of the dining room—where your counterparts see your "half" of the space on a similar screen. And multiway videoconferences allow the distribution of coordinated events over many locations; the members of a quartet, for instance, can perform from four different places.

Movies—like stage productions—are made for theaters, but a projection screen now replaces the proscenium, and performances are recorded so that the actors do not have to show up, repeatedly, at the same times as the audience. In other words, the audience's action of going out to the theater is no longer synchronized with the actions of the performers. Indeed, it is typically the case that there was no single, unified, original performance; the film is pieced together from shots made at many different times and places. This is the condition of asynchronous presence.

Finally, there may be no fixed performance time or place and no definite temporal or spatial relationship of performers and audience. The mass distribution of sound recordings and videotapes—which may be played anytime, anywhere—creates this highly decentralized condition. The growing feasibility of audio-on-demand and video-on-demand over digital networks goes a step further, and completely substitutes asynchronous telepresence for the old idea of a singular, unified, theatrical performance.

As the entertainment industry has discovered, one effect of the newer, electronically mediated possibilities is to create a larger overall demand for theatrical performances in their various guises. CDs create interest in concert tours, and concerts help to sell CDs; radio reaches places and audiences that live performances cannot, and so on. (The entire phenomenon of stardom is unthinkable without records, radio, and television.) And, in the context of this increased demand, potential audience members make choices among the four possible combinations of presence and telepresence, and of synchronous and asynchronous interaction. The different theatrical forms compete for audience share by exploiting their characteristic advantages. The result is some distribution of theatrical activity over the four cells of our table.

Thus, for example, audiences continue to be drawn by the exciting unpredictability of live theater and by the variation among performances—no two of which are ever exactly the same. Live broadcasts reach larger audiences while effectively retaining these qualities, but not the thrill of being on the spot, in the physical presence of renowned performers. Although you might see the same performance at home, on videotape, going to the movies is a social event; being part of a large audience, and sharing its collective reaction, is an important part of the fun. Video-on-demand at home is potentially inexpensive, extraordinarily convenient, and accessible to the infirm, the immobile, and the geographically isolated, but it lacks some of the dimensions of the live theater, and even of the movies.

Furthermore, although recording and telecommunications technologies erode the practical need for performances to unfold at particular times and places, they do not alter the fact that memorable times and places can inflect meanings and add to enjoyment in important ways. A performance of *Oedipus Rex* in the ancient Greek theater on the Athenian acropolis is different from a performance on Broadway. A performance of *A Midsummer Night's Dream* outdoors in a park, on a warm and sultry evening, carries a different weight from a performance in a downtown, air-conditioned, proscenium theater. And it is not even quite the same thing to see a movie at a great old movie palace, a drive-in, or a suburban multiplex. Settings do not end at the edge of a stage or the frame of a shot; context still matters—sometimes a little, sometimes a great deal.

Here, in rough summary, is how these respective advantages and disadvantages of "high presence" and "low presence" forms of theatrical performance stack up:

High presence	Low presence
High cost	Low cost
Fixed location	Flexible locations
Fixed performance schedule	Flexible performance schedule
Social event	Private event

Strong sense of occasion	Less sense of occasion
Unpredictable, varying	Standardized
Live contact with renowned performers	Indirect contact only
Contextualized	Decontextualized

It is obvious at a glance that the differing forms are not exact functional equivalents and therefore do not straightforwardly substitute for each other. We should expect, then, that traditional, "high presence" forms of theater will continue to thrive where their special advantages add substantial value to justify the cost and inconvenience of getting there. But where they cannot, less costly, more convenient, electronically mediated forms are likely to take over.

Libraries

If we extend the analysis from theaters to other cultural institutions, similar patterns of possibilities emerge. The following table, for example, summarizes alternative—traditional and emerging—forms of libraries.

	Synchronous	Asynchronous
Presence	Homeric epics	Noncirculating manuscript libraries
		Circulating libraries
Telepresence	Telephone reference desks	Lexis/Nexis, Dialog
	Broadcast poetry readings	WWW libraries

Before the invention of writing, libraries could only exist in the heads of bards and oracles (those who performed the social role of producing and preserving information), and literary works could only be extracted from them through direct, face-to-face contact. Thus, for example, the Homeric epics were memorized (and, apparently, sometimes transformed) by itinerant performers and transmitted by being spoken aloud.

Thus both libraries and theaters can be traced back to the ancient practice of memorizing information and then transferring it through face-to-face performance. (The modern idea of the lecture recalls this common ancestry.) But they began to diverge with the introduction of recording techniques—writing, in particular—which allowed preservation of information outside of human heads and the asynchronous transfer of that information.

Writing, together with associated technologies for preserving written texts, yielded manuscript libraries. By the seventh century B.C., the royal library at Nineveh had amassed more than ten thousand texts, assigned to different rooms according to a system of subject categories. And the Great Library of Alexandria collected nearly seven hundred thousand works. These, and their numerous successors, attracted scholars from afar and became, in effect, specialized sites for the asynchronous transfer of information from authors to readers. The scholarly communities that grew up at such sites eventually evolved into modern universities.

Closer to our own era, paper, printing, and efficient transportation systems combined to make reliance on manuscript libraries no longer necessary. Much more numerous and widely dispersed bookstores and circulating libraries now became the distribution points. Inexpensive print publications proliferated, and there is a large, literate public ready to consume them. So there was a massive decentralization of the process of transferring information from authors to readers.

Electronic telecommunications allowed texts to be separated from their material substrates and transmitted almost instantaneously to remote locations; they could be encoded and transmitted by telegraph or teletype, or (recalling Homeric practice) read aloud over the radio or the telephone. But the real revolution for libraries came when digital telecommunications combined with digital storage to yield fast, inexpensive, efficient systems for remote, asynchronous communication of textual information—store-and-forward electronic mail, FTP, Telnet, Usenet Newsgroups, Gopher, and the World Wide Web. Vast online libraries became feasible and attractive, and (despite difficulties in sorting out intellectual property issues) pioneering examples of these quickly appeared. Lexis/Nexis, Dialog, and other such services emerged to serve specialized professional audiences. Project Gutenberg made numerous out-of-copyright and out-of-print texts available online. Classicists converted a complete library of ancient Greek texts to digital form, published them (together with specialized access and search software) on CD, and eventually put them online through the Perseus project. The *Oxford English Dictionary*, the *Encyclopedia Britannica*, and other standard reference works appeared in online versions. New books began to be published simultaneously in hardback and WWW versions, and online scientific and technical journals began to compete with their print counterparts.

The practical advantages of online, digital libraries are impressive: storage space and costs are radically reduced; preservation and replacement issues are less critical; providing quick, efficient access to large numbers of scattered users becomes easy; a volume is never checked out or on the reshelving cart; sophisticated indexing, searching, filtering, and brokering services can readily be provided; and the resources of multiple sites can be combined electronically to create much larger collections than would otherwise be possible. So, provided that a reasonable consensus can be reached on how to deal with intellectual property rights in this context (which, by all indications, will not be easy) and that satisfactory remuneration mechanisms for authors and information brokers can be put in place, they seem assured of a rapidly growing role.

Does this mean that traditional, paper-based libraries will disappear—that bound volumes, bookstacks, and reading rooms will soon become a thing of the past? For several reasons this seems very unlikely.

First, there is a huge, worldwide stock of library books, and there has been massive investment in construction, equipment, and organizations to maintain it. Library buildings have become important civic monuments and have served to focus school, college, and university life. The scale of this commitment is so large that transition to a more electronic form is likely to be a lengthy process, and traditional libraries will retain at least a residual role for a very long time.

Even more importantly, print on paper continues to have its advantages over on-screen display and so remains—if nothing more—a useful alternative. (That is why computer systems have printers, after all.) It presents text in robust, inexpensive, high-resolution, high-contrast form, and it is readily adaptable to a wide range of sizes and formats. And when pages are bound into a well-made book, you get a nice, three-dimensional object that fits comfortably in the hand, has pleasant textures, smells, and even sounds as you turn the pages, is quick and easy to navigate, and provides visual and tactile feedback about where you are in the text. Electronic displays will continue to improve, no doubt, and some form of programmable "smart paper" may eventually blur the distinction between books and displays, but printed, bound books will continue to have a role in contexts where the pleasure of the act of reading matters more than sheer efficiency in accessing information. We will increasingly surf the Web to retrieve scientific, technical, commercial, and other data that we need, but we will still take printed, bound novels to the beach.

Physically embodied text also plays a role in certain religious, social, and legal rituals, and we cannot assume that digital versions could automatically substitute. You can swear on a printed Bible, but it isn't clear that you can do so on a downloaded file of the same text.

And finally, many scholars would argue passionately that the cultural significance of a text cannot clearly be separated from the history of its production and distribution in various forms—in manuscript (maybe multiple drafts), in print (multiple editions, perhaps), and in digital form. Although scanned digital images might play a useful role in making rare versions of texts available to a wider community, it is often necessary for scholars to go back to the originals. And collectors, of course, are at least as interested in the physical artifacts and their histories as they are in the abstract textual information that these artifacts carry. Context may matter, too; a book or manuscript may have added significance as part of some important collection, and that collection may be closely linked to some particular architectural setting. So, even in an age of inexpensive and convenient digital information, it remains important to conserve the physical fabric of books and manuscripts as well as their disembodied contents, to respect the integrity of significant collections, and to preserve relationships of texts and collections to particular architectural settings. Shakespearean scholars may welcome the wide availability of machine-processable digital texts and of high-resolution facsimiles of the folios, but they will not want to give up the Folger.

Once again, as follows, we can summarize by tabulating the respective advantages and disadvantages of traditional, "high presence" libraries that bring readers face to face with physical books and manuscripts, and more recently emergent, "low-presence" ones that store and distribute texts digitally:

High presence	Low presence
High cost	Low cost
Fixed location	Flexible locations
Fixed opening hours	Flexible opening hours
Large storage space requirements	Reduced storage space
Volumes unavailable when in use	Volumes never unavailable
Relies on on-site collection	Can combine dispersed resources
Preservation and replacement problems	Few preservation problems
Manual indexing, searching, filtering	Automatic indexing, searching, filtering
Originals	Reproductions
Pleasant to read	Less pleasant to read
Contextualized	Decontextualized

This suggests that digital libraries will not—despite their enormous advantages—completely replace traditional ones, as some apostles of the digital revolution have suggested. Manuscripts and printed documents—together with places to store and consult them—will retain a crucial cultural role because they add value to textual information in certain ways that digital formats and systems cannot. Physical and virtual will coexist and will complement each other.

Museums and art galleries

Museums and art galleries, like libraries, maintain collections. And like theaters, they put on shows—public events in which curators convey content by selecting and arranging artifacts and providing commentary. Shows may reach their audiences through face-to-face contact or telepresence, and in synchronous or asynchronous mode, as summarized below:

	Synchronous	Asynchronous
Presence	Live guided tour	Self-guided tour
		Audio-guided tour
Telepresence	Live broadcast tour	Printed catalogue
	Videoconference presentation	CD tour
		WWW virtual museum

A traditional, "high presence" approach—particularly common in the great art and archaeological museums—is for a docent to provide a live guided tour of the collection. Alternatively, visitors might take self-guided tours with the assistance of written captions or handheld audio players; this is less interactive, but it means that guides and visitors do not have to coordinate their schedules, and it makes fewer staff demands and allows visitors to proceed at their own pace. Video technology provides the possibility of conducting tours for remote audiences; QVC, the home shopping channel, has carried tours of the Metropolitan Museum of Art, in New York; the Smithsonian Institution, in Washington; and the Museum of Fine Arts, in Boston—paid for with merchandising tie-ins to the museum shops. And "virtual tours" can be provided through a variety of media: traditional printed catalogues, CDs, and WWW "virtual museum" sites.

One of the important draws of traditional museums is the thrill we experience from being face to face with important, unique objects; there is only one Mona Lisa, and even though one has to cope with hordes of people flashing their cameras at it and jostle for a spot in front of the glass-enclosed canvas, it is still exciting to be there. The object's importance may stem from its intrinsic quality as a work of art or invention, from its rarity (as with archaeological relics), or from its association with a notable person. For example, the Whirlwind at Boston's Computer Museum, which is among the first computers ever built, contains the first-ever use of magnetic core memory. The ability to see the first core memory stack and inspect an actual 32-by-32 core plane from any angle focuses the mind and is fascinating to anyone who understands the significance of this invention. Seeing the original helps conjure up an image of the inventors, the challenges that they had to overcome, and the realization that it could have worked out differently.

The possessions or creations of famous people also have an aura and a capacity to evoke associations of important past events that attract visitors. The prices fetched by objects used by U.S. presidents, for example, testify to this. Perhaps paradoxically, the value of such objects is increased, not diminished, by the widespread availability of reproductions. The more people know and care about an object through reproductions, the more they value the original.

The mechanisms of aura and evocation of associations can sometimes defy rational analysis—but the effects are no less powerful for that. Another source of instant fascination at the Computer Museum, for example, is the robot R2D2, used in the making of the *Star Wars* trilogy. This object is just a crudely made plastic costume for a very short actor. What are people thinking of when they gaze in awe at the "real" R2D2?

Catalogues, CDs, and online virtual museums can show superb reproductions of objects like the Whirlwind and R2D2. Indeed, in some ways, they can show them better—for example, by providing 3-D digital models that can be viewed from any angle and taken apart at will. Thus the Zentrum für Kunst und Medientechnologie in Karlsruhe has published a CD that shows one hundred chairs arranged in galleries laid out like spaces; you can look around with QuickTime VR and select a chair to see a work from different angles and read its label. This sort of thing has great value, but something is also lost; the aura, the sense of uniqueness and special connection to a historical moment, seems to be inseparable from the original and is filtered out in even the most accurate and beautifully made reproductions.

Another point where traditional and virtual museums differ is in their presentation of the scales of objects. As architects know particularly well, scale is important; we feel differently when we look at a distant view or see a mountain towering over us. Similarly, physical proximity to objects or reconstructed environments within museums creates an immediate impact based on scale, both large and small. Examples of awe-inspiring large-scale objects abound in museums: the brontosaurus skeleton, a fifty-foot totem pole, the walls of Nineveh. By contrast, the most precious objects from the Tutankhamen exhibition, blown up to enormous size on posters, were in reality only a few inches tall. Reconstructed exhibit environments that engulf the visitor can also derive much of their power from sheer scale; the giant heart at the Franklin Institute, the coal mine at the Deutsches Museum, and the Walk-Through Computer at the Computer Museum are all good examples.

Photographic reproductions and most digital simulations, on the other hand, tend to even scales out to fill the available display space; most of us probably recall the experience of seeing the original of some widely-reproduced painting for the first time and suddenly realizing that it was much larger or much smaller than we had thought. High-quality immersive display devices have the potential to remedy this deficiency, though, and even to provide effects of dramatic scale change—simulating motion through the human body at tiny scale, through the solar system at massive scale, or through an unbuilt work of architecture that would only otherwise be seen in small drawings, for example.

A closely related issue is level of detail. Digital reproductions, by definition, have finite, fixed, spatial and color resolution. Since paintings, for instance, may be very large and filled with intricate detail, and since doubling the spatial resolution of a digital reproduction quadruples the amount of information needed to encode it in uncompressed form, resolution limitations can be very serious even in contexts where storage is inexpensive and high-bandwidth networks are available. Furthermore, even the highest-resolution two-dimensional digital image "flattens" a painting; it captures little of the three-dimensional texture of brush strokes and canvas, of variations in specularity from matte to shiny, and of the buildup of transparent layers that produces subtly different appearances from different angles and under different lighting conditions.

Where digital virtual museums—both online and packaged on media like CD—really shine is in their capacity to widen access to collections. Even the most centrally located major museums of the traditional sort are geographically constrained in their capacity to attract visitors; they can never make themselves available to more than a tiny fraction of those who might be interested in them. And even the largest, organized as they now are for blockbuster shows, are limited in their daily throughputs. Even worse, many important art collections are housed in venues that are neither physically capable nor staffed to handle large numbers of visitors. And some sorts of exhibits, such as watercolor paintings, are so delicate that they cannot be put on view for extensive periods. But once a collection has been encoded digitally, network and server capacities are the only fundamental limitations on accessibility; an online virtual museum can inexpensively serve a huge, worldwide clientele seven days a week and twenty-four hours a day.

The other great advantage of digital virtual museums is the flexibility of exploration that they provide. In traditional museums, the grouping of exhibits into rooms imposes a fixed classification—sometimes a very tendentious and ideologically loaded one, and the circulation system is a hardwired access path. Such organizations may be changed from time to time, but the effort of doing so is significant. But through use of hyperlinking, sophisticated indexing, search engines, and so on, virtual museums can overcome these traditional limitations and allow visitors to explore collections in flexible and highly personalized ways.

These is a downside to this personalization, however; there is a loss of social interaction. People often go to traditional museums in groups; families, school parties, and friends can enjoy spontaneous and informal interaction while visiting an exhibit together. The simultaneity of experience stimulates the sharing of reactions and often leads to conversations that build from the shared experience. How many conversations about flight are started when visitors to the Smithsonian's Air and Space Museum are greeted by the Wright Flyer? Or about the Spanish Civil War when confronting Picasso's *Guernica* at the New York Museum of Modern Art? This sort of interaction is often the most valued part of the experience, and it occurs effortlessly in physical settings. Early forms of virtual museums have not provided it, though of course sophisticated shared virtual environments might.

As with theaters and libraries, then, the "high presence" and "low presence" forms of museums and galleries have their respective upsides and downsides. Here is the summary:

High presence	Low presence
High cost	Low Cost
Fixed location	Flexible locations
Fixed opening hours	Flexible opening hours
Limited numbers of visitors	Potentially unlimited numbers of visitors
Navigation on foot	Hyperlink navigation
Limited to on-site collection	Can combine resources of dispersed sites
Aura of the original	Aura is lost
True scale	Variable scale
Unlimited detail	Limited detail
Group experience	Individual experience
Contextualized	Decontextualized

Once again, we can expect that traditional and newer electronic forms will coexist in some mix. Indeed, the emerging electronic possibilities are already combining with established institutions and venues to yield some very interesting hybrids. At London's National Gallery, for example, visitors may begin a tour by entering a computer-filled room. Here they can explore a digital version of the collection at very high speed, without wearisome walking, using sophisticated navigation tools, and getting the benefit of lots of annotation and commentary. Then, when they have finished with this, they can print out a personalized guide to the particular works in which they have shown interest. They can follow this guide to enter the rooms of the physical museum itself, and confront the original works face to face. Thus many of the complementary advantages of the physical and the virtual are combined.

The infobahn, cultural institutions, and the city of the future

As these discussions have illustrated, the personal computer and the evolving infobahn have created a new economy of presence within which traditional cultural institutions—theaters, libraries, museums, art galleries, and others— must now attempt to define their roles.

Furthermore, there are numerous interesting opportunities for new sorts of institutions to emerge within this new economy of presence. As networks continue to extend their reach and coverage, as bandwidth burgeons, and as digital environments become more and more sophisticated—overcoming some of the current limitations that we have discussed—the competition from remotely accessible and asynchronous sites of cultural activity will be increasingly intense. What, then, are the prospects for cultural institutions? And what is their likely role in the city of the twenty-first century?

As the economy of presence matures, live theaters, book-filled libraries, and traditional museums will only be able to maintain their prime real estate and convince audiences and benefactors to cover their relatively high costs if they vigorously emphasize the unique kinds of value that physical space and face-to-face presence can add to an experience. By the same logic, museums without unique and important connections, libraries that only stock commodity books, and places that offer little architectural interest or opportunity for satisfying social interaction are unlikely to compete successfully with virtual environments that offer comparable services more conveniently and at lower cost. Paradoxically, then, the digital revolution may end up making successful institutions of this sort more physical, hands-on, and dependent on face-to-face interaction—not less.

At the same time, associated functions that do not intrinsically depend on physicality and face-to-face interaction will irresistibly be pulled into cyber-space. Recall the fate of card catalogues, for example; once they were unique facilities located in the reading rooms of libraries, and you had to go there to access them; then they were supplemented and sometimes replaced by data-bases and special computer terminals; and now they are increasingly available in digital form, anywhere, via the Internet and the World Wide Web. And it is easy to see that many of the computer-based, interactive exhibits that are so popular in science museums might as well be delivered, more widely and con-veniently, via the Internet. As a result of such shifts, many activities that once were centralized in cultural institutions will increasingly be dispersed to homes, schools, airplane seats, and other such locations.

In general, then, cultural institutions that add value to high levels of pres-ence will be the ones to survive—in physical form—in the city of the future. All three of the types of institutions discussed here have aspects that do indeed work best (or work at all) at high levels of presence; they will concentrate on those aspects in their physical manifestation, while carrying out their remain-ing functions more cost-effectively using lower levels of presence. On the one hand, they will create intense foci of hands-on, face-to-face experience. On the other, they will employ digital electronic means to deliver access to large, highly dispersed audiences and to broker information on an unprecedented scale.

There may be a lesson here for cities in general. As commerce, entertain-ment, education, governance, and other activities shift increasingly to cyber-space, there will be diminished motivation to locate these activities in high-cost urban centers. But cities will continue to provide appropriate contexts for cultural institutions that provide unique, valuable, face-to-face experiences, and these institutions will be key to the continued attraction and importance of those urban centers that can continue to maintain them. Paradoxically, then, the general decentralization of activity that seems likely to follow from the shift to cyberspace will enhance, rather than diminish, the importance of those urban centers that have genuine cultural significance.

DENNIS TSICHRITZIS

The Dynamics of Innovation

19

Research and innovation

Research always brings to mind the paradigm of an absent-minded scientist playing aimlessly with his pencil (and computer) seeking some universal truth. It is a paradigm that gave us, over the centuries, great progress in science, and it resulted in relative prosperity for mankind. The basis for this paradigm was and still is that the researcher is highly intelligent, self-motivated, and rather undisciplined. Can we go to the next millennium with this paradigm? In a society where everything is measured, quantified, and rationalized, how can researchers continue to live in an idealistic world? We already see the signs of trouble. Research budgets and research institutes are under pressure in both the public and private sectors. This is the time to revise our position, especially in the fast-moving area of information technology.

Research is not the goal but the means. Searching for something cannot be the goal; finding it is the goal. Research, like any other activity, is measured by its results. When the area of research is related to an economic sector, the results should be concrete and looked upon as "products." The product of computer science research is innovation. We constantly question existing knowledge in order to provide something new, to innovate in terms of concepts, methods, materials, or whatever.

This innovation is effective when it has three aspects:

(a) It provides a significance different from what it was known before; let's call it the *quality* of innovation.
(b) It becomes sufficiently widespread to make a real difference; let's call it the (audience) *penetration* of the innovation.
(c) It does so quickly; let's call it the *speed* of innovation.

Innovation is achieved in different ways. We will distinguish at least three: through ideas, through people, and through products.

Idea innovation

Idea innovation follows a well-known pattern of scientific research. On the basis of what is known, something is discovered by research, and it is documented through publications. In this way, the state of the art is advanced, at least in principle. Idea innovation is mainly based on originality. There is no need to discover the same result twice. Publication serves to make the results well known and avoid duplication. Publication itself is not a goal, it is only the means to inform other researchers so they can avoid duplication and collect the accumulated knowledge. It is a well-accepted principle that idea innovation is judged in terms of its *quality*. Penetration and speed of the innovation are important but not critical. Quality is paramount. How different and surprising is the new result is also relative to some extent on how difficult it was to achieve.

Idea innovation needs top talented people who can make contributions on very difficult and important problems. The newer the area of scientific activity, the better chance to get, with the same effort, a surprising result. Originality and quality have a better chance in new fields. On the other hand, new areas have a smaller audience of active researchers and fewer publication venues, so the penetration is less and it takes more time to develop. If the area expands quickly, then both speed and penetration of the innovation are well served. This is exactly what happened in the first fifty years of the ACM, where we saw new and rapidly expanding areas. Many people became famous on the basis of high-quality publications at the beginning of a new area. It is wonderful that many of these persons are still active and that they are authoring some of the papers in this book.

The question is, Can we go on like this for another fifty years? Not very likely. Many of the areas of computer science are not new and show signs of maturity. Results in many established areas are not so surprising anymore. Even new developments like the Web or agents or Java are recombinations of ideas that have existed for quite some time. Another sign of maturity is some reemergence of old ideas with new names. This attempt to provide surface quality through terminology is not significant in the long term. Some intellectual closure is at play. The global networks help propagate innovation, but they breed conformity. How can researchers get something new and significant if they are in constant communication? We are therefore in some kind of middle-age crisis. Is there a way out?

New areas are difficult to define, but they pop up at the boundaries of existing areas. Within computer science the boundaries, say, between databases, AI, and programming languages provided exciting fields. The new generations of computer scientists, however, know all these areas from school, and the previously artificial boundaries between different areas of computer science have disappeared. Computer science areas remain in journals and conferences and as circles of friends rather than as intellectually distinct domains.

If we want to achieve new, spectacular results, we have to move to new boundaries between computer science and other totally new areas within biology, medicine, chemistry, etc. This clash of scientific method and expertise may provide new opportunities. If we do not evolve rapidly, then the other areas will adapt our tools and move on. Scientific computing may end up a branch of physics, bio-informatics a branch of biology, medical informatics a branch of medicine, etc. With respect to overall scientific progress this development may be fine. We will, however, miss the challenging environments, and we will limit our area with disastrous consequences.

I believe that to achieve high-quality research in the next fifty years we have to move decisively in totally uncharted waters between computer science and other disciplines.

People innovation

A second way to innovation is through people. Many new ideas are transmitted through education and training to people who then go on to innovate the different processes in industry, institutions, and the economy in general. New ideas in education and course programs are introduced faster and more effectively if the teachers themselves are part of the research effort that produces the ideas. It is a well-accepted principle that good education is much related to some credible research effort. The idea is old (W. von Humboldt, 1767–1835), and it is widely propagated in all educational institutions.

In innovation through people one should bring the new ideas in the educational process gradually, and only when they are mature and well understood. In addition, good teachers need to be well up to date and do credible research by making significant contributions. They do not absolutely have to be very original.

Quality and speed of innovation are not critical. Penetration, however, is critical. We need to propagate the new techniques and ideas among a vast audience. The innovation has to be widespread to be effective, since it creates a new generation of experts who can change things wherever they go.

Research related to innovation through people should be widely spread to many institutions to keep everybody up to date. Small projects with minimum overhead and an effective communications network are effective. Publications are also important, not to advance the state of the art, but to clarify things and find the best possible way to transmit knowledge. Originality is not so critical as readability and packaging. Writing a book or putting together educational software gives more benefit than attempting to do original work on obscure, self-defined problems.

Teaching in computer science has evolved tremendously well over the past thirty years. The manner in which the curriculum was created was rather simple. Every few years a new area was identified based on original work. When the knowledge was organized properly in terms of scientific community, books, conferences, workshops, etc., the area was simply *added* to the computer science curriculum. We went from numerical analysis to adding theory and languages and computer systems and artificial intelligence and databases and graphics, etc. Can we go on like this for the next fifty years? Not very likely. The computer science curriculum is full. There is no more place for adding. In addition, some major changes are happening to what people need to learn to be effective in their future careers.

The first identifiable trend is that two major areas based on digital technology are becoming indispensable for computer science education: communications and media. The old idea of computer science education, "let's add the new to the program," does not work. The areas are too big in terms of ideas, communities of scientists, and commercial sectors. They cannot be absorbed. We need to completely redefine the program. The implication is that at least a third of the computer science program has to be phased out to make room for new courses. This will not be easy since some well-known and established areas will have to go.

The second trend, which is more general, is away from specialization and towards more general education. Changes occur so fast in economic activity and to people's careers that education needs to give them a solid basis rather than specialized knowledge soon to become obsolete.

This implies that computer science programs will have to open up to areas of general expertise: literature, philosophy, economics, psychology, law, etc. Enough room has to be left aside for students to learn some other interesting scientific area at their option. We need, therefore, alliances with other fields and many more educational programs of the form X-computer science, where X can vary.

Finally, the very existence of the Internet, the Web, teleconferencing, and other technological developments changes the nature of teaching. Professors are no longer major information providers. They are mere mentors, guides present to comment and place information in the appropriate contexts. Students are as up to date with the latest developments as their professors, since they get their information from the same source, the networks. In addition, geographical location and ease of travel do not play such an important role; nor do all the meetings and workshops that are mainly designed for information exchange. Teaching and training are "at any time," "at any place" and do not have to evolve in rigid schedules and classrooms. Communication and dialogue, not lectures, are important.

If we add to all these changes the need for a lifelong education to make innovation more active, we are embarking on a new era. We will have to change dramatically the educational programs and the way they are dispensed. Since our technology is the motor for all these changes, we should also be at the forefront, leading it rather than complaining about the changes. We need as never before our pioneering spirit that was present in computer science from the beginning.

Product innovation

Product innovation has only one goal, economic advantage. It is not that important to be original; an interesting combination of existing ideas is sufficient. It is also counterproductive to have a large audience penetration. On the contrary, the fewer people involved in exactly the same innovation the better it is. Market penetration is important, not the audience penetration of the exact innovation that your product is based on. Unfortunately, any innovation, unless it is heavily protected by patents, is not so difficult to replicate. Since patents, especially in software, are not very effective and rather expensive, the best protection is continuous product innovation. The speed, therefore, of product innovation is the most important aspect. If a company can innovate its products faster than anybody else, it has a decisive advantage.

Product innovation is demand-based and application-oriented. It does not fit exactly into any of the areas of computer science. It is interdisciplinary, and it is based on a good understanding of the market.

The traditional cycle of idea innovation, then people innovation, then product innovation in an independent and serial fashion is proving to be ineffective. The major problem is with speed. Ideas, even when quickly propagated, need some years to be sufficiently understood and accepted. To wait until the people in the companies absorb the new ideas and then base their products accordingly takes too long.

Since most research results are published, the competition can have access to the idea at about the same time. Only speed in product cycles gives a distinct advantage. Being close institutionally or geographically does not give such an advantage. It seems, therefore, that the best possible speed advantage comes when research, R & D, and product development are so interleaved that they are not distinct organizationally. This is precisely the advantage of small, dynamic companies, companies that have integrated research into their product development, or research institutions that have a product development effort through spinoff companies.

Another problem arising when research and product development are considered separately is the relative absence of feedback. It is one thing to get feedback for research results from a small number of experts at conferences, but it is a quite different thing to get feedback from thousands of users of a product. Innovation progresses faster and is better targeted if it is widely tested through products.

We see lately that the pace of innovation is increasing because nearly everyone is trying to gain in speed. Traditional universities and research centers, which avoid being close to product-oriented innovation, have a severe disadvantage. First, they are left behind since they do not have the same pressures. Second, they risk being irrelevant since they do not have sufficient feedback. We see more and more that real innovation comes from dynamic companies. There is nothing more dramatic for a researcher than to see his ideas already incorporated into a product before he even has had the chance to publish them. Fortunately, the publication procedures are so old-fashioned that they do not consider incorporation into a product as publication. In this way one can claim originality not by producing something new, but only by writing about it.

Concluding remarks

We have outlined three distinct areas of innovation in terms of ideas, people, and products. For idea innovation the major goal is *originality* and the major aspect is *quality*. For people innovation the major goal is *competence* and the major aspect is *penetration*. For product innovation the major goal is *economic advantage* and the major aspect is *speed*.

It used to be the case that three distinct kinds of institutions were involved in these separate aspects of innovation. Research centers were there mainly to innovate in terms of ideas. Universities were there to innovate in terms of people. Commercial companies were there to innovate in terms of products. A process has already started some years ago such that the boundaries are becoming fuzzy.

Research centers are also involved in education and training, partly through the rotation of people, partly through links with universities. In addition, through common projects and spinoffs they participate in innovation of products. Universities were always involved in idea innovation, and they sometimes have major research groups. In addition, they are now actively encouraging spinoffs and technoparks. Finally, companies always have some research effort. They also find it appropriate to support people innovation to keep their personnel up to date.

We are entering an era where it is not important what your label is. Universities, research centers, companies—whether private or public—all are striving to innovate. The goals and the means have to be clearly defined for a group, institution, region, and country. The right mix of ideas, people, and product innovation has to be present in every entity. In addition, the separation of research centers and universities as public institutions and companies as private entities is also blurred. Most successful efforts involve finding the right combination of both. Public institutions should get close to the market and private companies can start taking up functions that before were reserved for public institutions. The dissolution of all these boundaries is producing a great competitive environment. It will be beneficial in general for innovation, and it will give an advantage to those groups and institutions that can adapt to the new situation.

PETER J. DENNING

How We Will Learn

20

At the close of the twentieth century, higher education is facing a series of strong, sometimes contradictory pressures that will transform the two major missions of the university—teaching and research. On the teaching side, these pressures will be resolved by a new distinction between knowledge and information, between "knowing how" and "knowing about." This change will be accompanied by a strong alignment of graduate educational offerings with the needs and interests of working professionals, with a special emphasis on certifying competence in selected areas. This distinction will also foster a new commitment to offering broader perspectives that enable people to deal with complexity and uncertainty, act with wisdom, build powerful social relationships, and practice the skills of entrepreneurship. Digital media and Internet communications will transform learning practices from the sequential classroom curriculum to nonlinear hyperlearning environments. A new kind of teacher will emerge—the teacher who is a course manager and a coach rather than an information transmitter.

Private, for-profit organizations will offer educational services, especially brokerage services, often in competition with the universities; some universities will disappear because they cannot adapt. On the research side, a new social contract will be struck among universities, business, and government. University research will take on new roles. The two most notable will be partnerships with companies in applied research and research that leads to greater learning, to distinguishing the dross from the essential in all the information offered to us. Research will not wither for lack of funding, for universities will become entrepreneurial in finding sponsors. These new alignments will bring a new spirit of freedom and entrepreneurship that will kindle a renaissance of higher education. This renaissance will eventually spread to high school and secondary education.

Irresistable forces and immovable objects

For education at the end of the twentieth century, it is the best of times and it is the worst of times. More than ever, people see education as their great hope to help them overcome poverty, find good jobs, change careers, and live meaningful and fulfilling lives. At the same time, they are becoming more demanding with consumerist expectations: they want university faculty to be experts on all frontiers of knowledge, states of the arts, and histories of how things came to be as they are; they want more counseling and coaching, fewer large classes, and less bureaucracy; they want greater assurance that graduates will have practical skills and be rapidly employable; they want a broad education as citizens; and they want lower costs.

This paradox has been brought about by the explosive spread of information technology, which is changing people's practices of work and relationships and their expectations and hopes for education. The world's weekly production of over one billion microchips quickly finds its way into products everywhere. The ubiquitous microchip has spawned new markets that no one even imagined in 1990; it is birthing a new age of plenty, new market forces, and new political alignments. Through the CD/ROM, the cable TV channel, the modem, and the Internet, the microchip challenges the book, the library, and the classroom, offering new access to knowledge just in time to overcome the turmoil of the obsolescence it creates. Private businesses and educational brokerages are beginning to offer for-profit educational services. Traditional schools, colleges, and universities are having enormous problems coping with the changes.

Working people, parents, sons, and daughters have always looked to education as the key to jobs and a social position in a world dominated by technologies. In addition to their hopes, they are driven by their anxieties: (a) The world seems overwhelmingly complex. Intercontinental communications have made the billions of other human coinhabitants stunningly obvious. A hundred other countries regularly create problems or crises that affect us without warning. (b) Technological change is coming faster and with less warning. Not even the experts in the universities know about all the new technologies in advance; novices and experts alike learn of them from the newspapers. (c) There is too little time to deal with uncertainty and ambiguities. Business and career opportunities spring up without warning and demand action before they can be fully assessed. (d) No job is secure any more. Dozens of new professions are springing up and dozens of others are becoming obsolete. Jobs may disappear and people may be too old for retraining. The lifetime of many new professions will be much shorter than a person's career. (e) In this stew, it is easy to fall into a mood where you don't see many possibilities for yourself. Our governments seem out of ideas and money but are still hungry for our thinner paychecks. We want education to help us find a place to stand as the winds of change howl across our society.

Employers, business leaders, and government officials look to the educational system to cultivate citizens and to prepare and maintain workforces. They also have their anxieties: (a) The number of small businesses is growing rapidly. Business leaders want employees who understand entrepreneurship and are comfortable with it. (b) Business leaders sense that business success depends ever more on the quality of networking—meaning social networks facilitated by computer networks. (c) Customer satisfaction, loyalty, and adoption of products or services are essential for a business's success. Business leaders want employees whose actions inspire these assessments with customers and partners, and across national boundaries. (d) Business leaders have a growing sense that "information" does not lead to know-how. They want people working for them to understand the difference. (e) They worry about the growth of their economy relative to others. They want employees who value hard work, loyalty, and perseverance.

In the above we can see two broad, seemingly contradictory forces. On the one side is growing pressure for education to deliver more competence—which in our current understanding of competence sounds like more specialization, more commercialization, more "training," and less education. On the other side is the growing pressure for a general education that produces historical sensibility, wisdom, self-discipline, responsibility, and facility with relationships, citizenship, connections, and identities. This paradox cannot be characterized as a conflict between a business view and a traditional view of education. You will find students, parents, business leaders, government officials on all sides of these issues.

In response to these pressures, some institutions will surely divide, splitting into a part that deals with general education and a part that deals with professional education. Others will specialize in one or the other. But I think the vast majority, driven by the traditional desire to integrate education and research, will change themselves into a new breed of university that accommodates both these pressures without contradiction. When this happens, I expect a renaissance in higher education. In what follows, I will examine these claims in detail.

Universities in the twentieth century

In the past ninety years, higher education has moved from a concern of the family, church, and local community into a largely state-managed operation. The small classroom and personal involvement by parents and teachers have given way to mass production of diploma-holders. Buoyed by a public mood that low-cost education should be available to all citizens, nearly every state of the United States supports at least one large campus with student populations in excess of 20,000—larger than the hometowns many of us grew up in. Most of the growth has occurred since 1960, when university budgets totalled about $7 billion and students numbered nearly three million; in the mid 1990s, the budgets totalled about $170 billion and students number over thirteen million. This is a twenty-five-fold increase in budgets and a fourfold increase in students. In the United States, state residents typically pay less than half the cost of their education. Class sizes in required lower-division courses are often measured in the hundreds and in required upper-division courses in the many tens; fifty years ago, classes of one or two dozen were the norm. In many cases, the diploma is little more than a receipt for attending the prescribed classes and paying tuition.

Wilhelm von Humboldt, founder of the University of Berlin in 1809, did the most to spread the notion that universities are places of research. Previously their sole job had been to give students a broad education and to prepare them for careers in church or government. Humboldt argued that professors should be scholars and researchers as well as teachers. Over the next hundred years, Humboldt's idea spread to universities everywhere. The world over, universities became centers of scientific advancement and intellectual ferment.

During World War II, the U.S. government offered large contracts to some universities to engage faculty and students in questions helpful to the war effort. The practice was institutionalized with the creation of the National Science Foundation in 1950 and the Advanced Research Projects Agency in the early 1960s. Based on a 1945 report by Vannevar Bush of MIT called *Science, the Endless Frontier,* the legislation founding the NSF in effect established a social contract under which the government would pay scientists to engage in research of their own choosing on the understanding that significant benefits would come back to American society in the forms of military security, public health, and economic prosperity. In the 1980s, the objectives of federal support for university research were expanded to include international competitiveness and "National Grand Challenges," leading to the Human Genome Project, the Manufacturing Initiative, and the High Performance Computing and Communications Program. These new federal programs involve big monies; in 1993, for example, $800 million was allocated to high-performance computing, over half of which flowed to universities. After many years of generous government support for sponsored research, universities have made research a centerpiece of their public identities and offer faculty sure rewards for success at sponsored research.

The American university system has become the envy of the world. The ubiquitous, well-funded research programs are a major factor in this success. Many foreign students come with scholarships from their home countries, in the expectation that they will help their home countries on their return. "Exporting" American higher education has become such a big business that some economists believe it actually cancels much of the U.S. balance-of-payments deficit.

Yet something has happened to tarnish the image of research in universities. Despite its many successes, two major problems with academic research carry considerable weight among federal lawmakers, who question whether the massive spending on research produces the value claimed by the Humboldtian and Bushian adherents. One is the "publish or perish" syndrome. In the past half century, nearly every university has adopted the practice of tenuring or dismissing a new faculty member within six years; in the context of the near-universal quest for a research reputation, most junior faculty are induced into a mass frenzy to publish papers in prestigious journals, a habit many retain for life. Much of this research is mediocre or of no consequence. About two million scholarly papers in science and engineering are published each year by seventy-two thousand journals; the vast majority of these papers are read by a few hundred people at most; in most disciplines well over half the papers are never cited by another author. The "publish or perish" syndrome has devalued the original purpose of research in the university—education. The second problem with academic research is that it does not conform to the linear model envisaged by Bush, that ideas are born to researchers and wend their way through a pipeline of development, production, and marketing before becoming consumer products. Authors Bruno Latour and Stephen Kline, among others, have shown that the real processes of innovation are much messier, full of feedbacks and chaotic disturbances involving many players. It is maddeningly difficult to prove that an innovation actually began with a researcher; too many other people are involved.

The kinder critics of academic research say that publicly supported research should be limited to the professors who are genuinely good at it. The sharper critics say that research should be banished from universities. Neither of these will happen; but there will be a major restructuring of the nature and role of research in education.

In the past thirty years, the universities have, largely at the behest of the state, undertaken new goals such as cultural diversity, ethnic studies, affirmative action, and economic competitiveness, all founded in the belief that the state can forge a better society with less racial tension, less disease, less poverty, less discrimination, and less unemployment. These goals are administered by special offices, sometimes with large staffs. The effect has been to add much to the bureaucracy and to diminish the relative effort spent on teaching.

Columbia University Professor Eli Noam has argued forcefully that the Internet and digital library are making the university library and local community of scholars obsolete, while at the same time, e-mail, phones, fax machines, and jet airliners have made it easier for faculty to establish stronger loyalties to national professions than to local institutions. Information technology therefore threatens the university as historically constituted and lays the foundation for the new university.

Business designs

In his book *Value Migration,* Adrian Slywotzky speaks of a "business design." He refers to the overall framework in which a business is constituted—its style, approach, and basic assumptions. Most businesses have research, development, and marketing (RD&M) processes by which they invent and market new products and services. These processes are part of the company's business design. What happens if the business design itself becomes obsolete? Would that render the RD&M processes incapable of keeping the firm competitive?

Indeed, this happens frequently, sometimes spectacularly! The designs of IBM and Digital Equipment Corporation worked very well for many years until Microsoft introduced commodity software—and then Microsoft was challenged by the business designs of Netscape and Sun's Java. Maxwell House and Folgers coffees are now challenged by Starbucks. The Postal Service is challenged by FedEx and e-mail.

When a new company offers a better design, customers migrate to it. Because an older company's products and services are formulated within a context that the customers no longer find attractive, that company cannot seem to find products and services that will attract the customers back.

What happens if the institution with the obsolescent business design is a university? Private universities with obsolescent designs tend to respond quickly to declining enrollments. State-controlled universities are generally much slower. Customers of state universities who wish to migrate have two options: choose private alternatives (at a considerably higher price) or complain to the political process. After enough complaining, the political process responds by passing new laws to regulate the ailing schools, thereby freezing them more solidly in their current business designs, or by transferring budget monies to more popular programs.

Make no mistake about it, the market and political forces are conspiring to generate a new design for universities. The only questions are who's in, who's out, and what new competitors for students are going to show up? Today's universities are facing enormous threats not only to their traditional ways of doing business but in some cases to their very existence. At the same time, they are presented with enormous opportunities for significantly improved education that once again attains its aims of preparing people for productive careers and meaningful lives.

The pressures to change

The late twentieth-century university features a structure of four-year programs, large classes organized on semester (or quarter) schedules, midterm and final examinations, a small menu of degrees awarded after a student completes a certain number of credit hours with certain grades, a substantial research program that is accessible mainly to graduate students, and occasionally a continuing education program adjunct to the main academic offerings. This structure cannot accommodate the changes being forced upon the universities. For example, a graduate program leading to defined, certified competence doesn't fit because with the possible exception of Ph.D. dissertations, our conception of university doesn't accommodate courses of study in which students proceed at different rates toward a fixed outcome. Universities deal best with courses taking a fixed amount of time to produce variable outcomes.

The new expectations that students, parents, employers, and business executives have of universities are easy enough to see in their requests and complaints. They divide among three main categories.

(1) What we learn:
- Offer us a general education that affirms values central to our civilization, cultivates historical sensibility, facility in social relationships and social networking, and prepares us for responsible and meaningful careers, families, and lives.
- Accommodate those of us who are not fully prepared for the university curriculum by our high schools.
- Provide for those of us whose natural abilities can take us to much higher levels of performance than the average.
- Teach us about entrepreneurship in our respective fields.
- Teach us the wisdom we need to cope with the apparent rise of complexity in a world increasingly infused with technology.
- Offer us continuing professional education after the bachelor's degree.
- Offer us certification in certain professional fields, such as software engineering and network engineering.
- Offer us more content and worry less about process.
- Offer us programs of study in hot interdisciplinary areas such as bioinformatics.

(2) How we learn:
- Give us new learning environments that accommodate differences in our learning styles, backgrounds, working schedules, and interests.
- Adopt course formats that fit with our working schedules.
- Teach us more through apprenticeships.
- Certify our capacity to act (i.e., practical competence) rather than our ability to regurgitate information.
- Incorporate privately produced courseware, seminars, and educational services into your offerings.
- Restructure the curriculum for Internet delivery without taking away our access to the faculty.
- Give us teachers who can motivate, manage, inspire, and coach us.
- Assess teachers by the results we students produce rather than by their individual classroom or research performances.

(3) The social contract for research:
- Collaborate with industry on research leading to products.
- Involve undergraduates in research.
- Spend more time writing about your findings in ways we can understand and put to use.
- Teach us how to answer our questions when we are bombarded with information and cannot easily tell the dross from the essential.

The pressures for change in these areas are so intense that universities will change after huffing and puffing. They will restructure all the major components: general education, professional education including certification, the practices of learning, teaching, and research. As they do this, they will revise their interpretations of the nature of education, teaching, and research. The new interpretations will change the conventional wisdom and will resolve the paradoxes and contradictions that arise within conventional understandings. They are explored in the sections following.

There is no reason to suppose that all of today's universities will do these jobs. Some will transform themselves and be successful. Others will not. Some will disappear. Private organizations will be increasingly successful, and will probably take the lead in the educational brokerage business.

True knowledge

A recurrent theme in these requests is the call for competence. Students and employers ask for educational programs that confer and then certify definite skills. Given that so many people now view a college diploma as a ticket to a good job and that so many employers recruit directly from universities, this is no surprise. Yet it inspires derision from faculty who hear the world "competence" as a code word for vocational "training" and who argue strenuously that it is not the mission of a university to provide training. They view courses aimed at skills as steps in the direction of increasing specialization, an affront to the university's mission of general education.

Educators do not agree among themselves on this. There are many who argue just as strenuously for more proficiency-based courses, which means that students don't pass until they can *demonstrate* that they know the material and can act effectively with it. To reassure their colleagues, these educators say that they mean competence in a broad sense that ranges from operating a computer or building a large software system to public speaking, rhetoric and debate, critical thinking, analyzing history, working on and managing teams, and leading a group. The common theme is that competence in a field includes knowledge of its history, methods, goals, boundaries, current problems, relations to other fields, and an ability to meet or surpass standards defined by those already in the field. Certification is another name for the public demonstration of competence. In some cases, such as engineering, education, accounting, law, or medicine, certification can be quite specific and rigorous. Certificates are necessary or at least highly desirable for professional practice.

This debate is the first sign of an important change in our understandings of data, information, and knowledge. It is seeping into more people's consciousness that there are fundamental distinctions among these three, which may be described as follows: (1) Data are symbols inscribed by human hands or by instruments. (2) Information is the judgment, by an individual or group, that given data resolve questions, disclose or reveal distinctions, or enable new action. In other words, information is data that makes a difference to someone. Information thus exists in the eyes of the beholder; the same data can be nonsense to one person and gold to another. (3) Knowledge is the capacity for effective action in a domain of human actions.

Lewis Perelman likens these distinctions to a menu in a restaurant. The data are the symbols on the menu; information is the understanding of the restaurant's offerings; knowledge is the dinner. You don't go to the restaurant to lick the ink or eat the menu.

These distinctions are not practiced rigorously in the university. Most curricula are set up on the assumption that there is a body of knowledge (organized data about a field that conveys information to its beholders) that must be transmitted to the students. The teacher is the communication channel. Testing reveals whether the information survived transit intact. Universities are serving mostly menus. The call for competence is a cry from the hungry for dinner.

As we begin to heed this call, we will become increasingly aware of two kinds of knowledge. One is practical knowledge, the skills behind action. Over time, with practice and coaching, one's skill level will increase. There are six distinguishable levels: beginner, rookie, professional, expert, virtuoso, and master. Each level has its own standards for performance set by the practicing members of the domain. It can take years to advance to the higher levels. Apprenticeship is the most effective method of learning skills.

The other kind of knowledge is awareness of the observer one is. Each of us is filled with interpretations and biases that affect what we perceive. There are many things we cannot see—and we cannot see that we cannot see them. Thus the observer I am affects my ability to act in a specific situation because it affects my power to make distinctions and connections. Each of us has experienced moments when our observer shifted and new actions appeared to us. We call these paradigm shifts, "aha!" insights, eureka moments, and sudden realizations. Unlike skill acquisition, shifts of observer can happen suddenly and can affect performance immediately. Master teachers and coaches know this: they can help the student-apprentice acquire skills and judgment faster by assessing and shifting the student's observer at the right moments.

Although observing another person's observer is hard enough, observing one's own observer can be nearly impossible. This is why changing a community's paradigm—for example, a business design—is so difficult. Most people are not aware of how they see the world and are not open to the possibility that they are blind to the very possibilities that would solve their problems. It is the special skill of leadership that helps communities of people break out of their current blindness.

The growing awareness of these distinctions will engender significant shifts in education. The student-teacher relation of "apprentice-master" will become the most traveled path to knowledge. The teacher will need special skills, not at presenting information, but at observing and shifting how students see and bring forth their worlds. The apparent contradiction between general and professional education will disappear. General education seeks to produce a graduate who can act effectively by reading, writing, speaking, and listening, and who understands history, literature, philosophy, language, and social relationships. General education is the context in which a person can attain higher levels of competence.

Hyperlearning

In *School's Out*, Lewis Perelman vividly pictures the changes ahead for education in the presence of the forces enumerated above. He says that the resistance of current schools to make changes resembles the opposition of equestrian associations in the late nineteenth century to the arrival of the "horseless carriage" or of candle and gas associations to the arrival of the electric lamp. Automobiles eventually swept away the horse-drawn carriage, electricity the gas light. Perelman says that future historians will record that the school reform movements of the late twentieth century were as irrelevant to the new world of education as horse reforms were to the automobile: The learning revolution has already made the classroom teacher as obsolete as the blacksmith. He gives the name *hyperlearning* to the new kind of learning environment that is emerging. The prefix "hyper" here means nonlinear and multidimensional, as in a mathematician's hyperspace or an author's hypertext.

In the traditional model of school, a course is a sequence of topics covered in a series of lectures, held in classrooms at weekly intervals, with homework practice in between. This is a linear model of learning. It is designed to convey information in an orderly manner. All students proceed at the same pace regardless of their interests, prior experience, talents, or other demands on their time. At the end grades indicate the levels of achievement they were able to make in the fixed time period allocated for the course.

Imagine a new model. Instead of a classroom, see in your mind a large "learning room" with an entrance, an exit, and a number of learning stations (booths). You meet the teacher on entry. The teacher may place you into a small study or working group. The room's exit is guarded by a "certifier," whose job is to assess whether you have become competent at everything promised by the teacher, according to well-defined standards. You visit the stations to learn particular subjects or practices. Colored lines on the floor suggest paths among the stations. You can visit as many stations as you need to, and in any order consistent with your current knowledge, to prepare yourself for final certification. You can take trial certifications and then backtrack to the stations needed. You can take self-assessment tests at any time you like. You collaborate with other students in projects and study groups. You call on the teacher for help at any moment you are stuck. The teacher will offer guidance if you are heading in a wrong direction. In contrast to the linear model, everyone who exits gets the same "grade" (a certificate of completion or competence); the variables are the length of time and the path followed. While this image may not be the final hyperlearning model, it is a useful way to visualize the first kinds of hyperlearning environments that are now emerging.

It might seem that this paradigm makes all students be the same and does not leave room for talented or gifted students to develop their skills. This is not so. In fact, the talented student will complete a hyperlearning room faster than the others and go on to achieve more advanced certifications than the others.

An important technology in this picture is the certifier, which is a teacher-assisting agent that confirms when a student has met the learning objectives of a course and issues an authoritative declaration. The first generation of certifiers already exist and are not very powerful; they offer multiple-choice and short-answer tests for problems with algorithmically computable answers, such as occur in math, science, and engineering. Future generations of certifiers are likely to include intelligent agents, virtual-reality simulations, and interactive conferences with a panel of judges who can question and direct the candidate through a series of actions. The same technology can also be used to support self-assessment tests by which a student can tell how well prepared he or she is to enter a learning environment or to be certified. Eventually, we will get very good at designing hyperlearning environments that will prepare a person for practice in a profession or specialty.

Professional education

College curricula are organized for the undergraduate who comes straight from high school and earns a bachelor's degree in four years. The master's program covers one or two more years beyond that. Universities offer very few programs for the remaining forty-five years of a person's professional life. Most continuing education programs are not part of the regular academic program and are not staffed by the regular faculty.

A growing number of working professionals want certification in selected subjects valuable to them (and their employers) in the workplace. They want educational programs that promise and deliver specific, well-defined competence and skills. They want an evolving and growing portfolio of professional certificates. They do not want these programs to be isolated, but rather conducted in a framework that affirms and reinforces the basic disciplines of a general education. The desire for professional certificates will grow into a market force so powerful that it might supersede the formal graduate degree with an equivalent set of certificates.

Two kinds of education programs will meet these demands. These correspond to the two kinds of knowledge discussed earlier. One is a program that leads its students to certified competence in an area. Examples are network engineering, scientific computing, biomolecular engineering, corporate law, high-school math teaching, or statistical analysis. Such programs might take a typical student a year to complete. The other is a program that offers to change a student's observer. Examples are study of a timely question (e.g., "how can a business reduce cycle time to delivery of new products?"), a refresher of some aspect of general education (e.g., "how does linguistic philosophy inform us in the knowledge age?"), or an introduction to a field (e.g., "security and privacy in networks"). Such programs might take a few days to a few months to complete.

Some universities now have certification programs, which normally award the certificate to a student who has completed a specified set of courses with "A" or "B" grades. These certification programs do not meet the demand described above. Professional certification programs will promise specific competence and skills, include rigorous project work and testing, and will take as long as needed to deliver a given level of competence to those willing to persevere. Developing these programs and making them a regular part of the university's offerings will be a major challenge because they are based on a variable length of time to attain a given grade (the certificate) rather than a fixed length of time leading to a variable grade.

Professional education will be offered in new course formats consistent with the working schedules of employed people. They will feature occasional workshops, active working groups of students communicating via the Internet, projects, and public exhibitions and defenses of results. The regular weekly scheduled class will become a little-used option.

With a focus on competence and a clientele of working professionals, it will become possible to design educational programs offering higher levels of competence than we are able to offer now. These include the expert, virtuoso, and master levels, which we normally associate with later stages of a person's career. This will be fertile, virgin territory for universities.

The new teacher

The same pressures impelling us toward new curricula will compel a revolution in teaching. Our practices of teaching will change to fit the new university, its curricula, and its hyperlearning approaches. Two forces are driving this. One is the demand of students for a more customer-oriented relationship with the university. Faculty are going to master new skills in listening, trustworthiness, compassion, service, valuing diversity, communication, and historical sensibility—not only to interact effectively with their future students, but to teach these things to them.

The other driving force is digital media and networking. Faculty have been brought up in an environment where most teaching consists of presentation and testing. Teaching can be assessed by peer review—faculty can observe each other's performances in front of the classroom. As classrooms disappear and machines take over much of the presentations—often doing it much better than a live human lecturer—and as the machines take over testing and record-keeping, what will be left for the teacher to do?

I said earlier that the job of a teacher is to cultivate knowledge. This job can be elaborated in terms of the metaphor of the clearing—the space of actions available to a community of people. The metaphor recalls an opening in the forest; within it, movement is easy, but outside it movement is restricted by the underbrush. One aspect of a human clearing is its common sense—the shared beliefs and practices of its people. To move effectively in the clearing, the new person must learn those practices and be able to perform them effortlessly, without little or no thought. He must adopt and become part of the common sense. The person who defies the common sense can quickly become ensnared in the underbrush of resistance; he will be slowed down or, if others consider him a threat, will be put completely out of commission. The job of the teacher consists of three main aspects.

1. Sharpening the student's awareness of the common sense of the clearing into which the student seeks entry.
2. Showing the students what the framework of practices of the clearing is; this includes a historical account of how and why that framework came to be, its methods and practices, its goals, its boundaries, its current problems, and its relationships to other clearings.
3. Providing coaching and exercises that assist the student in learning to observe the clearing and engage successfully with its practices, so that these powers of observation and capacities for action become ingrained and skillful.

It should be obvious that teaching is not made obsolete by technologies for presentation, assessment, and record-keeping. To the contrary, the teacher will be expected to inspire, motivate, manage, and coach students. Few teachers have learned these skills because they never had to, and in any case there was no one to teach them. New and extensive development programs will assist them in learning how to be highly effective teachers. The topics that will be important in such a program include:

Educational goals
Data, information, and knowledge
The role of educational technology
How humans use language for disclosure, coordination, and information
Clearings
Reading
Communication
Listening
Seduction
Trust
Compassion
Fear and self-esteem
Service
Assessment
Diversity

Seriousness and humor
Invention and innovation
Historical sensibility
Games and simulations
New course management practices
Coaching
Designing exercises to help students observe and learn well

Unfortunately, a good training workshop in the above topics is not enough. Teaching practices are strongly connected with the curriculum. There is little room for some of these practices in today's curricula. Engineering curricula, for example, are structured as an intense presentation of topics in a well-defined order; the use of games and simulations or creation of milestones that can be passed only by proficiency demonstrations would not fit easily into this structure.

The two driving forces of customer-orientation and machine-aided presentation are moving us inexorably toward restructuring our curricula and teaching practices. The only unknown is the timing.

The prospect of this change is undoubtedly unsettling to many faculty members. Many will be offended by a move to treat students as customers who expect them to fulfill educational promises rigorously. Moreover, the end of presentation-oriented teaching will bring new methods of assessing teaching effectiveness. The situation will be a lot like that faced by the manager of a business project or the manager of a ball team. The manager's performance will be based on the performance of the team. Teachers will be assessed by how well their students perform. Nothing else will matter.

The New social contract for research

The fifty-year-old social contract about research has come to an end. What will replace it? Even as a German university gave birth to the modern research university, a German research institute may have discovered a formula for research in the twenty-first century. Writing elsewhere in this volume, Dennis Tsichritzis, the chairman of the German research institute GMD, is interested in innovations: shifting the standard practices of a community of people so that they are more effective at what they do. He proposes that we regard research as a path to innovation. The modern research university is hampered by a belief that the discovery of new ideas is the only path. There are at least four processes leading to innovation:

1. Generating new ideas. Powerful new ideas shift the discourse, in turn shifting the actions of those practicing the discourse. Research consists in formulating and validating the new ideas. It places a great deal of emphasis on originality and novelty. The scientific publication process aims to certify originality and novelty through peer review.

2. Generating new practices. A teacher initiates people into the practices of a new discourse. Research consists of selecting, clarifying, and integrating the principles relevant to the practices. It places a great deal of emphasis on understanding that produces widespread competence.

3. Generating new products. New tools enable the new practices, producing an innovation; the most successful are those that enable people to produce their own innovations in their own environments. Research consists in evaluating and testing alternative ways of building a tool or defining its function. It places a great deal of emphasis on economic advantage.

4. Generating new business. Successful firms continually improve their business designs. Research consists in testing markets, listening to customers, fostering offbeat projects that explore notions defying the conventional wisdom, and developing new narratives about people's roles and identities in the world. It places a great deal of emphasis on market identity, position, and exploring marginal practices.

Although Tsichritzis does not explicitly mention the fourth kind of innovation, he clearly practices it his leadership of GMD.

The first two kinds of research are done primarily in universities, the last two primarily in companies. The third kind is most common in industry R & D and is occasionally encountered in university-industry collaborations. Most innovations familiar to the public have come directly from the third kind of research and indirectly from the first.

The second kind of research is often overlooked or downplayed, yet it plays an extraordinarily important role in developing individual and corporate competencies. Many faculty members are highly competent practitioners of this kind of research. Through their scholarly work they investigate questions, compile results, integrate their findings, bring clarity to a subject, generate new interpretations, and offer the new narratives needed for others to understand the subject. They produce popular articles, books, simulators, tools, and software. By participating in the research process, writing scholarly papers, building software, and attending conferences, they stay sharp, teach students competent investigative practices, and maintain credibility as experts knowledgeable about the leading edges of technology or thought.

In the academy, the first kind of research is by tradition accorded the greatest prestige; those most successful at it receive the highest honors. Yet not everyone is good at it; others try mightily but succeed only occasionally. In time, tradition will give way to economic reality. As universities adapt to shrinking federal funding for basic, "curiosity-driven" research, the first kind of research will be performed mostly in well-equipped labs by those who are genuinely good at it: the creative thinkers, mavericks, offbeat inventors, troublemakers, and others with a talent for finding answers to basic questions. The second kind of research will rise in stature because it will be directly tied to the educational mission of the new university. The third kind will become more popular as universities come to grips with their own entrepreneurialism, discovering that they can realize income by helping businesses with their directed R & D, and discovering that this kind of research attracts students.

University research will be restructured, broadened, and enriched, but not eliminated. The research mission is too deeply ingrained into the university's ethos.

The new university

Although information technology, networking, and digital media may be undermining the basic assumptions behind our universities, we must look to the movements of the marketplace and political processes for guidance on how to respond to the changes. These are precisely the forces exerting the greatest pressures. I have sought here to analyze these forces and to suggest the great opportunities presented to the universities who respond.

The teaching function of the university will be reshaped by new expectations from students concerned about the return on their investment in education—from business leaders seeking graduates with practical competence and from politicians who want more efficient and effective education for the state's subsidies—and by new technologies and competition from private firms. The traditional linear classroom will give way to hyperlearning environments. Professional training and certification will become a new and lucrative line of business in graduate education. Curricula will be restructured to account for new understandings of the distinctions between knowledge and information. And a new kind of teacher will emerge who is good at inspiring, motivating, managing, and coaching, and who is evaluated on the performance of their students.

The research function in the university will be reshaped around a new social contract that places more emphasis on research leading to competence and on research partnerships with companies. (The latter, it should be noted, will be bolstered by industry's disinvestment in its own research.) Research will be funded less by the federal government and more by the university's own entrepreneurial actions.

Universities today are beset by many social controversies such as affirmative action, special treatments for certain groups, harassment policies, speech codes, and political correctness. How these will turn out is unknown. The outcomes will not affect the movement toward the new university, because the forces driving these controversies are not as strong as the forces driving the changes in what we learn, how we learn, and how we will conduct research.

Those who do respond will be rewarded with enriched educational programs, more competent graduates, satisfied employers, an enlarged repertoire of ways to engage in research, programs in professional educations, and new teaching practices. Education has a bright future indeed.

Readings

In *School's Out* (Avon Books, 1992), Lewis Perelman discusses in great detail his vision of the future of education, a paradigm he calls hyperlearning. Definitely read this. If you like the traditions of the university, you are likely to find this book deeply disturbing. Perelman comments on his philosophy of knowledge and learning in an interview published in the online *Journal of Bionomics*, September 1996 (http://www.bionomics.org).

In *Value Migration* (Harvard Business School Press, 1995) Adrian Slywotzky discusses at great length the concept of business design and gives many examples of customers migrating to new business designs that offer them greater value.

In *Post Capitalist Society* (Harper Business, 1993), Peter Drucker lays out a vision of what teaching and learning for the knowledge worker will entail. This expands on an earlier version of his vision in *The New Realities* (Harper & Row, 1989). Drucker's works often give readers a sense of understanding and serenity in the face of complexity because he is so good at revealing the historical forces that are always at work and showing their implications.

In *Science in Action* (Harvard University Press, 1987) Bruno Latour differentiates between "ready-made science" and "science in the making" to show the cacophony, controversy, and chaos that litter the trail to scientific truth.

In *Conceptual Foundations for Multidisciplinary Thinking* (Stanford University Press, 1995) Stephen Jay Kline demonstrates that the processes of innovation are highly nonlinear and punctuated by many feedbacks and hiccups;

he casts doubts on the notion that most innovations begin as ideas in researchers' minds.

Andy Grove's account of his leadership of Intel in *Only the Paranoid Survive* (1996) reveals much about the processes of research and innovation in a successful high-tech company.

Beginning with Charles Sykes's *ProfScam* (St Martin's Press, 1988), various authors have written best-selling, iconoclastic books about disease and corruption in the academy. Even if you don't accept the premises of these books, they were bestsellers, and hundreds of thousands of people paid $24.95 to own one or more of them. If nothing else, they give good insight into what ails the current business design of universities.

Not normally given to comments on university research, the *Economist* (24 August 1996, p. 14), said that the "publish or perish" syndrome is devaluing education by taking faculty energy away from teaching. Much of what faculty have accomplished is mediocre.

Eli Noam gave his views on the demise of the university in a commentary for *Science* magazine in October 1995 and again for *Educom Review* in May/June 1996. He spoke specifically about the way information technology is undermining the traditional assumptions of the university.

Eliott Soloway has written repeatedly about the need for effective teaching and teacher development, most recently in "Teachers are the key" in *Communications of the ACM,* June 1996.

Andy Whinston and two colleagues have written about educational brokerages in "Electronic markets for learning: education brokerages and the Internet," *Communications of the ACM,* June 1996.

I have written several articles exploring some of these themes. You can find them in the *Communications of the ACM:* (1) "Educating a new engineer," December 1992; (2) "Designing new principles to sustain research in our universities," July 1993; and (3) "The university's next challenges," May 1996. See also "Business Designs for the New University" in *Educom Review,* November 1996.

With Daniel Meanscé I have produced prototype hyperlearning environments in the Center for the New Engineer (http://cne.gmu.edu). The CNE maintains a library of learning modules and workbenches; the math and statistics refresher modules contain prototype certifiers.

Paul W. Abrahams

Paul W. Abrahams, Sc.D., CCP, is a past president of the Association for Computing Machinery and an ACM Fellow. As a consulting computer scientist, he specializes in programming languages, design and implementation of software systems, and technical writing. He is the author of the book *TeX for the Impatient* and the lead coauthor of *UNIX for the Impatient*. Dr. Abrahams received his bachelor's degree in mathematics from the Massachusetts Institute of Technology in 1956 and his doctorate in mathematics from the same institution in 1963, studying artificial intelligence under Marvin Minsky and John McCarthy and writing his dissertation on "Machine Verification of Mathematical Proof." He is one of the designers of the first Lisp system and also the designer of the CIMS PL/I system, which he developed while a professor at New York University. He also participated in the design of the Software Engineering Design Language (SEDL), developed at the IBM T.J. ~ Watson Laboratories. Currently he is working on the design of SPLASH, a Systems Programming Language for Software Hackers and on a new book, *OS/2 for the Impatient*.

Dr. Abrahams resides in Deerfield, Massachusetts, where he writes, hacks, hikes, forages for wild mushrooms, and listens to classical music. His Internet address is abrahams@acm.org.

Franz L. Alt

Franz L. Alt is the oldest surviving president of the ACM (1950–52) and the first editor of the *Journal of the ACM*. Born in 1910 in Vienna, Alt earned a Ph.D. in mathematics from the University of Vienna in 1932, with research in set-theoretic topology and logical foundations of geometry. Alt left Austria after the *Anschluss* in 1938 and came to New York, where he worked at the Econometric Institute. He served in the 10th Mountain Division of the U.S. Army during WWII.

While in the Army, he became acquainted with early automatic computers, then under development, and did programming before their completion. After 1946 he resumed working on computers, briefly at Aberdeen Proving Ground; mainly at the National Bureau of Standards; finally at the American Institute of Physics, in New York. After he retired in 1973, he volunteered his services to peace and justice organizations.

Alt was one of the first members of the Association for Computing Machinery (ACM), and he organized its first national meeting (Aberdeen Proving Grounds, 1947). He wrote one of the first books on computers, *Electronic Digital Computers* (Academic Press, 1958) and numerous technical papers. In 1962, he wrote "Fifteen Years ACM" (*Communications of the ACM* 5 no. 6). He edited *Advances in Computers* for its first eleven years. Alt is a recipient of the ACM Distinguished Service Award and was inducted as an ACM fellow in 1994.

Gordon Bell

Gordon Bell is a senior researcher at Microsoft and a computer-industry consultant at large, having spent twenty-three years at Digital Equipment Corporation as vice president of R & D, where he was responsible for various mini- and time-sharing computers and led the development of DEC's VAX. Bell has been involved in the design of many products at Digital and a score of startup companies. As the first assistant director for computing at NSF, he led the National Research Network panel that became the NII/GII, and was an author of the High Performance Computer and Communications Initiative. Bell is the author of books and papers on computers and high-tech startups and a member of various professional organizations, including the National Academy of Engineering and the American Academy of Arts and Sciences. He received The 1991 National Medal of Technology.

John Seely Brown

John Seely Brown is the chief scientist of Xerox Corporation and the director of its Palo Alto Research Center (PARC). At Xerox, Brown has been involved in expanding the role of corporate research to include such topics as organizational learning, ethnographies of the workplace, complex adaptive systems, and techniques for unfreezing the corporate mind. His personal research interests include digital culture, ubiquitous computing, user-centered design, organizational and individual learning. A major focus of Brown's research over the years has been in human learning and in the management of radical innovation.

Dr. Brown is a cofounder of the Institute for Research on Learning, a non-profit institute for addressing the problems of lifelong learning. He is a member of the National Academy of Education and a fellow of the American Association for Artificial Intelligence. He also serves on numerous advisory boards and boards of directors. He has published over sixty papers in scientific journals and was awarded the Harvard Business Review's 1991 McKinsey Award for his article "Research that Reinvents the Corporation." Brown was an executive producer for the award winning videotape "Art • Lunch • Internet • Dinner," which won a bronze medal in the Ethnic/Cultural category at Worldfest '94, the Charleston International Film Festival.

Brown has a B.S. in mathematics and physics from Brown University and an M.S. in mathematics and a Ph.D. in computer and communication sciences from the University of Michigan.

James Burke

In 1965 James Burke left teaching to work with BBC TV. For over thirty years he wrote and presented prize-winning television series for BBC and PBS such as "Connections," "The Day the Universe Changed," "After The Warming," and "Connections 2." He has authored a number of best-selling books. His most recent are *The Axemaker's Gift*, written with psychologist Robert Ornstein and published by G. P. Putnam's Sons in 1995, and *The Pinball Effect*, an "interactive" book published by Little, Brown in September 1996. Burke also wrote and hosted a CD ROM game called "Connections—a Mind Game" released by Discovery Communications in February 1996. He is a frequent keynote speaker on the subject of technology and social change to audiences such as NASA, Microsoft, MIT, the European Parliament, and the World Affairs Council. He writes a monthly column for *Scientific American* and is at present in production on a new, ten-hour technology/history series for The Learning Channel. He is also building a large "knowledge web," which he hopes to put online in the near future. Burke was educated at Oxford and also holds honorary doctorates for his work in communicating science and technology. He lives in London, Nice, and airplanes.

Vinton G. Cerf

Vinton G. Cerf received a B.S. in mathematics from Stanford in 1965 and an M.S. and Ph.D. in computer science from UCLA in 1970 and 1972, respectively.

He is senior vice president for data architecture at MCI Telecommunications, where he is responsible for the design of MCI's data services, including its Internet service offerings. He was president of the Internet Society from 1992–95 and vice president of the Corporation for National Research Initiatives from 1986–94.

He served as vice president of the MCI Data and Inform from 1982–86. He served as program manager and principal scientist in the ARPA Information Processing Techniques Office; where he was responsible for the Internetting program, packet communication technologies program, and network security program. Before 1982, he was an assistant professor at Stanford University in the computer science and electrical engineering departments; there, he led the development of the TCP/IP protocols and with Robert Kahn designed the basic architecture of the Internet. Prior to Stanford, he served as a member of the ARPANET team at UCLA's Network Measurement Center.

Cerf is a fellow of the IEEE, National Academy of Engineering, American Association for the Advancement of Science, the American Association for the Arts and Sciences, and the Association for Computing Machinery. He is the recipient of several ACM and IEEE awards. In 1995, he received the Silver Medal of the International Telecommunications Union.

He is married, has two sons, and has an abiding interest in fine foods, wine, and mind-rotting science fiction.

Don Chamberlin

Don Chamberlin is an ACM Fellow, a research staff member at the IBM Almaden Research Center, and an adjunct professor of computer engineering at Santa Clara University. He is co-inventor of the SQL database language and a recipient of the ACM Software Systems Award for contributions to the design and implementation of database systems. He holds a B.S. degree from Harvey Mudd College and a Ph.D. from Stanford University, and he has recently published a book entitled *Using the New DB2: IBM's Object-Relational Database System*.

Peter J. Denning

Peter J. Denning is Associate Dean for Computing and Chair of the Computer Science Department in the School of Information Technology and Engineering at George Mason University. He is also director of the Center for the New Engineer, which he founded at GMU in August 1993. He was formerly the founding director of the Research Institute for Advanced Computer Science at the NASA Ames Research Center, was cofounder of CSNET, and was head of the Computer Science Department at Purdue. He received his Ph.D. from MIT and BEE from Manhattan College. He was president of the Association for Computing Machinery from 1980 to 1982 and is now chair of the ACM publications board. He has published three books and 250 articles on computers, networks, and their operating systems and is working on two more books. He holds two honorary degrees, three professional society fellowships, two best-paper awards, two distinguished service awards, and the prestigious ACM Karl Karlstrom Outstanding Educator Award.

Edsger W. Dijkstra

Edsger W. Dijkstra was born in Rotterdam, where he lived until 1948. He then studied mathematics and theoretical physics at the University of Leyden until he graduated in 1956. In September 1951 he was introduced to programming in Cambridge, England, and in March 1952, at the Mathematical Centre, he became the first professional programmer of the Netherlands. In 1959 he got his Ph.D. in computing science at the University of Amsterdam. In 1962 he was appointed full professor of mathematics at the Eindhoven University of Technology. In 1973 he became a research fellow of Burroughs Corporation, a position he enjoyed until his immigration to the USA in 1984, when he was appointed to the Schlumberger Centennial Chair in Computer Sciences at the University of Texas at Austin.

He is known for early graph-theoretical algorithms (shortest path and shortest spanning tree), the first implementation of ALGOL 60 (completed in August 1960), the first operating system composed of explicitly synchronized sequential processes, the invention of a number of seminal problems (such as mutual exclusion, the dining philosophers, distributed termination detection, and self-stabilization), the invention of guarded commands and of predicate transformers as a means for defining semantics, and for programming methodology in the broadest sense of the word. His current research interests focus on the formal derivation of proofs and programs and the streamlining of the mathematical argument in general.

He has been elected the first distinguished fellow of the British Computer Society (together with Christopher Strachey), member of the Royal Netherlands Academy of Arts and Sciences, 1972 recipient of the ACM Turing Award, 1974 recipient of the AFIPS Harry Goode Memorial Award, foreign honorary member of the American Academy of Arts and Sciences, and honorary doctor of sciences of The Queen's University of Belfast.

Larry Druffel

Larry Druffel is the president of SCRA, an organization engaged in economic development through science and technology.

He was the director of the Software Engineering Institute from 1986 to 1996. Before that, he was a vice president of Rational Software.

Druffel was on the faculty at the USAF Academy. He later managed research programs in advanced software technology at DARPA. He was founding director of the Ada Joint Program Office, then served as director of computer systems and software (research and advanced technology) in the Office of the Secretary of Defense.

He is a coauthor of a computer science textbook and of thirty-five professional papers. He has a B.S. in electrical engineering from the University of Illinois, an M.Sc. in computer science from the University of London, and a Ph.D. in computer science from Vanderbilt University.

Druffel is a fellow of the IEEE, a fellow of the ACM, and a member of the board of the Oak Ridge Associated Universities. He chaired the AF Science Advisory Board Study on Information Architecture and cochaired the Defense Science Board study on Acquiring Defense Software Commercially. He has served on numerous AFSAB, DSB, and National Academy studies dealing with information warfare and the use of information technology for defense.

Bob O. Evans

Bob O. Evans worked for IBM from 1951 through 1984, in positions that included vice president of development, data systems division (1962–64); president, federal systems division (1965–69); president, systems development division (1969–73); president, system communications division (1973–77); and IBM vice-president, engineering, programming, and technology (1977–84). Among many other activities during that time, Evans helped develop IBM's first electronic computer system, the 701 Defense Calculator; organized and led the team that conceived, developed, and released into production the IBM Model 360; and initiated the IBM-Comsat partnership that later grew into Satellite Business Systems. His last post at IBM was as its "chief engineer," responsible for the company's worldwide engineering, programming, and technology activities. After retiring from IBM in 1984, Evans joined Hambrecht & Quist Venture Partners (the name was later changed to Technology Strategies & Alliances), where he is today the managing partner. Evans has served as a consultant to the Defense Department and to the Republic of China; as a trustee of the New York Public Library and of the Rensselaer Polytechnic Institute; as a director of several high-technology corporations; and on many advisory committees and task forces. He has been awarded the NASA Public Service Award, the NSA Meritorious Service Award, the IEEE Edwin H. Armstrong Achievement Award, and the National Medal of Technology for his work on IBM System 360.

Fernando Flores

Fernando Flores, considered by some to be one of the most outstanding scholars in the management field today and one of the pioneers of workflow technology, has founded and led various organizations in Chile and in the United States. Among these are Action Technologies, Inc., which holds patents for the development of software for managing communications in digital networks, and Business Design Associates, Inc., an international management consulting company that specializes in business process design, implementation on new practices, computer and networking technology, strategy, and leadership. Dr. Flores is a coauthor of one the leading books in the field of computer science—*Understanding Computers and Cognition: A New Foundation for Design*. He is also a coauthor of the (MIT Press) *Disclosing New Worlds: Entrepreneurship, Democratic Action and the Cultivation of Solidarity*. He holds a Ph.D. from the University of California at Berkeley. He also holds a degree in industrial engineering from Universidad Católica de Chile. Prior to moving to the United States, Dr. Flores held important academic and cabinet positions in Chile.

Bob Frankston

Bob Frankston has long been interested in the possibilities of computers and the assumption that there must be something useful about them. He is best known for implementing VisiCalc (along with Dan Bricklin), the first electronic spreadsheet and the first program to make the personal computer a required business tool. At MIT he cofounded the Student Information Processing Board to make computing more accessible to students and wrote a master's thesis on selling services on information systems (now known as microtransactions). He cofounded Software Arts (with Dan) and was later at Lotus Development and Microsoft, where he has continued to develop products and services. He has received the lifetime achievement award from PC Magazine and is an ACM Fellow. Having started with punched card computers (the IBM1620) and mainframes, and having experienced creation of on-line services, the Internet (the ARPANET), minicomputers, the PC, and the Web, he looks forward to the disappearance of the computer into the woodwork.

David Gelernter

David Gelernter is professor of computer science at Yale, where his research centers on artificial intelligence, parallel programming, and information management, among other things. The programming language called "Linda" that he developed with Yale colleague Nicholas Carriero sees use worldwide for parallel programming. (Linda and its central idea, called "tuple spaces," forms the basis of the "JavaSpaces" extension to Java recently described by JavaSoft.) He has published lots of technical articles in the usual places and two text-books, *Programming Linguistics* with Suresh Jagannathan and *How to Write Parallel Programs* with Nicholas Carriero. His 1991 book *Mirror Worlds* (Oxford, translated also into German and Japanese) laid out a net-based computing future similar to the Web-based internet world that has since emerged. His 1994 *Muse in the Machine* (Free Press) dealt with emotion, dream-logic, and artificial thought; the forthcoming *Beauty and the Heart of Computing* (on aesthetics and software) is his contribution to Basic Books's "Master Classes" monograph series. He is one of the thirty-three technologists, thinkers, entre-preneurs, etc. who the author of the just-out *Digerati* claims (albeit question-ably) constitute the "cyber elite." In the nothing-to-do-with-computers de-partment, he's the author of the semi-novel *1939* (Free Press, 1995), is art critic and contributing editor at the *Weekly Standard,* contributing editor at the *City Journal* and *National Review,* and has also published (among other publications) in the *New York Times, Washington Post, Commentary, The New Republic, Scientific American,* and the net-magazine "Feed."

James N. Gray

James N. Gray is a specialist in database and transaction processing computer systems. At Microsoft his research focuses on scalable computing: building super-servers and workgroup systems from commodity software and hard-ware. Prior to joining Microsoft, he worked at Digital, Tandem, IBM, and AT&T on database and transaction processing systems including Rdb, ACMS, NonStopSQL, Pathway, System R, SQL/DS, DB2, and IMS-Fast Path. He is editor of the *Performance Handbook for Database and Transaction Processing Sys-tems* and coauthor of *Transaction Processing Concepts and Techniques.* He holds a doctorate from Berkeley and is a member of the National Academy of Engi-neering, a fellow of the ACM, a member of the National Research Council's Computer Science and Telecommunications Board, editor in chief of the *VLDB Journal,* trustee of the VLDB Foundation, and editor of the Morgan Kaufmann series on Data Management.

Richard W. Hamming

Richard W. Hamming has been an adjunct professor and senior lecturer at the Naval Postgraduate School in Monterey, California, since 1976, where his overriding goal has been to teach his students an attitude of excellence toward science, not just technical skills. His most recent book, *The Art of Doing Science and Engineering: Learning to Learn,* published in 1996 by Gordon & Breach Science Publishers, explores the concept of effective thinking as an art that engineers and scientists can be taught to develop. Professor Hamming was president of the Association for Computing (ACM) from 1958–1960. In 1968, he received ACM's most prestigious award, the A. M. Turing Award, for his work on error-correcting codes at AT&T Bell Laboratories, where he worked for thirty years on numerous research projects.

William J. Mitchell

William J. Mitchell is professor of architecture and media arts and sciences and dean of the School of Architecture and Planning at the Massachusetts Institute of Technology. He teachers courses and conducts research in design theory, computer applications in architecture and urban design, and imaging and image synthesis. He consults extensively in the field of computer-aided design and was a cofounder of a California software company.

Mitchell's most recent book, *City of Bits: Space, Place, and the Infobahn,* examines architecture and urbanism in the context of the digital telecommunications revolution and the growing domination of software over materialized form. Published by the MIT Press in 1995, it is also available on the World Wide Web <http://www-mitpress.mit.edu/City_of_Bits/>. In *The Reconfigured Eye: Visual Truth in the Post-Photographic Era* (MIT Press, 1992), Mitchell examined the social and cultural impact of digitally altered photographs and synthesized photorealistic scenes.

In addition to numerous articles, Mitchell is also the author of *Digital Design Media,* with Malcolm McCullough (Van Nostrand Reinhold, second ed., 1995; orig. publ., 1991); *The Logic of Architecture: Design, Computation, and Cognition* (MIT Press, 1990); *The Poetics of Gardens,* with Charles Moore and William Turnbull (MIT Press, 1988); *The Art of Computer Graphics Programming,* with Robin S. Liggett and Thomas Kvan (Van Nostrand Reinhold, 1987); and *Computer-Aided Architectural Design* (Van Nostrand Reinhold, 1977). With Patrick Purcell and Malcolm McCullough he edited, and contributed essays to, *The Electronic Design Studio* (MIT Press, 1990).

A Fellow of the Royal Australian Institute of Architects, Mitchell came to MIT in 1992 from the Graduate School of Design at Harvard University, where he was the G. Ware and Edythe M. Travelstead Professor of Architecture and director of the Master in Design Studies program. From 1970 to 1986 he was on the faculty of the School of Architecture and Planning at the University of California, Los Angeles, where he headed the Architecture/ Urban Design program and was associate dean. He has also taught at Yale, Carnegie-Mellon, and Cambridge Universities. Mitchell holds a BArch from Melbourne University, a Master of Environmental Design from Yale University, and an MA from Cambridge University. He was awarded an honorary doctorate of humane letters by the New Jersey Institute of Technology in 1992.

Mitchell is chair of the editorial board of the MIT Press and also a member of the press's management board. He serves regularly on the juries for the Chrysler Awards for Innovation in Design and the *ComputerWorld* Smithsonian Awards.

Abbe Mowshowitz

Abbe Mowshowitz received the Ph.D. in computer science from the University of Michigan in 1967 and has been professor of computer science at the City College of New York since 1984. He has also held academic appointments at the University of Amsterdam, Erasmus University-Rotterdam, Rensselaer Polytechnic Institute, University of British Columbia, University of Toronto, and University of Michigan. Mowshowitz began his research career in information theory and discrete mathematics but shifted to organizational and social implications of computers some twenty years ago. He was awarded the 1990 Tinbergen Professorship at Erasmus University-Rotterdam in partial recognition of his work on computers and organizations. He has published about twenty books and reports (including *The Conquest of Will: Information Processing in Human Affairs,* 1976) and over fifty articles on the social impact of computing. Recently, his interests have shifted to the economics of computer-based information and to organizational theory. He has been investigating the cost effects of "information commodities" and managerial aspects of "virtual organizations." A book on *virtual feudalism* is in progress. In addition to teaching and research, he has acted as consultant on the uses and impacts of information technology (especially computer networks) to a wide range of public and private organizations in North America and Europe.

Donald A. Norman

Donald A. Norman is vice president of the Apple Research Laboratories at Apple Computer and professor emeritus at the University of California, San Diego, where he was founding chair of the Department of Cognitive Science. He was one of the founders of the Cognitive Science Society and has been chair of the society and editor of its journal, *Cognitive Science.* He is a fellow of the American Academy of Arts and Sciences, and in 1995 he received an honorary degree from the University of Padua.

Norman is the author of twelve books, with translations into twelve languages. His most recent books are *The Design of Everyday Things, Turn Signals Are the Facial Expressions of Automobiles,* and *Things That Make Us Smart,* all three collected together on a Voyager CD-ROM—"Defending human attributes in the age of the machine"—complete with video talks, demonstrations, collected papers, and even examination questions.

Oliver Strimpel

Oliver Strimpel joined the Computer Museum in 1984, becoming its executive director in 1990. He led the development of several permanent exhibitions, beginning with *The Computer and the Image* (1984) and *Smart Machines: Robots and Artificial Intelligence* (1987). Subsequent to these, he spearheaded the creation of the next generation of major exhibits at the museum: *The Walk-Through Computer* (1990), *People and Computers: Milestones of a Revolution* (1991), and *Tools and Toys: The Amazing Personal Computer* (1992). His plan to establish a set of cohesive cornerstone exhibits on computing history, technology, and applications culminated in the 1994 opening of *The Networked Planet: Traveling the Information Superhighway.*

Strimpel was formerly the curator of mathematics, computing, and data processing at the Science Museum, London, where he helped develop the exhibition *Science in India* (1982) and led development of *Information Technology* (1982) and *Photography and Beyond: Seeing the Invisible* (1983) at the then newly formed National Museum of Photography, Film and Television. He holds a B.A. in physics from Cambridge University, an M.Sc. in astronomy from Sussex University, and a D Phil. in astrophysics from Oxford University.

Dennis Tsichritzis

Professor Dr. Dennis Tsichritzis is chairman of the board of GMD, the German National Research Center for Information Technology. He is also currently president of ERCIM, the European Consortium on Informatics and Mathematics, and a member of various advisory boards in information and communication technology. Professor Tsichritzis received his academic degrees from the Universities of Athens and Princeton. From 1968 to 1985 he was professor of computer science at the University of Toronto, and since 1985 he has been professor of informatics at the University of Geneva. Professor Tsichritzis has worked in several fields of computer science, including theory, software, database management, engineering, office automation, object-orientation systems, and multimedia. He is the author of numerous scientific papers and books on various topics in computer science.

Sherry Turkle

Sherry Turkle is professor of the sociology of science at the Massachusetts Institute of Technology and author of *Life on the Screen: Identity in the Age of the Internet* (Simon and Schuster, 1995). She specializes in the study of people's relationships with technology, in particular computers. Her most recent research focuses on the psychology and sociology of computer-mediated communication.

Professor Turkle has pursued her research with support from the National Science Foundation, the MacArthur Foundation, the Guggenheim Foundation, and the Rockefeller Foundation. Her work on computers and people has been widely reported in both the academic and popular press, including *Time*, *Newsweek*, and *U.S. News and World Report*. She has been featured on the covers of *Wired* and *Technology Review* and has been named "Woman of the Year" by *Ms.* Magazine as well as a member of "America's New Leadership Class" by *Esquire*. Professor Turkle has spoken on many radio and television shows about the impact of the computer, including "Nightline," the "Today" show, "20/20," and the "CBS Morning News."

Professor Turkle's other publications include *The Second Self: Computers and the Human Spirit* (Simon and Schuster, 1984; Touchstone paperback, 1985) and *Psychoanalytic Politics: Jacques Lacan and Freud's French Revolution* (Basic Books, 1978; MIT Press paperback, 1981; second revised edition, Guilford Press, 1992).

Professor Turkle holds a joint Ph.D. in sociology and personality psychology from Harvard University. She is a graduate and affiliate member of the Boston Psychoanalytic Society and a licensed clinical psychologist.

Mark Weiser

Mark Weiser is the chief technologist at the Xerox Palo Alto Research Center (PARC). Weiser has no bachelor's degree; his Ph.D. is in computer and communications sciences from the University of Michigan (1979). Weiser was assistant and associate professor and associate chair in the Computer Science Department at the University of Maryland from 1979 to 1987, when he joined Xerox PARC as a member of the technical staff, then heading the Computer Science Laboratory for seven years. He has started three companies. His over seventy-five technical publications are in such areas as the psychology of programming, program slicing, operating systems, programming environments, garbage collection, and technological ethics. Weiser's work since 1988 has focused on ubiquitous computing, a program he initiated that envisions PCs being replaced with invisible computers imbedded in everyday objects. Weiser is the drummer with the rock band Severe Tire Damage, the first live band on the Internet.

Terry Winograd

Terry Winograd is professor of computer science at Stanford University, where he directs the teaching and research program on Human-Computer Interaction Design. He has written two books and numerous articles on natural language understanding by computers. His book *Understanding Computers and Cognition: A New Foundation for Design* (Addison-Wesley, 1987, coauthored with Fernando Flores) took a critical look at work in artificial intelligence and suggested new directions for the design of computer systems and their integration into human activity. He coedited a volume on usability with Paul Adler, *Usability: Turning Technologies into Tools* (Oxford, 1992). His most recent book, *Bringing Design to Software* (Addison-Wesley, 1996) brings together the perspectives of a number of leading proponents of software design. Winograd was a founder of Action Technologies, a developer of workflow software, and was a founding member of Computer Professionals for Social Responsibility, of which he is a past national president. He is also a consultant to Interval Research Corporation and serves on the national advisory board of the Association for Software Design and on the editorial boards of numerous journals, including *Human-Computer Interaction* and *Computer-Supported Cooperative Work*.

AI: *See* **Artificial intelligence**

Algorithm: a sequential logical process sufficient to the solution of a well-defined problem, such as the instructions comprising a computer **program.**

Artificial intelligence (AI): the use of computers, suitably programmed, to simulate acts of human intelligence.

Biological computer: a system of neurons, artificially grown, capable of problem solving via biologically real, brain-like operations.

Browser: a type of computer **software** which allows the user to view selected files or datasets, private or public, as on the **Internet.**

Calculation: broadly, the formal manipulation of uninterpreted symbols; sometimes, however, restricted to mean merely the performance of routine numerical computations.

Calm technology: technology which, somewhat like an efficient computer operating system, moves smoothly between central and peripheral data sources in the process of routine problem solving.

Chip: a microcircuit embedded on a base less than one square inch in area, typically performing logical functions of increasing **complexity.**

Complexity: in a basic sense, simply the number of components in a system; in a larger sense, the number and type of connections among such components must also be taken into account. As complexity increases (in most cases), so does intractability.

Corbato's law: states that the number of lines (i.e, amount) of code required to program an **algorithm** (for computer **software**) is independent of the computer **language** used.

Cyberspace: term from a novel by W. Gibson, to describe a computer meganetwork with which people literally connected their brains. Now used to refer to the **Internet,** or to the computer world at large.

Cycling through: a psychological disposition, observable in children, to employ overdetermined (ambiguous) words in each of several senses in close succession.

Dangling String: an analog display, composed of an elongated plastic strip and variable electric fan, which visually displays the amount of traffic on a computer system or a network.

Digital libraries: large libraries of books, stored via **digital technology** and accessible via a computer network, such as the **Internet.**

Digital technology: in general, computerized systems in which information transfers are reduced to strings of binary (0/1) digits. An increasingly broad range (visual, acoustic, etc.) of phenomena can be thereby simulated.

Embedded commands: computer instructions automatically inserted within other **programs,** in response to particular user requests, in order to render such systems more "**user friendly.**"

Ethernet: currently, the most widely used **LAN** (local area network).

Expert systems: problem-solving software systems which simulate human expertise.

Fifth Generation Project: a research program sponsored by the Japanese government with the goal of engineering radical computer enhancements of daily human life.

File Transfer Protocol (FTP): a basic set of instructions controlling access to (log on) and manipulation of files on a computer network, such as the **Internet.**

FTP: *See* **File Transfer Protocol**

Gigabytes: one billion bytes of computer storage, each byte of eight bits (binary digits) typically representing a symbol such as a decimal digit (0–9), alphabetic character (A–Z), etc.

Graphical user interface (GUI): software which permits users to interact with the computer via visual displays of icons representing various program choices.

GUI: *See* **Graphical user interface**

Home page: the initial page addressed in a given **World Wide Web** site, usually containing **hypertext** indexes to further options available to the user.

Hyperlearning: an expanded learning environment in which **hypertext** linkages among educational media are used to facilitate individual learning processes.

Hypertext: computer linkages among stored texts via keywords which are indexed (often bold faced or underlined) as such in each of the texts.

Information appliances: devices for converting a TV set into a **World Wide Web browser.**

Information hiding: the removal of system details from interface function, facilitating user interaction and thereby rendering the system more "**user friendly.**"

Internet: a global network of over 40,000 local networks of various types; the "information superhighway."

Internet Relay Chat (IRC): the use of the **Internet** communications system for multiuser conferencing.

Internet service providers (ISPs): generally speaking, organizations which are capable of providing physical (electronic) access to the **Internet.**

IRC: *See* **Internet Relay Chat**

ISPs: *See* **Internet service providers**

"Just in time" principle: a manufacturing practice, originating in Japan, in which the delivery of required materials from outsources is tightly scheduled so as to reduce wait time and the need for maintaining extensive inventories.

LAN: *see* Local area network

Language: in computer science, one of a number of formal symbolisms used in writing **programs** to control the operations of computers.

Leibniz's dream: after the 18th century German Enlightenment philosopher G. Leibniz, who expressed the hope that human discourse might someday be so completely rationalized that all debate (philosophical, political) might be reduced to mere **calculation.**

Local area network (LAN): communications networks confined to small areas, such as individual buildings.

Machine language: the base **language,** or instruction set, of a computer into which all other instructions must be translatable.

Microchip: *See* **Chip**

Mobots: mobile robots

Moore's law: a technological estimate by Intel's G. Moore that the number of transistors on a **microchip** would approximately double every one and one-half years.

Morphing: in general, the rapid change of form, such as "shape shifting" in the film "Terminator II."

MUDs: multiuser games played on the **Internet.**

Multicomputer: a computer composed of a system of computers, operating simultaneously.

Multiuser programs: computer **programs** which accept simultaneous input from a number of separate users.

Netscape: a **browser** software program which enables users of certain types of computers to view selected datafiles on the **Internet.**

Network computer: an inexpensive stripped-down PC designed for accessing a computer network.

Nondeterminism: the absence of, or freedom from, strict rules of casual determination as described in classical physics.

OLTP: *See* **Online transaction processing**

Online transaction processing (OLTP): immediate computer response to the receipt of data in business operations; e.g., the continuous, realtime, updating of inventory records.

Operating system: the master control **program** of a computing system with which all other programs must communicate.

Programming/programs: in general, creating an ordered set of instructions adequate to a formal **calculation,** establishing thereby control over the operation of a computing device; the design of **software.**

RAM: *See* **Random access memory**

Random access memory (RAM): bytes of computer memory directly accessible and routinely erased, which thus provide an open workspace for **program** operations.

Real time interrupt: immediate interuption of computer operation upon user input or environmental stimulus, thus allowing quick response.

Smart machines: in general, a reference to enhanced automation, with user-oriented features (e.g., voice recognition) and which is environmentally sensitive (cybernetic).

Software: the sets of instructions that control computer operations, usually based on **algorithms.**

Spreadsheet: a type of computer **software** which simulates the layout of an accounting worksheet, e.g., for budget analysis.

Teleconferencing: the use of sophisticated electronic communications technologies (video, fax, **e-mail,** etc.) for conferencing among respondents geographically separated; e.g., **virtual companies.**

Telepresence: "being there while being here at possibly some other time"; the user's presence and movement in **cyberspace** via, e.g., **e-mail, Internet, teleconferencing,** etc.

Turing test: after A. Turing, a British mathematician, who asserted that the criterion for the ascription of (human) intelligence is the inability of the investigator to determine otherwise.

Uniform Resource Locator (URL): the system of addressing used on the international **Internet.**

UNIX: currently considered by many to be the most advanced multi-user **operating system** for large-scale transaction processing.

URL: *See* **Uniform Resource Locator**

Usenet newsgroups: a categorized **e-mail** bulletin board service publically accessible through the **Internet.**

User friendly: broadly, any system featuring enhanced user compatibility, or ease of use, via such features as iconic menus, voice recognition, etc.

Virtual communities: interactive computer networks of geographically separate users linked through a wide range of common interests, whether business or pleasure, research or recreation.

Virtual companies: business organizations functioning largely in **cyberspace,** using **e-mail,** fax, **teleconferencing,** etc. for communications with geographically separate employees and customers.

Virtual office: a working environment extended beyond the traditional space defined by physical structure; cf. **virtual companies.**

Virtual reality (VR): a simulation system which, by means of computer-generated sensory input, creates an illusory "reality", or simulated physical environment.

Virus: a set of self-replicating computer instructions hidden inside a **software** program; when activated, the replication of the "virus" can overwrite and thereby destroy essential program files, rendering entire computer systems inoperative.

VR: *See* **Virtual reality**

WAN: *See* **Wide area network**

Wide area network (WAN): a communications network covering a large geographic area (e.g., a state, region, or country).

Windows: a sophisticated computer **software** interface which facilitates program selection and operation by the use of graphics and variable screen formats.

Word processing program: software for the creation of literal documents, or texts, with a computer; **Microsoft Word** is currently the most frequently used such program.

World Wide Web (WWW): a system enabling access to all documents stored on the vast **Internet** system by means of **hypertext** linkages.

WWW: *See* World Wide Web

Yahoo: a **World Wide Web** directory of addresses for Web sites.

INDEX

Abrahams, P., 90, 287
ACM. *See* Association for Computing
Action Technologies, 183
Advanced Research Projects Agency, 271
Affordance, 80
AI. *See* Artificial intelligence
Algorithms, 47–48, 67, 70. *See also* Programming
Allen, P., 151
Alt, F., 89, 287–288
Analogy, 121–122
Anarchy, ix
Androids, 100
Anxiety, 103
Architecture, 158–159
ARGUS software, 201
ARPANET, xii
Art, 144, 253–257
Artificial intelligence (AI), xii, 127–135, 154–155
Artificial objects, 98
Association for Computing (ACM), xi, xiv
Automotive design, 157–160

Babbage, C., 7
BAN. *See* Body Area Network
Bell, A. G., xiii
Bell, G., xiii, 1, 288
Berkeley, E., 136
Biological life, 100
Bionomics (Rothchild), 236
Biotechnology industry, 105–110, 115–116, 176

Body Area Network (BAN), 2, 24, 29
Books, F., 49
Brain, 6, 109, 111. *See also* Artificial intelligence
Brooks, R., 99
Brown, J. S., 3, 288–289
Burke, J., 289
Bush, V., 7, 271
Business structure, 163–169, 213, 272–273, 285

Cable TV, 18
Cache memories, 67
Calculation, 63, 94–95. *See also* Programming
Calm technology, 75–85
Cary, F., 172
Cerf, V., 2, 289–290
CERT Coordination Center, 195
Chamberlin, D., 165, 290
Chaining, 124
Chess, xii, 128, 132
Children, 88
    computers and, 93–102
    cycling through, 102, 104
    hyperlearning, 277–279
    language and, 97–98
    memories, 121
Chips. *See* Microchips
Clarke, A., 154
Clusters, 11, 25–26
Codebreaking, xi, 70, 200
Cognitive science, 88, 117–119
Cohrane, P., 6
Coleridge, S. T., 122